The God of the Bible
A Study of the Father, Son, and Holy Spirit

by David E. Pratte

Available in print at
www.gospelway.com/sales

The God of the Bible:
A Study of the Father, Son, and Holy Spirit

ISBN-13: 978-1494498900
ISBN-10: 1494498901
Imprint: Independently published

Note carefully: No teaching in any of our materials is intended or should ever be construed to justify or to in any way incite or encourage personal vengeance or physical violence against any person.

"He who glories, let him glory in the Lord" – 1 Corinthians 1:31

Other Acknowledgements
Unless otherwise indicated, Scripture quotations are generally from the New King James Version (NKJV), copyright 1982, 1988 by Thomas Nelson, Inc. used by permission. All rights reserved.

Scripture quotations marked (NASB) are from *Holy Bible, New American Standard* La Habra, CA: The Lockman Foundation, 1995.

Scripture quotations marked (ESV) are from *The Holy Bible, English Standard Version*, copyright ©2001 by Crossway Bibles, a publishing ministry of Good News Publishers. Used by permission. All rights reserved.

Scripture quotations marked (MLV) are from Modern Literal Version of The New Testament, Copyright 1999 by G. Allen Walker.

Scripture quotations marked (NRSV) are from the New Revised Standard Version of the Bible, copyright 1989 by the Division of Christian Education, National Council of the Churches of Christ in the United States of America.

Scripture quotations marked (NIV) are from the New International Version of the Holy Bible, copyright 1978 by Zondervan Bible publishers, Grand Rapids, Michigan.

Scripture quotations marked (HCSB) are from the Holman Christian Standard Bible, copyright 2008 by Holman Bible publishers, Nashville, Tennessee.

Other Books by the Author

Topical Bible Studies

Why Believe in God, Jesus, and the Bible? (evidences)
True Words of God: Bible Inspiration and Preservation
"It Is Written": The Authority of the Bible
Salvation through Jesus Christ: Basics of Forgiveness
Grace, Faith, and Obedience: The Gospel or Calvinism?
Growing a Godly Marriage & Raising Godly Children
The God of the Bible (study of the Father, Son, and Holy Spirit)
Kingdom of Christ: Future Millennium or Present Spiritual Reign?
Do Not Sin Against the Child: Abortion, Unborn Life, & the Bible

Commentaries on Bible Books

Genesis	*Proverbs*	*Ephesians*
Joshua and Ruth	*Ecclesiastes*	*Philippians &*
Judges	*Gospel of Matthew*	*Colossians*
1 Samuel	*Gospel of Mark*	*1 & 2 Thessalonians*
2 Samuel	*Gospel of John*	*Hebrews*
1 Kings	*Acts*	*James and Jude*
2 Kings	*Romans*	*1 and 2 Peter*
Ezra, Nehemiah, Esther	*Galatians*	*1,2,3 John*
Job		

Bible Question Class Books

Genesis	*Ecclesiastes*	*2 Corinthians and*
Joshua and Ruth	*Isaiah*	*Galatians*
Judges	*Daniel*	*Ephesians and*
1 Samuel	*Hosea, Joel, Amos,*	*Philippians*
2 Samuel	*Obadiah*	*Colossians, 1&2*
1 Kings	*Gospel of Matthew*	*Thessalonians*
2 Kings	*Gospel of Mark*	*1 & 2 Timothy,*
Ezra, Nehemiah,	*Gospel of Luke*	*Titus, Philemon*
Esther	*Gospel of John*	*Hebrews*
Job	*Acts*	*James – Jude*
Proverbs	*Romans*	*Revelation*
	1 Corinthians	

Workbooks with Study Notes

Jesus Is Lord: Workbook on the Fundamentals of the Gospel of Christ
Following Jesus: Workbook on Discipleship
God's Eternal Purpose in Christ: Workbook on the Theme of the Bible
Family Reading Booklist

Visit our website at <u>www.gospelway.com/sales</u> to see a current list of books in print.

Other Resources from the Author

Printed books, booklets, and tracts available at
www.gospelway.com/sales
Free Bible study articles online at
www.gospelway.com
Free Bible courses online at
www.biblestudylessons.com
Free class books at
www.biblestudylessons.com/classbooks
Free commentaries on Bible books at
www.biblestudylessons.com/commentary
Contact the author at
www.gospelway.com/comments

Table of Contents

(Due to printer reformatting, the above numbers may be off a page or two.)

Notes to the Reader

You may find that major topics of this material will repeat topics or concepts covered elsewhere. This serves to emphasize these points and allows each major topic of study to be complete of itself (so major sections can be studied independently).

Unless otherwise indicated, Bible quotations are from the New King James Version. Often – especially when I do not use quotations marks – I am not quoting any translation but simply paraphrasing the passage in my own words.

To join our mailing list to be informed of new books or special sales, contact the author at
www.gospelway.com/comments

God of the Bible

God's Power

Introduction:

1 Peter 5:6 says to "humble yourselves under the mighty hand of God."

Many Scriptures affirm the greatness of God's power.

Jeremiah 32:17 – There is nothing too hard for You.

Revelation 19:6 – God is called "Almighty." (1:8; 4:8; 21:22; 2 Corinthians 6:18; etc.)

Mark 14:36 – Father, all things are possible for You.

Job 42:2 – I know that You can do everything, and that no purpose of Yours can be withheld from You.

Job 26:14 – The thunder of His power who can understand?

(2 Chronicles 20:6; Matthew 19:26; Jeremiah 32:27; Psalm 115:3; 135:6; Genesis 18:14; Isaiah 43:13)

The purpose of this study is to consider "the mighty hand of God."

We want to learn to appreciate the greatness of God's power and why He deserves worship and honor. This should strengthen our faith. God demonstrates His power so we can trust Him to guide and care for us. This then will encourage us to obey God. He deserves our service because of His great works.

Note the greatness of God's power as shown by His works.

Only God Had the Power to Create the Universe.

Men of every generation have wondered about the origin of the universe: the sun, moon, stars, earth, plants, animals, and man.

God Simply Spoke All Things into Existence in 6 Days.

This is recorded in Genesis 1.

Jeremiah 32:17 – You have made the heavens and the earth by Your great power and outstretched arm.

Hebrews 11:3 – By faith we understand that the worlds were framed by the word of God, so that the things which are seen were not made of things which are visible.

Karen and I once saw a planetarium presentation about our Universe. It showed our sun and planets, describing the size of our solar system. Then it compared our sun to other stars in our galaxy: one star is so large that hundreds of our solar systems could fit inside it!

Then it pictured the Milky Way galaxy with millions of stars. But this is just one of millions of galaxies. One area of space has so many galaxies they appear as many as the stars in our sky! Finally, it pictures the whole Universe to the extent man knows it today.

God spoke all this into existence on one day, the fourth day of creation (Genesis 1:14-19). The Bible account simply says, "He made the stars also."

Psalms 147:4 says He not only knows how many there are, but "He calls them all by name."

Imagine the power necessary to do this.

(Compare Psalm 33:6-9; Exodus 20:11.)

Creation Proves the Existence and Power of God.

Romans 1:20 – The creation demonstrates the power and Godhead of the invisible God.

Many scientists deny creation. They say living things evolved over millions of years. Many believe someday man will become smart enough to create life. The fact is that man has never created the simplest form of life, let alone all the plants, animals, and man.

Consider an imaginary event in which the world's greatest scientists gather before God and tell Him they have become wise enough to make a man. So, God challenges them to a showdown to see who is powerful enough to make a man. But God says, "You must make man just like I made Him at Creation." The scientists agree.

The day comes and all the scientists gather before God. The showdown begins, and God reaches down to grab a handful of dirt. The scientists also grab up some dirt. God says, "No, no! This is my dirt. I made all this dirt at the beginning. You go make your own dirt, like I did!"

Man has made some amazing things, but we always start with things that already existed. We can't even make dirt without having something to start with, let alone can we duplicate the living things we see in nature. The Bible says God made everything in nature starting with nothing.

One who could make the Universe could do anything He set His mind to. Creation proves nothing is too hard for God.

(Acts 17:15; 17:24; Job 36:26-33)

Only God Has the Power to Rule the Universe.

God Rules Over All He Created.

Acts 17:24,25,28 – God rules the universe because He made it.

Only He had the power to make it. Therefore, He alone has the power to rule it, and He alone deserves to rule it.

When a man invents a machine, he makes it so he can control it. If he makes an airplane or rocket, he makes computers and switches to tell it what to do. If one goes off course and refuses to obey commands, men have the power to destroy what they created.

So God made the universe, including us. He deserves to rule us, and we ought to respect that power.

1 Chronicles 29:11,12 – God rules as Head over all.

Many people are guilty of Humanistic thinking. We act like we are the highest beings in existence, so we have the right to determine for ourselves how we will live.

But the fact is that everything in nature came from the Creator of the universe. Everything in Heaven and Earth belongs to Him. Every blessing is a gift from Him.

Throughout history God has asserted His right to control the universe, and has punished men who refused to accept His authority. (2 Chronicles 20:6)

People Should Worship and Praise God for His Power.

Revelation 19:4-6 – Give praise and worship to God, for the Almighty reigns. In eternity, those who recognize God's power will praise Him forever. In order to be among that number, we must understand and appreciate God's power enough to praise Him regularly on earth.

Matthew 28:18-20 – Jesus has all power in heaven and on earth. So all people should be taught to obey His commands.

Do you appreciate God's power enough to honor God and worship Him regularly?

(Genesis 17:1; Revelation 4:10,11; 14:7; 11:16,17; 15:3,4)

Only God Has the Power to Perform Miracles.

God has used human agents through whom to do the miracles, but the power comes from God.

Old Testament Miracles

Jeremiah 32:17,20-22 – Nothing is too hard for God. He showed this by the great miracles He did to lead Israel out of Egypt.

God brought great plagues on Egypt: water turned to blood, frogs, darkness, and especially the death of the firstborn. Yet Israel was protected from the plagues.

God caused the Red Sea to part, so Israel crossed on dry ground. Pharaoh's army tried to cross and was drowned.

People think we are powerful, but can we do miracles like these? Such accounts should humble us to appreciate God's greatness. (Psalm 135:6ff)

New Testament Miracles

Hebrews 2:3,4 – As with the Old Testament, so God confirmed the New Testament by powerful miracles.

Examples of miracles

* Jesus walked on water and calmed a storm (Matthew 14:22-33; 8:23-27).

* He fed multitudes with a few loaves and fish (Matthew 14:13-21; 15:32-39).

* He and His apostles instantaneously and completely healed all kinds of diseases, including leprosy, withered hands, deafness, blindness (from birth), and lameness (from birth). (John 4:46-54; 5:1-9; 9:1-11,30-38; Acts 3:1-20; 4:22; 14:8-10; 5:12-16; 19:11,12; 9:32-35; Mark 2:1-12)

* They raised the dead (John 11:17-44; Acts 9:36-42).

God of the Bible

The purpose of miracles was to confirm God's message and show God's power.

John 20:30,31 – By the time the New Testament was written, God had powerfully proved in the Old Testament that He is God. But people still needed proof that Jesus was Deity and that the men who spoke the New Testament were guided by the Holy Spirit. That was the purpose of the miracles.

Consider the power required to do these miracles. Who today can walk on water or raise the dead? We think men have done well when they invent a cure for tuberculosis or polio. Imagine the power it takes to bring someone back from the dead!

God has unquestionably proved His power.
(Mark 16:20; Acts 14:3; 2:22; 4:7,10; John 5:36)

The Resurrection of Jesus

Romans 1:4 – Jesus was declared to be the Son of God with power ... by the resurrection from the dead.

Jesus claimed He was the Son of God, He possessed Deity, and all men must believe in Him or perish (Matthew 16:15-17; John 20:28,29; 8:24,31,32).

Such claims must be backed up by powerful evidence. What proof could be more powerful than resurrection from the dead? We know that Jesus really was raised, because we have a written record of the eyewitness testimony of many people who saw Him alive after His death (1 Corinthians 15:4-8).

1 Corinthians 6:14 – God raised up the Lord ... by His power.

We have considered the power needed to create life in the first place. With all our abilities, we cannot do that. How much less can we give life to one who has been dead three days? If God could raise Jesus, who can doubt that He can do anything He chooses to do?

God has demonstrated His power, so that we will believe in Him, worship Him, and obey Him. Do you believe in the power of God? Do you worship and obey Him faithfully?

Only God Has the Power to Reward Men Eternally.

After This Life, We Will Be Raised and Judged for Our Lives.

God has the power to raise us from the dead.

1 Corinthians 6:14 – The same power that raised Jesus from the dead will also raise us.

(1 Corinthians 15; John 5:28,29)

We will then be judged for our deeds.

Acts 17:30,31 – Having said that God had the power to create us (verses 24,25) and to rule the universe (verse 24) and to raise Jesus (verse 31), Paul said God also has the power to judge us. Whatever God determines to do, He has the power to do. This is why we need to repent (verse 30).

Many people claim they believe in God, yet they continue in sin without repenting. They may believe in "once saved, always saved" or they justify their sin some other way.

This denies the truth of the Bible, or else the power of God, or both. If we believe in the power of God and in the word of God, then we must believe God will raise us from the dead and judge us for our lives. That means we need to get ready for judgment.

We Will Be Rewarded or Punished Eternally.

Jeremiah 32:17-19 – The God who has such great power, also knows everyone's deeds and will give everyone according to his works.

Matthew 25:31-46 – At the judgment, those who obey God will receive eternal life. Those who disobey will receive eternal punishment.

There is no value in studying the power of God unless we are willing to make application to our lives. God's power proves that He can do whatever He determines to do. He says He will raise us, judge us, and reward or punish us eternally. If we believe in His power, we need to repent and prepare for judgment. Are you ready, or are there things you need to do to correct your life?

Only God Has Power to Save Men from Sin.

God has the power to punish or reward. He would prefer to reward. But the problem is that all men have sinned and need to be punished (Romans 3:23; 6:23). Man cannot save Himself by His own power, so again we need the power of God.

Jesus Has the Power to Save All Men from Sin.

Hebrews 7:25 – He is able to save to the uttermost those who come to God through Him. To make this possible, He had to die as a sacrifice, suffering punishment for us. (1 Peter 2:24; John 3:16)

Mark 2:7 – Who can forgive sins but God alone? No one. But Jesus was God in the flesh, the sacrifice for our sins. Salvation is available only in Him.

(Acts 4:12; Matthew 19:23-26; John 14:6)

To Receive Forgiveness Men Must Believe Enough to Obey.

Matthew 28:18-20 – Jesus has all power (authority). So He commands all men to be baptized and then obey all His commands.

Mark 16:15,16 – The parallel account says we must hear the gospel, believe, and be baptized to be saved.

Acts 17:30 adds that we must repent.

Romans 10:9-17 says we must also confess Christ with our mouths.

The only power that can save from sin is the blood of Jesus Christ. When people truly believe in God's power to save, they will obey and serve Him. Who can imagine people, who really believe in the power of the God we have studied, yet who presume to disregard or to pervert His instructions?

If God is the God of power, then only He can save us from our sins. And if He has the power the Bible describes, no one would dare to change what He says to do to be saved. But His word says that Jesus' blood saves conditionally. We must hear, believe, repent, confess, and be baptized. Then we must live a faithful life.

Conclusion

Behold, the mighty hand of God!

Matthew 19:26 – Truly, with God all things are possible.

But that incredible power can either work for us or against us. If God is against us, His power will punish us eternally. If for us, He will reward us eternally.

Who would dare to stand against the God of the Bible? Those who truly appreciate God's power will serve Him faithfully. Do you appreciate God's power? Are you serving Him?

God's Wisdom

Introduction:

Consider the wisdom of God as described in these verses:

John 16:30 – Jesus' disciples said to him, "Now we are sure that You know all things." Nothing is beyond the ability of God to know.

Psalms 139:6 – Such knowledge is too wonderful for me; It is high, I cannot attain it. No man can attain to the level of knowledge God possesses. We cannot even conceive such wisdom, let alone possess it ourselves.

(1 John 3:20; Isaiah 40:28)

The purpose of this lesson is to study the wisdom and knowledge of God.

This is one of many characteristics of God that we can never fully understand because the infinite God is beyond the ability of finite man to understand. Yet considering His wisdom will help us appreciate how great He is.

Note that the infinite wisdom of God follows as a consequence of His infinite power. If God can ***do*** anything He chooses to do, then it follows that one thing He can do is to ***know*** anything He chooses to know. An all-powerful God must necessarily be an all-wise God.

Consider the wisdom of God as demonstrated in these areas:

God Has Demonstrated His Wisdom in the Past.

God Created Everything in Nature in Six Days.

Consider all that God made according to Genesis 1:

Day	Verses	Things created
#1	Verses 3-5	Light and darkness (day and night)
#2	Verses 6-8	Firmament; divided the waters
#3	Verses 9-13	Dry land, seas, plants
#4	Verses 14-19	Sun, moon, & stars
#5	Verses 20-23	Fish, birds
#6	Verses 24-28	Land animals, man

Consider the incredible wisdom required to create these. Man cannot make any one of them in a lifetime. God made them all in six days, and made them so they could all function together. All that He made was "very good" (verse 31).

God's Creation Demonstrates His Wisdom.

The stars

Proverbs 3:19 – The Lord by wisdom founded the earth; By understanding He established the heavens. The creation took great power, but it took equally great wisdom.

Psalms 147:4-5 – He counts the number of the stars; He calls them all by name ... His understanding is infinite.

Before the invention of the telescope, men thought they knew about how many stars there were. But every time we make a stronger telescope, we find more stars. Now scientists admit that they cannot begin to count the stars. But God not only counts them, He has a name for everyone. That is infinite understanding.

God's wisdom is so great that, not only can man not make things greater than God's creation, we cannot duplicate the things He has made, and in many cases cannot even understand how the things He made work!

Life and birth

Ecclesiastes 11:5 – As you do not know what is the way of the wind, or how the bones grow in the womb of her who is with child, so you do not know the works of God who makes everything.

Consider the birth of a child. Few events are more amazing. Since the beginning of time, men and women have known what to do to have a baby. Yet no man can invent a machine, a factory, or a process that can create a new human. In fact, we cannot even make the simplest of cells and make it come alive.

The average congregation seems to have more women who are faithful than men. Could this be influenced by the fact women personally experience the growth of a new human within their own bodies? How could anyone experience that and then doubt God's existence and wisdom?

Imagine the wisdom God needed to create all that exists in nature. After years of study by thousands of scientists, there are yet many mysteries of nature that man has not been able to understand even after God made them, let alone could we have made them ourselves. (Psalms 104:24)

God Has Demonstrated His Wisdom Regarding the Future.

Only God Can Know the Future with Certainty.

Man cannot predict the future in detail with certainty.

Proverbs 27:1 – Do not boast about tomorrow, for you do not know what a day may bring forth. Who can speak with certainty about the future?

We have plans about what we hope to do. How often has even one day gone exactly as you planned it? Every day I have planned what I hope to do, but rarely have I accomplished it all by night. Even the most definite of plans can be completely upset.

James 4:14 – You do not know what will happen tomorrow. For what is your life? It is even a vapor that appears for a little time and then vanishes away. Man does not even know he will be alive tomorrow, let alone know what he will do tomorrow.

God can know and predict the future.

Isaiah 41:21-23 – Jehovah challenges the idols to prove they are gods. God can show us what will happen, declaring things to come hereafter. Man cannot, but God can. If idols cannot, then they are not gods.

Isaiah 42:8,9 – God declares new things before they spring forth. This proves He deserves to be honored as God. That honor should go to no one else.

No man can know what will happen in the future, but God proves His wisdom and His Deity by doing so.

God of the Bible

God Predicted Many Details of Jesus' Life.

God has made many predictions that have come true. Some concerned the destiny of nations or cities. Some of the most important predictions concerned the life of Jesus. Here are just a few of them:

Prophecy	Subject	Fulfillment
Micah 5:2	Place of birth: Bethlehem	Matthew 2:1-6
Jeremiah 23:5	Lineage: Seed of David	Acts 13:22,23
Isaiah 7:14	Virgin Birth	Matthew 1:18-25
Deuteronomy 18:17-19; Psalm 110:1-4	Prophet, priest, & king	Acts 3:20-23; Hebrews 7:17; 8:1
Isaiah 40:3,4	Fore-runner: John Baptist	Luke 3:2-5
Zechariah 9:9	Triumphal entry	Matthew 21:1-9
Psalm 22:16-18; 34:20	Death by crucifixion	John 19:18-37
Isaiah 53:4-12	Died for others' guilt	1 Peter 2:21-25
Isaiah 53:9	Buried in rich man's tomb	Matthew 27:57-60
Psalm 16:10	Resurrection	Acts 2:24-32

How could a person know these things ahead of time by human wisdom? You might guess one or two by chance, but you could never be sure. The combination of them all would be impossible.

God's wisdom is proved by the fact God knew them all and predicted them hundreds of years before Jesus was even born. How can we doubt His wisdom?

The purpose of these prophecies is to convince us to believe in God and in Jesus, so we will obey them. If God can so predict the future, then surely He knows the best way for you and me to live. The man who disobeys God is saying, in effect, that He does not believe God is wise enough to tell us the best way to live.

God Assures Us of His Wisdom Regarding the Present.

Awesome as God's demonstrations of His wisdom has been in the past and regarding the future, for us personally, some of the most important applications come from His knowledge of the present.

God Knows Our Problems and Our Needs.

God knows our problems.

Revelation 2:9 – I know your works, tribulation, and poverty (but you are rich); and I know the blasphemy of those who say they are Jews and are not, but are a synagogue of Satan.

When we suffer, especially for serving God, we wonder, "Does God really see? Does He know what's happening to me?" Faith in the wisdom of God will assure us that He sees, and He will provide everything we need to remain faithful (1 Corinthians 10:13; Philippians 4:13).

God knows our needs.

Matthew 10:29-31 – God knows everything that happens even to the birds. The very hairs of your head are all numbered. Do not fear therefore; you are of more value than many sparrows.

Often we worry about the future. What will happen? Will we have what we need? The God who had the wisdom to create us and all the animals, also has the wisdom to know what is happening to us, and He has promised to provide what we need.

If He can take care of birds, can He not take care of us? What bird ever possesses more than just a nest made of twigs and mud? Yet they don't need to worry about the future. They live one day at a time and fill the world with song. We live in big houses with nice furniture, nice clothes, nice cars, and a refrigerator full of food, yet we worry about the future!

Matthew 6:8,32 – God knows everything we need, and He knows even before we ask. Do we believe that He knows our needs and knows how to answer prayer and give us what we need?

I worry about our society, about our rulers. Will we have leaders that will provide a world where my family will be safe, or will we face even more dangers, more immorality, even persecution? But God knows all about that. We should do what we can about it, but God knows what we need.

My real problem is, I'm just not sure God agrees with me about it! I'm not sure He's going to give me what I think I need! When I worry like that, I don't really trust His wisdom!

If we truly believe that God had the wisdom to make the world and the wisdom to predict the details of Jesus' life, how can we doubt that He has the wisdom to know how to provide what we need?

When we doubt that God knows our needs or will answer our prayers, when we worry about the future, we need a fuller appreciation of the wisdom of God.

(Exodus 3:7; Deuteronomy 26:6,7; Psalms 69:19)

God of the Bible

God Knows Our Words, Deeds, and Thoughts

God knows everything we do and everything we say.

Often we don't know what other people say and do. They may not know what we do. So we somehow think God does not know. We think He can be fooled like people can.

Psalms 139:1-4,7-12 – God knows everything we say and do. Anywhere we go, God still sees us. No one can hide from God or escape His knowledge. The all-wise, all-knowing God always knows everything about us.

"You can fool all of the people some of the time and some of the people all the time." But you can't fool God any of the time.

God knows everything we think.

1 Corinthians 2:11 – No man knows the thoughts of another man. You know what's in your heart, but you can't know what's in my heart unless I tell you.

1 Chronicles 28:9 – Serve Him with a loyal heart and with a willing mind; for the Lord searches all hearts and understands all the intent of the thoughts. God not only knows our words and deeds, He knows our thoughts.

1 Kings 8:39 – Give to everyone according to all his ways, whose heart You know (for You alone know the hearts of all the sons of men). Only God knows what is in our hearts. He not only knows, but He will judge it. He alone is qualified to judge.

This is one of the most frightening aspects of God's wisdom. We cannot escape it. He knows everything about us, and He will judge us on that knowledge. Nothing you have ever done, said, or thought, is beyond the knowledge of God.

This can also be comforting because God knows, not only the bad we do, but also the good. We sometimes wonder if God will reward us. If God could be mistaken or forget, He might overlook the fact we repented of wrong and corrected it. God will not be ignorant of either our evils or our righteousness.

The same God who had the wisdom to make the world and to predict in detail the life of Christ, also watches over our needs and will judge us for our lives. We should trust Him to do right and be sure our lives are acceptable.

(Jeremiah 17:10; 23:24; Psalm 33:13-15; 44:21; John 2:24,25; Revelation 2:23; Proverbs 15:3; Hebrews 4:13; Acts 1:24; Ezekiel 11:5)

Conclusion

Romans 11:33,34 – Oh, the depth of the riches both of the wisdom and knowledge of God! How unsearchable are His judgments and His ways past finding out! "For who has known the mind of the Lord? Or who has become His counselor?"

So great is God's wisdom that no one can search it, let alone give Him advice. The wisest and most intelligent scientists and philosophers on earth do not even know many things God has done, let alone do they understand how He did them. How could we possibly improve what He has done or advise Him what He ought to do?

Isaiah 55:8,9 – "For My thoughts are not your thoughts, nor are your ways My ways," says the Lord. "For as the heavens are higher than the earth, so are My ways higher than your ways, and My thoughts than your thoughts."

Far too often we fail to do God's will because what God says does not please us. Somehow we believe we have a better way. But there is no such thing as a better way than God's. No one can improve on any plan of God. Our only choice is to submit to His will.

People who respect God's wisdom will not try to change His ways or improve on them. Instead we will simply obey. Are you obeying Him?

God's Love

Introduction

1 John 4:8,16 – God is love.

Love is so essential to the nature of God that we are told "God is love." This does not deny the other characteristics of God, such as mercy, justice, righteousness, etc.

1 John 1:5 says God is light.

Hebrews 12:29 says God is a consuming fire.

Psalm 84:11 says God is a sun and shield.

1 John 5:6 says the Spirit is truth.

John 14: 6 says Jesus is the way, the truth, and the life.

These statements are intended, not to deny that God possesses other qualities, but rather to emphasize the quality that is mentioned. In this case, the purpose is to emphasize how important God considers love to be.

Ephesians 3:17-19 – We should know the love of God that passes knowledge.

We can "know" that God possesses love, because the Bible tells us He does and because He has demonstrated love in many ways. Yet God possesses such a depth of love that the degree or depth of it is beyond our ability to know: it "passes knowledge."

The purpose of this study is to examine several aspects of the Bible teaching about God's love.

Love is active good will: a sincere concern for the wellbeing of others that leads us to be willing to work for their good.

We seek to develop a greater appreciation of God's love. And we seek to learn how we ought to respond to that love.

Evidence that God Loves Us

God Gives All Physical Blessings.

Matthew 5:44,45 – God sends sunshine and rain on the just and the unjust. Context shows this is an expression of God's love.

We often take physical blessings too much for granted.

We often fail to see how much we need them, so we fail to show appreciation for them. This is especially true in a wealthy society like ours, where obtaining physical needs, and even luxuries, is so much easier than in many other places.

Consider living somewhere, like the moon or desert, where water was scarce or nonexistent. Would you like living there? Could you live there?

Consider living somewhere where there was too little sunshine, such as at the South Pole or on a distant planet. Temperatures there are so cold that we would not or could not survive.

Acts 14:17 – God does good, giving rain and fruitful seasons to fill our hearts with joy. We need God's physical blessings so we can have food and the necessities of life.

God's love is especially amazing because He provides these for all men.

Jesus said He sends rain and sun on the just and unjust. God does have many special blessings for those who serve Him as His people, but many of His physical blessings are given to all men: friends and enemies alike. This shows that God loves all people.

Acts 17:25,28 – God gives to all life, breath, and all things. For in Him we live and move and have our being.

James 1:17 – Every good and perfect gift is from above and comes down from the Father.

God Gives Guidance and Reproof.

Scriptures

Psalms 25:6-12 – Because of God's lovingkindness (verse 6), He teaches and instructs us (verses 8,9) and guides us (verse 9). It is an act of love on God's part to tell us how to live to please Him.

Revelation 3:19 – As many as I love, I reprove and chasten. God's love includes telling us when we are wrong! This does not seem pleasant to us. Many think that God rebukes us out of concern just for Himself, so He can get His way and please Himself regardless of what is good for us. But consider:

(Hebrews 12:6)

Why is this referred to as "love"?

Imagine serving a God who created you, He demands you serve His purposes, and He will judge you for your life. But suppose He never tells you what to do to please Him. Would that be love?

Jeremiah 10:23 – The way of man is not in himself, so we can't figure out by ourselves what is best or what God wants. Suppose God gave us no revelation at all but just left us to figure out entirely by ourselves the best way to live life. We would have no way to know what is best, because we are not wise enough to know by human wisdom. What would be the consequences?

Consider the consequences we can observe now in the lives of many people around us. Even though God has revealed His will, many people reject it. The result is violence, immorality, war, wickedness, selfishness, disregard for others, grief, and crime. This is the state everyone would face if God had not revealed His will.

A loving father wants his child to do what is best for the child; so if he really loves the child, he will guide the child so he knows the best way to live. This is exactly how God deals with us.

God Sacrificed Jesus to Save Us from Sin.

John 3:16 – God so loved the world that He gave His only begotten Son. How does this demonstrate God's love?

God's love led Him to offer us the gift of eternal life.

God so loved that whoever believes should have "**everlasting life**."

The greatness of a gift is often measured by its value. For me to give $1 would not be a great gift, but to give $1000 would be. Imagine offering someone the gift of eternal life. That would require great love!

God's love led Him to offer this gift to everyone.

God so loved "**the world**."

The greatness of a gift is also indicated by the number of people who receive it. To give $1000 to one needy person would show love, but to give that amount to every needy person you meet would show much more love. God offers eternal life to the whole world!

God's love led Him to pay an incredible price to offer this gift.

The price God paid so we could have eternal life was the life of His Son. He so loved the world that He "**gave**" His Son.

John 15:13 – Greater love has no man than to lay down his life for his friends.

Giving one's **life** is the supreme sacrifice. No one has a greater gift to give. What would you be willing to give your life for? Jesus showed His love by giving His life so we could have eternal life.

God's love led Him to give His only begotten Son.

God so loved the world that He gave "His **only begotten Son**."

To allow anyone you loved to die in someone else's place would require great love. But to allow your **son** – especially your **only** son – to die in someone else's place would require the greatest love. For what cause would you allow your only child to die?

God's love led Him to give His Son for sinners.

Romans 5:6-9 – It would be an amazing act of love if a person died in the place of some dear loved one who was a good man. But to give your life for sinful people, who were in fact your **enemies**, that takes great love!

The Bible says that, when we are in sin, we are God's enemies. Yet He gave His Son for us.

God's love led Him to make us members of His family.

1 John 3:1,2 – God bestowed such love on us that we should be called "**children of God**."

The blessing of being in a family depends on what family it is. Who is the father in the family, and who else are members of the family? There are some families which I have no desire to be part of! Can't you think of some? But there are other families that, to be a member of them would be a great honor.

Think what it means to be a member of **God's** family. Think of God's offering the life of His only begotten Son so that you and I could be His children and live with Him forever, even though we were His enemies and ought to be punished forever. How much love would that take?

(Galatians 2:20; Ephesians 2:4; Revelation 1:5)

Our Response to God's Love

Ephesians 5:2 – The love of God teaches us the meaning of love and how we ought to love. How should God's love reflect itself in our lives?

God's Love Should Lead Us to Love and Obey Him.

Matthew 22:37,38 – The greatest command of all is to love God with all our heart, soul, and mind.

John 14:15,21-24 – We ought to love everyone, but there is a special love we have for family. So God loves everyone, but He especially loves His children who love and obey Him. To benefit from God's love, we must love and obey Him.

1 John 4:19 – We ought to love Him because He first loved us.

1 John 5:3 – This is the love of God that we keep His commands. Many people talk about love, but don't obey. God's love for us demonstrates that real love must be *active*. We must do what is best for others.

Compared to God's love for us, how does our love for Him measure up? Do we really love God? Does it show in how we live?

(1 John 2:15)

God's Love Should Lead us to Love Our Families.

Ephesians 5:25 – Husbands should love their wives as Christ loved the church. Jesus' love is the standard that shows us how we ought to love. Most husbands would claim to love their wives, but do we love as Jesus loved? Do we express love for our wives by what we say and by what we do?

Titus 2:4 – Wives should also love their husbands and children.

Ephesians 6:1-3 – Children should honor and obey their parents.

What about your home? Is it a place of love or a place of screaming, quarreling, bickering, and strife? Do you give of yourself and share generously as Christ gave to share with you, or are you selfish and determined to have your own way? Is your home characterized by the kind of love God has for you?

God's Love Should Lead Us to Love Other Christians.

John 13:34,35 – We must love one another as Jesus loved us. This is the sign of discipleship. A disciple must follow his Master. Jesus, our Master, set the example of love, and we must follow. Do we honestly think, speak, and act in love for our brethren?

1 John 4:7-11; 4:20-5:2 – God's love teaches us to love one another. If we had more love for our brethren, would we have less bickering, gossiping, strife, hard feelings, and stubborn self-will?

Do you love your brethren as Jesus loved you?

(1 John 3:16-18)

God's Love Should Lead Us to Love Even Our Enemies.

Matthew 5:44-48 – God loves even those who hate Him, and He blesses them with good.

We too must love our enemies. We must not seek vengeance or harm to those who harm us. We must hope that they will receive good, and we must be willing to work for their salvation.

Do we treat those who hate us with the same love that God treats His enemies?

Conclusion

If you are not a child of God, do you love God enough to obey Him so He can forgive you and make you His child?

Romans 6:3,4; John 3:5 – To become a child of God, love and faith must lead us to be baptized into Christ.

If you are a child of God, have you been serving Him with love, even as he loved you?

God's Holiness and Righteousness

Introduction:

Ancient Israel was surrounded by nations that worshiped heathen idols. The first-century church was also surrounded by worshipers of the false gods of ancient Greece and Rome. Those gods were often guilty of evil: hatred, greed, selfishness, war, violence, materialism, immorality, deceit, and even sexual immorality. Often they were worshiped by drunken feasts followed by lasciviousness and fornication.

The God of the Bible is described as holy and righteous.

Understanding what God is like helps us to respect and appreciate Him. This in turn motivates us to serve Him.

"Holiness" is the same as "sanctification," both terms being translated from forms of the same word. To be holy means to be sacred, set apart or separated from sinful things. People are holy if we are dedicated and devoted to God's service, set apart from the world to serve God. Because we sin, we need to be forgiven in order to become holy. However, God is holy by virtue of being inherently good: He never commits sin.

"Righteousness" is the quality or character of being right or just. Men can be right by doing what God teaches to be right or by being forgiven when we fail to do right. But God is inherently right simply because He never does anything wrong or evil.

The two terms fit together because both emphasize that God is right, not wrong. He refuses to do what is evil or corrupt.

The purpose of this study is to examine passages that describe God's holiness and righteousness.

Consider lessons we may learn that give us greater understanding and appreciation of God.

God Deserves Honor Because He Always Does Right, Never Wrong.

Sometimes people think or act as though God does what is wrong. Some blame Him because we experience suffering and death. Some think He is harsh and cruel if He punishes men for sin. Others disagree with requirements of the Bible. Jesus was often accused of evil and sin when He lived on earth.

The Bible Often States God Does Right, not Wrong.

Consider these Scriptures.

1 Samuel 2:2 – No one is holy like the Lord.

Psalms 145:17 – The Lord is righteous in all His ways.

Revelation 4:8 – The four living creatures say, "Holy, holy, holy, Lord God Almighty, Who was and is and is to come!"

Revelation 15:4 – Who shall not fear You, O Lord, and glorify Your name? For You alone are holy. For all nations shall come and worship before You.

Sometimes humans do not understand why God's ways are right.

That is not because God is wrong, but because we are not infinitely holy and right so we do not understand. If we had perfect knowledge and holiness, then we would always understand that God's ways are right.

Consider, for example, why people accused Jesus of sin. It always happened, either because people did not understand what was right, or because they themselves were evil. Ignorant, sinful men often fail to appreciate God's goodness.

When we are tempted to blame God for our problems or even to fail to respect Him as a good God, we should realize the failure lies in us. We lack the wisdom or the goodness to recognize His holiness.

(Isaiah 6:3; Zephaniah 3:5; Exodus 15:11; Psalms 7:7; 33:4; 48:10; 99:9; Isaiah 5:16; Jeremiah 23:6; 11:20; Mark 1:24; Luke 23:47; Hebrews 1:8)

God of the Bible

God's Name Is Holy and Should Not Be Profaned.

God's name is holy.

God's name represents Him. It stands for Him and describes Him. Since He is holy, we should hallow His name: respect it as holy.

Psalms 105:3 – Glory in His holy name; let the hearts of those rejoice who seek the Lord!

Matthew 6:9 – Our Father in heaven, hallowed be Your name.

If we respect God as holy, then we must respect His name and speak respectfully when we use it.

(Psalms 145:21; 1 Chronicles 16:35; Psalms 30:4; 103:1; Isaiah 29:23)

We should not profane His name.

Exodus 20:7 – You shall not take the name of the Lord your God in vain, for the Lord will not hold him guiltless who takes His name in vain.

Leviticus 22:32 – You shall not profane My holy name, but I will be hallowed among the children of Israel. To profane God's name is to fail to respect God's holiness.

Many use God's name disrespectfully as an expression of anger, disgust, or surprise. We hear this everywhere: not just in entertainment, but often in public places. Even children when mildly surprised casually say, "Oh, my ..." and use God's name without respect. This is so common that people in social media and texts abbreviate it as OMG. People who do so need to learn to respect the holiness of God!

But we will see that there are many ways we might be guilty of profaning God's name. In fact, if we claim to be His people who wear His name but we fail to live in ways that give Him glory, then we have profaned His name.

The fact that someone makes something does not inherently prove that the maker is good. For example, people sometimes make things that we expect to serve us, but we are surely not always good. So God is God simply because He is the Creator. We must serve Him because He made us. But the fact that God is our Maker does not inherently mean that He would necessarily have to be good. Many heathen gods were very evil.

So God deserves our service because He made us. But an incredible additional blessing is that the God who made us is always good and right.

Do we always think, speak, and act in ways that show respect for God and His name? Do we need to learn to be more respectful?

(Leviticus 21:6; Ezekiel 36:20,22,23; 39:7)

God's Word Is Always Right.

This follows from God's righteousness. If everything God does is right, then it must be that everything He **says** is right.

Passages Stating God's Word Is Right.

Psalms 19:8,9 – The statutes of the Lord are right, rejoicing the heart; the judgments of the Lord are true and righteous altogether.

Psalms 33:4 – For the word of the Lord is right, and all His work is done in truth.

Psalms 119:138 – Your testimonies, which You have commanded, are righteous and faithful.

God deserves to be our authority, He deserves His word to be respected, because He is holy. You can always be sure His word is right, because God never does anything wrong.

(Isaiah 45:19; Psalms 25:8; 119:128,142; 60:6; 108:7; Isaiah 48:17; Hosea 14:9)

Men Do Not Always Realize God's Word Is Right.

Sometimes people speak or act as if God's word might contain mistakes. Some openly find fault with His word, claiming it contradicts science or history. Some say it contains "thousands of errors" or it contradicts itself, so they refuse to follow teachings with which they disagree.

Others may claim to believe the Bible, but they follow religious practices that come from human wisdom instead of the Bible. Whether or not they realize it, they are acting as though their ideas are better than the Bible. They are not just disrespecting the men who wrote the Bible, their actions imply that God's word is not right. This is a failure to respect God's righteousness.

When we say the word of God is right, sometimes people expect us to **explain** to their satisfaction why each statement in the Bible is right. Sometimes we may do so, but other times we may not. Just because we sometimes cannot explain why the Bible is right, that does not mean the message is wrong. It only means we are limited in wisdom or goodness. We are not always right, but God always is. So even when we cannot explain why His word is right, we must have faith to trust it to be right.

Imagine what it would be like to follow a god whose words might not be right. Imagine the confusion and uncertainty that would result. We would never know when to trust God's word and when not to.

Do we appreciate the fact that we have a revelation of God's will that is always right and never wrong? Do we sometimes follow human desires or wisdom instead of God's word, or do we trust it to always be right?

God's People Must Be Holy and Righteous.

Because God Is Holy and Righteous, He Cannot Tolerate Sin.

Some people seem to think God will tolerate almost any kind of conduct. They act as though He opposes little or nothing. Such a view contradicts the holy, righteous character of God.

Psalms 11:7 – For the Lord is righteous, He loves righteousness.

Psalms 5:4,5 – Because He is God, He does not take pleasure in evil but hates iniquity.

Hebrews 1:9 – You have loved righteousness and hated lawlessness.

When a person truly loves what is right, He must hate evil because evil is opposed to righteousness. God's holiness and righteousness compel Him to hate and oppose evil. When people believe God will just tolerate and overlook evil conduct, they need to learn to appreciate God's holiness and righteousness.

(Psalms 33:5; Daniel 9:7)

To Be God's People, We Must Be Holy.

Some people think God will accept them as His people even if they continue living in disobedience. They believe God will save them regardless of their sins.

Others think God's people should not speak out against the sinful conduct of others. In this age of "political correctness," every form of evil is tolerated. About the only people not tolerated are those who respect goodness enough to oppose evil. But just as God's holy, righteous nature requires that He reject evil conduct, so it also requires that His people must not accept evil, either in ourselves or in others.

Leviticus 20:26 – You shall be holy to Me, for I the Lord am holy, and have separated you from the peoples, that you should be Mine. We must not live like the world, because we belong to a holy God.

Hosea 14:9 – For the ways of the Lord are right; the righteous walk in them, but transgressors stumble in them. Those who are righteous rejoice in what is right. Only evil people oppose God's ways and defend evil.

1 Peter 1:15,16 – As He who called you is holy, you also be holy in all your conduct, because it is written, "Be holy, for I am holy."

Because God is holy, He cannot tolerate sin. If we seek to be the people of God, we must be holy. We must separate ourselves from evil and dedicate ourselves to living according to His righteous teachings.

When we are tempted to rationalize sin or to think that God will overlook people's sins, we need to think seriously about the holiness and righteousness of God. The idea that God's people should tolerate sin is a violation of the holy, righteous character of God.

(Psalms 119:128; Leviticus 19:2; 11:44,45; 21:6)

Yet God Offers Forgiveness to Those Who Repent.

God's righteousness requires Him to oppose our sins. But because He is righteous and we are not, only He has the power to forgive us when we sin.

So on the one hand, God's righteousness requires Him to oppose our evil; but on the other hand, that same righteousness compels Him to offer us a way to become right. And since He cannot simply overlook sin, if we wish to receive His forgiveness we must determine to turn away from sin and live right.

Romans 3:25,26 – God sent Jesus as a propitiation by His blood to demonstrate His **righteousness**, that He might be just and justify those who have faith in Jesus. Notice that God's willingness to forgive demonstrates His righteousness. But He must justify us in harmony with His just and righteous character. So, there are conditions we must meet.

1 John 2:1 – John wrote to teach us not to sin. But if we do sin, we have an Advocate with the Father, Jesus Christ the **righteous**. So Jesus can forgive us, because He is righteous. He was the sinless sacrifice for our sins. But to be forgiven, we must commit ourselves to overcoming sin in our own lives.

So long as we are content to continue practicing sin, we cannot be the people of a holy God. Only when we are willing to turn away from our sins by faith and strive diligently to be holy and righteous, only then can He forgive our sins and accept us as His people.

Do we have sins in our lives that we must turn from to become God's holy people? Or have we repented, committed ourselves to righteous living, and received His forgiveness through Jesus' blood?

(Philippians 1:11; 1 Corinthians 1:30; Daniel 9:16)

Conclusion

Imagine what it would be like to serve a god that you could never trust to do what is right or just. Many of the false "gods" of heathen idolatry were often wicked and selfish. Such a god might harm us for His own selfish purposes. He might not reward us even if we served Him faithfully. We might never be able to trust Him to do what is good for us.

What a blessing to know that our God always does what is good and right! We should always think, speak, and act in ways that show respect the holiness and righteousness of God. This requires us to respect His word as right and to ourselves live holy, righteous lives.

God of the Bible

Have you committed yourself to a life of holiness in serving this holy God? Are you one of His children? Are you serving Him faithfully?

God's Justice and Righteousness

Introduction:

Imagine what it would be like to worship a god who is not just and righteous. No one would ever know what rules to follow or how to please God. Today you might be punished for the same thing you were rewarded for yesterday. Everyone would live in constant fear that they might anger god without knowing why or what to do about it.

The Bible repeatedly affirms that God is just and righteous.

Revelation 15:3 – "Great and marvelous are Your works, Lord God Almighty! Just and true are Your ways..."

Zechariah 9:9 – Jesus' Triumphal Entry was prophesied: "Rejoice greatly, O daughter of Zion! Shout, O daughter of Jerusalem! Behold, your King is coming to you; He is just and having salvation..."

Isaiah 45:21 – ...There is no other God besides Me, a righteous God and a Savior; there is none except Me.

Psalms 145:17 – The Lord is righteous in all His ways.
(Psalms 11:7; 106:1; 119:68; 100:5; 86:5)

The purpose of this lesson is to study the Bible teaching about the justice and righteousness of God.

Righteousness means God always does what is right, never what is wrong. Justice means fairness: treating people properly according to the standard of right and wrong, so that those who do wrong are properly punished but those who do right are rewarded.

God of the Bible

Psalm 89:14 says these characteristics are fundamental to God's government of the universe. They are the foundation of His throne. We will see how important this is as we proceed.

God's Justice Goes Hand-In-Hand with His Righteousness.

Psalms 89:14 – Righteousness and justice are the foundation of Your throne...

Deuteronomy 32:4 – For all His ways are justice, a God of truth and without injustice; righteous and upright is He.

Zephaniah 3:5 – The LORD is righteous within her; He will do no injustice. Every morning He brings His justice to light; He does not fail.

Psalms 119:137 – Righteous are You, O Lord, and upright are Your judgments.

Note how righteousness and justice go together. Some translations even translate "righteous" where others have "just."

Notice how these two characteristics of God are inseparable. God is just because He is righteous. Both are essential to one another and to the character of God.

(1 Samuel 2:2; Psalm 99:9; Hebrews 4:15)

Because He is righteous, God knows the law.

John 12:48 – The word that I have spoken will judge him in the last day.

A just judge must know the law. Imagine standing to be judged in a court of law by a judge who had no knowledge of right and wrong according to the law. If he did not obey the law and did not care about the law, he might declare you guilty of a crime even when you had obeyed the law.

But a judge who himself lives by the law, is a judge who knows the law. God's knowledge of the law is perfect, because He is the giver of the law. The law is based on God's righteous character.

Human judges may make mistakes because they do not properly understand the law, but ignorance of the law can never cause injustice in God's court. God knows what is right and wrong because He always does what is right.

Because He Is Righteous, God Reveals the Law by Which We Will Be Judged.

2 Timothy 3:16,17 – The Scriptures profitably instruct us in righteousness. There is no lack of revelation of God's will. He tells us

how we can be right, and he gives guidance that warns us if we do wrong. His word provides us to all good works.

Acts 17:11 – Furthermore, that revelation can be understood. The Bereans were able to search it and know what was true. We too can know God's will if we search diligently with honest hearts.

Imagine standing in court to be judged according to a law when you had absolutely no way of knowing the law: not just that you did not know it, but it was impossible to know it.

Sometimes human laws are so complicated that, try as we will we cannot understand them. Or perhaps the law is on the books but is not explained to the citizens so they can understand it.

It would be unjust to condemn people for violating a law that they had no way of knowing. It may happen in human courts, but never with God. It would not be right, and God always does right. So He has insured that truth is available by revealing it in the word.

Because He Is Righteous, God Shows No Partiality.

God judges without partiality.

Romans 2:11 – There is no partiality with God.

Acts 10:34-35 – God shows no partiality. But in every nation whoever fears Him and works righteousness is accepted by Him. The reward we receive from God is determined by how we live according to the standard of His will. (1 Peter 1:17)

Sometimes human judges take bribes or allow people to escape punishment simply because they are wealthy, influential, or powerful. People who are poor or weak are sometimes oppressed. But we know this is not right. It is not just.

We need not fear that, after we have served God diligently for a lifetime, He may choose to punish us anyway because we were not rich or tall or handsome or of a certain nationality or some other characteristic that we cannot control or that is irrelevant to our obedience.

On the other hand, don't think you can live in disregard to His will and expect Him to save you because you are rich or handsome or famous, etc.

Because He is righteous, God rules fairly. To rule unfairly would be to do wrong, and God never does wrong.

We should appreciate the justice of God.

People who know the Bible have become accustomed to thinking of God as righteous and just. But have you ever thought about the fact that there is no guarantee that the God who made us would turn out to be a good God?

Consider the fact that many animals have owners that are cruel and unjust. They have no choice about it, nor is there anything they can do about it. In the same way, many of the gods worshiped in idolatry and mythology were certainly not good gods. What if, in fact, we had been made by such a God? We would have absolutely no control over that!

Imagine serving a God who was cruel and unjust. No matter how hard your tried to please Him, He may determine to punish you. He might invent cruel tortures just because He wanted to.

What a blessing it is to us that, completely beyond our control, it turns out that the God who made us is perfectly righteous and perfectly just! Do we really appreciate the importance of the fact our God is righteous and just?

God's Justice and Righteousness Require That Wicked People Be Punished.

Some people believe that God is too loving to punish the wicked in hell. God is a loving God, but these people need to consider the justice and righteousness of God.

God Has Punished Wicked People in the Past.

If God is so loving that He will not punish sin, then He must not punish any sin at all, no matter what the sin may be. But there is no need to wonder whether or not God will punish the wicked. He has already proved He is willing to do so.

Genesis 6:5-7 – The people in Noah's day were so corrupt God destroyed them all by a flood.

Genesis 19:24,25 – The people of Sodom and Gomorrah were guilty of exceedingly great sin (13:13; 18:20), including homosexuality. God rained fire and brimstone on them.

Numbers 14:30-34 – When the people of Israel refused to enter Canaan, God required them to wander in the wilderness forty years till the older generation all died. During that period, God brought various curses upon them in which many died.

In the same way, the Bible clearly records that God has brought punishments upon nations for their wickedness, including sending people into captivity and even wiping out entire civilizations.

Was God a loving God in these days? Yes, but did that keep Him from punishing these people? No. Love leads God to offer men opportunity to repent and be forgiven, but His justice and righteousness still requires Him to punish those who will not repent.

God Has also Promised to Punish People Today Who Are Wicked.

The Scriptures clearly teach that God will punish the wicked.

Often human judges fail to punish those who do wrong. This can happen because the true facts are not revealed, or because of some legal loophole, or because of respect of persons. Such judges make good people angry. We tire of seeing crooks set free to steal, murder, and rape again. Righteous people want to see justice done. A just and righteous God will punish the wicked.

Hebrews 2:1-3 – The people whom God punished in the Old Testament are a warning to us. God punished then because His justice and righteousness demanded that they be punished. But His character is no different today. He is still just and righteous, and His character still demands that wicked people be punished.

Matthew 25:41,46 – There is a day coming when all men will be judged and rewarded for their lives (verses 31-33). Those who are wicked will be punished with eternal fire, eternal destruction.

Matthew 13:40-43 – The wicked will be cast into a furnace of fire.

God's verdict will be just and righteous, because His character is just and righteous.

Notice these Scriptures.

Psalms 119:137 – Righteous are You, O Lord, and **upright** are Your judgments.

Acts 17:31 – He has fixed a day in which He will judge the world in **righteousness** through the Man whom He has appointed, having furnished proof to all men by raising Him from the dead.

Romans 2:5,6 – Your hardness and impenitent heart are treasuring up for yourself wrath in the day of wrath and revelation of the **righteous** judgment of God, who will render to each one according to his deeds.

2 Thessalonians 1:6-9 – It is a **righteous** thing with God to repay with tribulation those who persecute God's people. Those who do not know God and do not obey the gospel will suffer vengeance in flaming fire, punished with everlasting destruction.

Romans 1:32 – According to the **righteous** judgment of God, those who practice the sins listed in the context are deserving of death. Not only should we not practice such things, but we also should not approve of those who practice them.

Revelation 16:5,7 – An angel said: "You are **righteous**, O Lord ... because You have judged these things." Another said, "True and **righteous** are Your judgments."

(Proverbs 29:27)

God of the Bible

Punishment of sin is righteous and just.

In this life, wicked people sometimes are not punished for their wrongs. Good people often suffer as much or more than evil people. If wicked people are not punished after this life, then justice has not been done.

People who violate the law do not want justice. But imagine what it would be like to serve a God who is not just. Suppose evil of all kinds went unpunished even after this life. Who would do right? Would we want to live in a world in which evil never had any penalties?

Some think the God of the Old Testament is a God of justice, but the God of the New Testament is a God mercy and love. Not so. God has always been a God of justice and mercy and love. His nature does not change (Hebrews 13:8; James 1:17).

Men may not understand how God's judgment is righteous, but that is because of our limited wisdom and righteousness. Whether or not we understand His justice, we can be sure every judgment of God will be right because He is always right and never wrong. Those who criticize God's judgments are impugning His righteousness and justice.

God loves us. This is why He sent His Son to die on the cross to save us from sin. If we yet refuse to repent and serve Him obediently after that great sacrifice, then God's justice demands that we be punished.

God's Justice and Righteousness Require that Good People Be Rewarded.

Justice demands, not just that the wicked be punished, but also that the righteous be rewarded.

God Has Rewarded Righteous People in the Past.

Note these examples from Hebrews 11 showing God's rewards to the righteous.

Verse 4 – Abel was counted righteous because of his excellent sacrifice.

Verse 7 – Noah was spared from the flood and became an heir of righteousness because he built the ark.

Verses 29,30 – Israel passed through the Red Sea, entered the promised land, and captured Jericho because of their faith.

Verse 31 – Rahab did not perish with Jericho because she protected the spies.

God has always made a distinction between the righteous and the wicked. Justice demands that the wicked be punished, but it demands just as surely that the righteous be rewarded.

God Has Also Promised to Reward People Today Who Are Righteous.

Often human judges punish those who are innocent. This can happen because the true facts are not revealed, or because of some legal loophole, or because of respect of persons, etc. When this happens, we are angered. Righteous people want to see justice done.

A just God will punish the wicked, but will reward the righteous. He rewarded people in the Old Testament who obeyed Him. But His character has not changed. He is still just, and His justice still demands that righteous people be rewarded.

Matthew 25:46 – At the judgment, the righteous will go into eternal life.

Matthew 5:10-12 – Those who are persecuted for righteousness sake will have a great reward in heaven.

1 Peter 1:3,4 – God has begotten us to a living hope, an inheritance incorruptible and undefiled, that does not fade away, reserved in heaven.

Again, in this life righteous people often suffer, sometimes because they have done right. If there is no reward after this life, then justice will not be done.

Imagine what it would be like to serve a God who would not do justice for the righteous. We might serve Him all our lives, yet in the end be punished as severely or more severely than those who lived their whole lives in sin. Who would serve God? Who would want to live in such a world?

A righteous person always respects righteousness in others. God must reward righteousness because He Himself is infinitely righteous. He can no more fail to reward righteousness than He can fail to punish evil.

Because He loves us, He has given us the opportunity to be forgiven of sins through His Son's death. If we will repent and obey Him based on our faith, He will reward us eternally because He is just.

(Romans 2;7,10; 6:23)

Conclusion

Rather than being reasons why God would **not** punish evil men, God's holiness and righteousness are the very reasons why we can be sure He **will** punish evil men. He will punish the wicked and reward the righteous, because His own righteousness and justice compel Him to do so. If He failed to punish evil and reward righteousness, then He Himself would be unrighteous!

Do we truly appreciate the great blessing of having a just God? Those who worshipped Greek, Roman, and other heathen "gods" admitted that their gods were not always just. They were like super-humans, yet they sometimes perverted justice by mistake or selfishness or whim.

Those are false gods, not really god at all. A great blessing given us by the true God is that He is always just and loving, righteous and merciful.

Will we make use of His mercy and obey Him in faith so we can be saved eternally by His justice? Or will we continue in sin and be punished eternally by His justice?

God's Faithfulness

Introduction:

Notice some passages about God's faithfulness to His word:

Numbers 23:19 – God *is* not a man, that He should lie, nor a son of man, that He should repent. Has He said, and will He not do? Or has He spoken, and will He not make it good?

Psalms 89:1,2,5 – I make known Your faithfulness to all generations ... Your faithfulness You shall establish in the very heavens ... Your faithfulness also in the assembly of the saints.

Titus 1:2 – In hope of eternal life which God, who cannot lie, promised before time began

Revelation 19:11 – Now I saw heaven opened, and behold, a white horse. And He who sat on him *was* called Faithful and True, and in righteousness He judges and makes war.

(Lamentations 3:22,23; 1 Corinthians 1:9; Psalm 119:90; Hebrews 6:18; Romans 3:4; Deuteronomy 32:4; 1 Samuel 15:29; 1 Thessalonians 5:24)

The purpose of this study is to examine God's faithfulness to His word.

"Faithful" means "strict or thorough in the performance of duty ... true to one's word, promises ... steady in allegiance or affection ... reliable ..." (*Random House College Dictionary*).

God is faithful in all aspects of this definition, but in this study we want to focus on God's faithfulness to His word, especially His promises. God always speaks the truth and always keeps His promises. His promises are "reliable" because He "strictly performs" what He says He will do.

People often fail to keep their promises. All of us can think of instances in which someone made a promise to us, then failed to keep their word. We know how disappointing this is. But God has never broken His word.

We will consider some examples of promises God has kept, we will discuss His faithfulness even in some cases in which some people deny that He has kept His word, then we will consider some promises that He has made to us.

Some Old Testament Examples of God's Faithfulness

We have read verses claiming that God is faithful, but He has not left this as a matter of doubt. He has often proved His faithfulness to his word.

Adam and Eve

The promise

Genesis 2:17 – But of the tree of the knowledge of good and evil you shall not eat, for in the day that you eat of it you shall surely die. God promised that eating the forbidden fruit would lead to death. Did God keep that promise?

The fulfillment

Genesis 3:19 – God told Adam: In the sweat of your face you shall eat bread till you return to the ground, for out of it you were taken; for dust you are, and to dust you shall return. People die physically because of sin.

Genesis 3:22-24 – God also drove Adam and Eve from the garden. As a result, they could not eat the tree of life and live forever. This was physical death. But they were also sent away from God's presence: this separation from God was spiritual death.

Romans 5:12 – This spiritual death passes on all men, because everyone sins (Ephesians 2:1-5,11-19; 1 Timothy 5:6). This death came on Adam and Eve "in the day that they ate." All of us also become separated from God (spiritually dead) when we become guilty of sin.

God kept His promise.

Noah

The promise

God promised that everything on the earth that breathed would die because of sin, but Noah and his family would be spared by means of the ark.

Genesis 6:17-18 – God told Noah: I Myself am bringing floodwaters on the earth, to destroy from under heaven all flesh in which is the breath of life; everything that is on the earth shall die. But I will establish My covenant with you; and you shall go into the ark; you, your sons, your wife, and your sons' wives with you.

The fulfillment

Genesis 7:23 – So He destroyed all living things that were on the face of the ground: both man and cattle, creeping thing and bird of the air. They were destroyed from the earth. Only Noah and those who were with him in the ark remained alive.

God kept His promise to Noah.

Abraham and Sarah

The promise

Genesis 18:9-15 – God promised Abraham's wife Sarah would have a son. Since Sarah was beyond the age of having children, she doubted God's promise. God asked if anything is too hard for God. Then He rebuked Sarah for doubting God's promise.

We must learn to trust God's word. To doubt Him is to deserve rebuke.

The fulfillment

Genesis 21:1-3 – God fulfilled the promise when Abraham was one hundred years old (verse 5). Sarah conceived and bore a son, whom they named Isaac. God knew this promise could not be fulfilled by natural process but would require a miracle. Yet God kept the promise, proving that nothing is too hard for God.

When people make promises, sometimes they do not intend to keep them. Sometimes they intend to keep them but later find out they are not able. When God makes a promise, He always intends to keep it, and nothing is too hard for God.

God's Covenant regarding Abraham's Descendants

God has proved that He always keeps His word. Yet some people claim that there are specific promises that He has not kept. Unintentionally, they are denying the faithfulness of God. One example is the special covenant God made regarding Abraham's descendants.

The Covenant Promises

Genesis 26:4 – And I will make your descendants multiply as the stars of heaven; I will give to your descendants all these lands; and in your seed all the nations of the earth shall be blessed.

This promise concerning Abraham's descendants was repeated many times (see Genesis 12:1-3,7; 22:15-18; etc.). It consisted of three parts:

1. **The nation promise:** Abraham's descendants would become a great nation (like the stars of the heaven).

2. **The land promise:** His descendants would receive Canaan to dwell in.

3. **The seed promise:** In Abraham's seed all nations of the earth would be blessed.

Premillennialists deny that the land promise has been fulfilled. They say Israel never received all the land God promised, so God will give them the land when Jesus returns. This denies plain Bible statements.

The Fulfillment

The nation promise was fulfilled.

Exodus 1:7 – But the children of Israel were fruitful and increased abundantly, multiplied and grew exceedingly mighty; and the land was filled with them. (1 Kings 4:20)

The land promise was fulfilled.

Joshua 21:43 – So the Lord gave to Israel all the land which He had sworn to give to their fathers, and they took possession of it and dwelt in it.

Joshua 21:45 – Not a word failed of any good thing which the Lord had spoken to the house of Israel. All came to pass.

Joshua 23:14 – And you know in all your hearts and in all your souls that not one thing has failed of all the good things which the Lord your God spoke concerning you. All have come to pass for you; not one word of them has failed.

Premillennialists, who deny that Israel inherited the land, directly contradict these plain Bible statements.

The seed promise was fulfilled in Jesus.

Galatians 3:16 – Now to Abraham and his Seed were the promises made. He does not say, "And to seeds," as of many, but as of one, "And to your Seed," who is Christ.

Acts 3:25-26 – You are sons ... of the covenant which God made with our fathers, saying to Abraham, "And in your seed all the families of the earth shall be blessed." To you first, God, having raised up His Servant Jesus, sent Him to bless you, in turning away every one of you from your iniquities. (13:32,33)

So Christ was the "seed" through whom the promise to Abraham was fulfilled. The blessing to come through the seed was forgiveness of sins. This was fulfilled when Jesus died for all men and sent the gospel to preach salvation to all.

You and I can receive the fulfillment of this promise, for the blessing of forgiveness comes even to us. The Bible claims both the land and the seed promises have been fulfilled.

(Galatians 3:26-29; Mark 16:15,16)

The Promise of God's Kingdom

The Promise

Daniel 2:36-44 – God promised that He would establish His kingdom in the days of the Roman Empire. Again, premillennial folks say this promise has never been kept, but that God will establish this kingdom at Jesus' second coming. This view also denies the faithfulness of God.

The Fulfillment

Mark 1:14,15 – Jesus came to Galilee, preaching the gospel of the kingdom of God, and saying, "The time is fulfilled, and the kingdom of God is at hand." Was the time "fulfilled" or not? Was the kingdom "at hand" or not?

Mark 9:1 – And He said to them, "Assuredly, I say to you that there are some standing here who will not taste death till they see the kingdom of God present with power."

Jesus promised that some standing there would not die till they saw the kingdom present. If so, then the kingdom must have begun centuries ago. To deny this is to say that God is not faithful to His word. Note that the **kingdom** would come "with **power**."

Acts 1:3-8 – Discussing the time of the coming of the kingdom, Jesus promised the apostles that the **power** would come when the **Holy Spirit** came. He had already said that would be in Jerusalem "not many days hence." So, the **kingdom** would come when the **power** came, but the **power** would come when the **Holy Spirit** came.

Acts 2:1-4,29-36 – The power of the Holy Spirit came on the apostles enabling them to speak in tongues. Peter preached that Jesus was reigning on David's throne at the right hand of God.

So, the **power** and the **Holy Spirit** came. It follows that the **kingdom** had come. This was in the lifetime of those to whom Jesus had made the promise. As a result, Peter said Jesus was then on David's throne.

God of the Bible

Colossians 1:13 – He has delivered us from the power of darkness and conveyed us into the kingdom of the Son of His love. God has fulfilled His promise. Jesus' kingdom came in the first century, and people were then in it.

There are many problems with the doctrine that denies this, but one problem is that it denies the faithfulness of God. To imply that He has broken any promise is to deny His faithfulness.

We can be sure God will never break His promises because He never has and because He never lies.

(Hebrews 12:22-29; Revelation 1:9; 1 Corinthians 15:22-26)

God's Promises to Us

If we believe in God's faithfulness, then we must accept every promise He has made to us as being true. Many of these promises involve blessings and punishments. To receive the blessings, we must meet conditions. If we fail to meet the conditions, we receive the punishments.

Consider these promises:

Knowledge of Truth

God has promised that the Scriptures will reveal everything we need to know to be saved eternally.

Psalms 25:12 – Who is the man that fears the Lord? Him shall He teach in the way He chooses.

2 Timothy 3:16,17 – All Scripture is given by inspiration of God, and is profitable for doctrine, for reproof, for correction, for instruction in righteousness, that the man of God may be complete, thoroughly equipped for every good work.

Do you believe these promises? Some people claim God has not fully revealed His will, or that we need something in addition to the Scriptures to know God's will. These views deny the faithfulness of God. If you believe God is faithful, you must study God's word to know His way.

(Matthew 5:6; 13:13-16; James 1:5)

Forgiveness of Sins

This is the blessing God promised through Abraham's seed. Jesus' death fulfilled this promise, making salvation available to all.

Hebrews 7:25 – He is also able to save to the uttermost those who come to God through Him...

Mark 16:16 – He who believes and is baptized will be saved; but he who does not believe will be condemned.

1 Peter 3:20,21 – In the days of Noah ... a few, that is, eight souls, were saved through water. There is also an antitype which now saves us – baptism ...

God kept his promise to Noah, saving him from the flood. But many people did not believe God's promise; those people died in the flood.

Now God has promised we can be forgiven if we believe Jesus enough to be baptized. Many people today likewise do not believe that baptism is necessary to salvation. Those people are denying the faithfulness of God's word just like people who did not believe they needed to be in Noah's ark to be saved.

Do you trust God's word enough to obey Him in baptism? (Colossians 1:12-14)

Overcoming Temptation

God has promised that we can overcome every temptation.

1 Corinthians 10:13 – No temptation has overtaken you except such as is common to man; but God is faithful, who will not allow you to be tempted beyond what you are able, but with the temptation will also make the way of escape, that you may be able to bear it.

Some people claim that they cannot help sinning. They claim that man is born totally depraved or with a sin nature, so certain temptations are beyond their ability to resist. They say they can't help committing homosexuality or fornication, doing drugs, smoking, telling lies, etc.

All such ideas deny the faithfulness of God. God says every sin can be overcome by trusting God and taking the way of escape He provides.

Do you trust God's word enough to turn away from sin? (2 Thessalonians 3:3; Philippians 4:13; Ephesians 3:14-20; 6:10-18; Hebrews 13:5,6)

The End of the World and Judgment

2 Peter 3:3-7,9 – Some deny that Jesus will come to judge and punish the wicked and end this world. Others say He will come but, instead of the world being destroyed, the righteous will live forever on the earth. All this denies the faithfulness of God's word.

God promised to flood the world in Noah's day, and He kept His promise. The same God has promised to destroy the world by fire. Then will come the judgment and the destruction of evil men.

To doubt this is to say that God is slack in His promise. Instead, the world still stands because God is giving men opportunity to repent (verse 9). Will you make use of the opportunity? To act as though wicked men will not be punished is to deny the word of God. (Romans 2:6-11)

God of the Bible

Eternal Life for the Righteous

The same God who sent His Son to forgive us, has also promised eternal life to those who serve Him faithfully.

Titus 1:2 – In hope of eternal life which God, who cannot lie, promised before time began...

2 Timothy 2:11-13 – This is a faithful saying: For if we died with Him, we shall also live with Him. If we endure, we shall also reign with Him. If we deny Him, He also will deny us. If we are faithless, He remains faithful; He cannot deny Himself.

God's faithfulness says that, if we give our lives in His service, He will allow us to live and reign with Him in eternity. But if we deny these promises, we will be denied the right to that reward.

Titus 1:16 – They profess to know God, but in works they deny Him... Some people think they have not denied God because they believe in God and Jesus. But God says disobedience is a form of denial.

If you have a true faith in God, you will obey Him (Hebrews 10:39; chap. 11). Those who do not obey have no promise of eternal life.

Conclusion

God has been faithful to every promise He ever made. Do you truly believe in His promises? If so, you will obey Him.

Revelation 2:10 – Be faithful until death, and I will give you the crown of life.

Jesus will be faithful to that promise. But the promise is conditional. We must be faithful to Him.

Have you received the forgiveness Jesus promised to those who believe, repent, and are baptized? Have you been living faithfully to receive His reward?

God's Providence

Introduction:

Many people are unfamiliar with the life of Esther, yet it is one of the richest, most beautiful, and most encouraging studies in the Bible.

Many are also unfamiliar with Bible teaching about God's providence, yet it too is one of the most beautiful and encouraging doctrines in the Bible.

Our purpose in this study is to study the story of Esther and learn the important lessons it teaches about the providence of God.

Interestingly, the book never directly names God or the word "providence." Yet we will see that these are major themes of the book.

The Life of Esther

Background of the Book and Esther Chosen as Queen - Chapters 1 and 2

The story occurred in Shushan, the capital city and palace of the empire of the Medes and Persians (1:3).

Nebuchadnezzar, king of Babylon, had defeated Jerusalem and carried many Jews into captivity. The Persians then defeated Babylon, and some Jews returned to Palestine. Our story concerns some who were still in Persia in Sushan (located north from west end of Persian Gulf - see a **map**).

God of the Bible

The king is called Xerxes in modern history, but was called in Hebrew Ahasuerus (1:1). He ruled from 486 to 465 BC, and our story occurs in the third to twelfth years of his reign (1:3; 3:7).

The story begins when queen Vashti refused to obey the king and was removed from being queen (chapter 1).

The new queen chosen was Esther (chapter 2). She was a Jew, but did not reveal this (2:10). She was also an orphan who had been raised by her cousin Mordecai, of the tribe of Benjamin (2:5-7).

In 2:21-23 Mordecai learned about two men plotting to overthrow the king. He revealed this through Esther, the plot failed, and this was recorded in the chronicles of the empire.

Haman's Rise to Power and His Decree against the Jews - Chapter 3

The villain of the story is Haman, who was second in authority in the empire.

The king commanded everyone to bow to Haman, but Mordecai refused.

The only reason given why he refused is that he was a Jew (3:1-6). Perhaps bowing was considered worship to deity (Acts 12:21ff).

Haman used his Influence with the king to decree that, on a certain day, every Jew in the empire should be slain (3:7-15).

Note the egotism of Haman. It was not enough to be second in the kingdom and nearly everyone bowed. He must have even Mordecai bow or he would slay him and all his nationality!

Esther's Appeal on Behalf of Her People - Chapters 4-7

Mordecai urged Esther to speak to the king on the Jew's behalf (4:8).

She replied that people could see the king only at his request. If she went to see him uninvited, she would be killed unless he held out the scepter (4:10-11).

Mordecai reminded Esther she was a Jew and should use her influence to speak out on their behalf, or she too would perish. Esther called on Jews to fast three days, then she would go in (4:13-16).

The king allowed Esther to speak, so she asked him and Haman to attend banquets with her the next two days. This made Haman feel even more exalted. But he was so angry Mordecai wouldn't bow to him that he decided to build gallows and ask the king for permission to hang Mordecai (chapter 5).

That night, the king couldn't sleep, so he had the chronicles of the kingdom read.

He heard how Mordecai had saved him from a conspiracy, but Mordecai hadn't been rewarded. He asked Haman for advice about how to reward a man who had pleased him, but did not tell who the man was. Haman figured the reward was for himself, so he suggested what he wanted: a "ticker-tape" parade riding on the king's horse in the king's clothes. The king said to do that ... to Mordecai.

Haman had gone to ask permission to hang Mordecai, but ended up leading Mordecai's horse in the parade (chapter 6). (Ever had one of those days when everything went wrong?)

Chapter 7 – At the second banquet, Esther asked the king to spare her life and her people.

The king didn't know she was a Jew, so he asked who would kill her and her people. She identified Haman. Haman fell before her to plead for his life, and the king thought he was trying to attack her. A servant informed the king of the gallows Haman built for Mordecai, so the king had Haman hung on it.

The Victory of the Jews Over Their Enemies - Chapters 8-10

Mordecai was exalted to second in the kingdom in place of Haman (8:1,2).

The decree to kill the Jews could not be reversed (8:8), but they were allowed to defend themselves and the rulers would help them. As a result, they defeated their enemies (chapters 8,9).

The Jewish feast of Purim was instituted to commemorate this event (chapter 9).

Lessons Regarding the Providence of God

Providence is "that preservation, care and government which God exercises over all things that He has created, in order that they may accomplish the ends for which they were created" – *International Standard Bible Encyclopedia*, page 2476. It is the work by which God "provides" for His will to be accomplished.

His will is for men to be saved and have eternal life. So, providence is the means He uses to **provide** for His people to be forgiven and be blessed, so they can be faithful and enter eternal life.

Note the lessons we learn about providence from the story of Esther:

God of the Bible

(The noun "providence" is not used in reference to God in Bible, but the verb "provide" is: Genesis 22:8; 1 Samuel 16:1; Hebrews 11:40; Job 38:41; Psalm 65:9; 78:20; 132:15.)

God Works in Human Affairs for the Good of His People and for the Ultimate Accomplishment of His Will.

God used Esther to preserve His people from death.

God had promised a descendant of Abraham and of David would be a blessing on all nations and a ruler of God's people. Haman's plan to annihilate the Jews would have defeated this plan.

Esther 4:14 – Mordecai clearly states the essence of providence: deliverance **will arise** for the Jews. God's purpose will not fail.

As a result, in spite of his great power, Haman failed so miserably that, while not one single Jew died, Haman was slain in the very way he wanted to kill Mordecai.

The Bible gives many other examples in which God provided for His will to be accomplished.

In the flood, wicked people were destroyed, yet Noah was saved.

Joseph, deserted as a lad in a foreign land, became governor to save Abraham's descendants.

Moses led Israel from Egyptian slavery to Canaan.

Likewise, God promises to provide for our needs so we can do His will.

Like Mordecai and Esther, we may face hindrance and opposition. God has not promised to remove all our problems. He has promised to provide everything we need to be faithful and receive eternal life, *if* we are determined to serve Him faithfully at all costs.

* Do you face hardship, temptation, and discouragement? Are you tempted to give up serving God? God will provide a way of escape (1 Corinthians 10:13).

* Do you face poor health, the death of a loved one, or mistreatment by others? God does not promise to remove the problem, but He promises peace and strength to endure (Philippians 4:6,7).

* Are you burdened by the guilt of sin and fear of eternal torment? God is able to save to the uttermost and give the hope of eternal life (Hebrews 7:25).

God Can Accomplish His Will Through Natural Law Without Miracles.

Some people think all God's influences on earth are miraculous. But Bible miracles are **impossible** by natural law or human ability: walking on water, calming storm, raising dead, etc.

Through Esther God's purpose was accomplished with no miracles at all.

There is not one miracle in the book. Each event, viewed at the time it occurred, was a reasonable, natural occurrence. But God directed and combined them so as to amazingly accomplish His will. Consider several events:

* Vashti was deposed for disobeying the king. That can happen naturally.

* Esther was chosen to take her place. Someone had to be chosen.

* Mordecai reported the plot against the king. This was just doing his duty.

* Esther spoke to the king on behalf of the people: this was difficult but not impossible.

* The king could not sleep on the night before her request, so he had the chronicles read.

Today also, God accomplishes His purposes through natural law.

The purpose of miracles was to confirm that a message or messenger was inspired by God (Mark 16:20; Hebrews 2:3,4).

Miracles were essential while the message was being delivered. Now that it is completely delivered, recorded, and confirmed, we read the Bible to learn truth and produce faith (2 Timothy 3:16,17; John 20:30,31). Supernatural gifts, by which truth was revealed and confirmed, are no longer needed so they have ceased (1 Corinthians 13:8-10; Jude 3; Acts 1:20,21).

Some people think every blessing they receive is a "miracle."

If a man is pronounced terminally ill but gets better, people say that's a "miracle." When we deny it, they say, "You don't believe God heals the sick, answers prayer, and exercises His power today?" They see only two choices, but there is a third alternative.

Did God bless His people and demonstrate His power in the story of Esther? Yes. Did He do miracles? No, He acted through natural law. Likewise today, He answers prayer, heals the sick, and blesses people through natural law.

God has designed His universe in such a way that He can control the laws of nature to do amazing things. The story of Esther is amazing. But nothing that occurred was miraculous: ***impossible*** by natural law.

People Often Cannot Understand How God's Providence Works or What God Is Doing or Why He Is Doing It.

Some people think anything they can't understand must not be true!

They deny God exists and works in the world because they don't understand **how**. But there are many things in life we believe but don't understand: What is life? How does your brain function?

The story of Esther shows that God worked for His people, but they did not understand how, what, or why He did what He did.

4:14 – "**Who knows** whether you have come to the kingdom for such a time as this?" When Esther became queen, no human could have predicted the service she would render. Even in the face of disaster, Mordecai was not sure God would use **this** means to deliver the people: maybe it would be this way, maybe another way. **Who knows?**

4:16 – Esther agreed to speak to the king, but concluded, "If I perish. I perish." She had no way of knowing what would happen. Maybe the king would grant her request, maybe he would ignore her, maybe he would **kill** her. God's people often have been martyred for speaking out for God's will.

Deuteronomy 29:29 – "The secret things belong to the Lord our God, but those things which are revealed belong unto us." How providence works is a "secret thing."

(Note other examples in 2 Samuel 12:22; Hebrews 11:17-19; Genesis 45:4-11; 50:15-21.)

So, we often don't know how God is working, why He does what He does, or what the outcome will be.

But we must believe He will work for our eternal salvation according to His will, **if** we are determined to remain faithful.

* We face sickness or death in the family. What will the outcome be? "Who knows?"

* We are persecuted and opposed. Maybe we are sued in court or imprisoned. How will God work that out? "Who knows?"

* We are trying to convert someone. Will they obey? "Who knows?"

* You are considering taking a new job in another city. What job and what city would be the best? "Who knows?"

* We face trying financial problems. How will it work out? "Who knows?"

* We have conflict in the church or in our family. What will the outcome be? "Who knows?"

We don't know **how** God will resolve these problems, **who** He will use, or **what** events will occur. These are not revealed in the Bible.

What we can know for sure is that God will work for our ultimate salvation, and He can help us be faithful in every circumstance *if* we are willing to be.

Romans 8:28 - "All things work together for good for them that love God."

So, we must not interpret events as a message to tell us what God wants us to do.

Some people search everyday events to find "signs" from God.

* Some event happens and people say, "I knew the Spirit was leading me to..." or "God must be trying to tell you something."

* Dr. James Dobson says one way to know God's will is by looking for open or closed doors. Hindrances to some plan mean God is telling us not to pursue that plan. But if barriers are removed, that means He wants us to go ahead.

Example: A man wanted to run for public office so he suggested he should try it and see if things worked well. If so, God must have wanted him to do that.

A woman tried to enter America illegally. She concluded that, if she arrived safely, that was a sign that she had done what God wanted her to do.

This uses providence as an avenue of revelation from God.

There are two problems: First, we don't understand what God is doing, so how can anything be revealed by it? Second, the **devil** is working in our lives too. How do we know whether any event is from God or from Satan?

Examples:

* When Mordecai refused to bow to Haman, serious problems resulted. Did this prove God wanted him to bow?

* Esther saw many barriers hindering her from talking to the king. She could have died. Should she have concluded God wanted her to keep quiet?

* Joseph was sold as a slave and then imprisoned. Did this mean his course of action was wrong? No, he later understood all this occurred to accomplish God's will.

* Job faced all kinds of hindrances. Was this as a sign he was doing something wrong? No, it was a temptation from the Devil! But Job did not know this. He faced the problems because his conduct was **right**, not because it was **wrong**.

The idea that you can look for signs in your life to tell you what God wants you to do is frankly a superstition. It is looking for omens like people do in the Occult. It is entirely subjective and proves nothing. ***Providence is not revelation!***

God of the Bible

When people begin to interpret events in their lives as signs from God, the proper response is that of Mordecai: "**Who knows**?"

The way to learn what God does or does not want you to do is, not by looking for signs in your life, but by searching the **Scriptures** (2 Timothy 3:16,17). When God's word does not reveal a thing to be acceptable or unacceptable, then we must use our best judgment and trust God to bless our lives to work for good in His service.

God's Providence Uses People to Accomplish His Purposes, Yet It Respects Man's Free Will.

Some people think that, if God has determined to work things out according to His will, this means people don't have a choice in what they will do.

The story of Esther shows people are free to choose good or evil. The decision they make determines what reward God will give them.

Esther had a choice – 4:8,14

Mordecai urged her to defend the Jews. She did and God rewarded her.

Mordecai realized Esther could refuse to help. If she did, she would perish, but God would still accomplish His promises.

Haman had a choice.

God did not force Haman to be evil. God tempts no man (James 1:13). Haman was evil because he gave in to his own sinful pride (1 John 2:15-17; James 1:14,15). Because he chose to sin, he was punished.

But despite Haman's sin, God accomplished His purpose. If Haman had chosen to be righteous, God would still have accomplished His purpose.

Likewise, we today may choose to do good or evil. Either way God will accomplish His purposes. But our choice will determine whether we are rewarded or punished.

Joshua 24:15 – Joshua challenged the people to **choose** whether or not to serve God.

Revelation 22:17 – **Whosoever will** may take of the water of life freely.

Mark 16:15,16 – The gospel should be preached to all. He who believes and is baptized shall be saved. He who does not believe will be condemned.

Like Esther and Haman, we have the power to choose to obey God or not. If we obey, He can use us for good in accomplishing His will, just as He used Esther. And we will be eternally rewarded. If we disobey, He will still accomplish His purposes, just as He did regarding Haman. But we will be punished eternally.

Conclusion

God does work in this world to accomplish His purpose. But each of us has a choice to make. Will you choose to obey God so He can use His providence to bless your life and strengthen you to receive eternal life?

God of the Bible

The Number of Individuals in the Godhead

Introduction:

The Bible repeatedly teaches that there is only ONE true God.

This God is "one" in contrast to the many warring, conflicting, different gods of heathen idolatry (Deuteronomy 4:35,39; 6:4; 32:39; Psalm 86:10; Isaiah 43:10-13; 44:6-8; 45:5,6,21-23; Matthew 4:10; Mark 12:29).

However, the Bible also mentions three beings each of whom is called "God," or other such terms used for God.

The Heavenly Father – Matthew 16:16,17; John 6:27,44,45; 20:17; Romans 1:7; 1 Corinthians 1:3; 2 Corinthians 1:2; Ephesians 1:3; etc.

Jesus, the Son – John 1:1,14; 20:28,29; Philippians 2:6-8; Hebrews 1:8,9; Colossians 2:9; Isaiah 9:6.

The Holy Spirit – Acts 5:3,4; Ephesians 4:30; 1 Thessalonians 4:8.

Some people conclude that "one God" means God is just one individual or personal being. So, they conclude that the Father, Son, and Holy Spirit are all the same individual or personal being. They claim that these are just different titles used to refer to the one individual, or that the different terms refer to different parts of the one individual ("Son" = the fleshly body, "Father" = the Divine Spirit that inhabited the body, etc.). This one individual is named Jesus, so the position is often called "Jesus only."

The purpose of this study is to show by Scripture that the Father, Son, & Holy Spirit are three separate and distinct living personal beings or individuals.

To illustrate what we mean by separate and distinct beings or individuals, consider various existing kinds of living intelligent beings:

Angels are intelligent spirit beings or individuals – Hebrews 1:13,14.

Satan and his servants (demons) are intelligent spirit beings or individuals – Matthew 4:1-11; 12:43-45; Mark 1:21-27.

Humans are intelligent beings or individuals (before death a human consists of body and spirit, but at death the spirit departs from the body) – Genesis 1:26,27; 2:7; James 2:26; etc.

The Bible teaches that the Father, Son, and Holy Spirit are individual beings **separate & distinct** from one another, like these various other intelligent beings are separate and distinct from one another. We do not claim the Father, Son, and Holy Spirit are physical beings, like humans, though Jesus did have a body on earth. Nor do we claim they are like these other beings in character, authority, etc. We simply say that these other living beings **illustrate the concept of separate and distinct individuals** or personal beings. The Father, Son, and Holy Spirit are each an individual, distinct from one another like angels are distinct from one another, etc.

The Father is not the same individual being as the Son, the Son is not the same being as the Spirit, etc. However, each possesses all the characteristics and privileges of Deity, so each is part of the Godhead. Therefore, the one true God consists of three separate and distinct individual divine beings.

We do not claim to understand all about God, nor can we answer all possible questions about the number of individuals in the Godhead. Some things are simply not revealed; limited, finite humans simply cannot understand all about the infinite, unlimited God (Deuteronomy 29:29; Job 26:14; 36:26; 37:5,23; Isaiah 55:8,9). Nevertheless, regardless of whether or not we understand all about it, we must believe and teach that there are three separate and distinct individuals in the Godhead, because the Bible says it.

God of the Bible

Evidence for Three Separate & Distinct Individual Beings in the Godhead

Evidence that the Father and the Son Are Distinct Individuals

A father and his son must be separate individuals

Consider the following references:

Matthew 3:17 – This is **My** beloved **Son**.

Matthew 16:16,17 – **You** are ... the **Son of the living God ... My Father** in heaven revealed this.

Matthew 17:5 – This is **My** beloved **Son** (spoken by God the **Father** – 2 Peter 1:16-18).

John 3:16 – **God** gave **His** only-begotten **Son**.

John 5:17 – **My Father** has been working, and **I** work.

Hebrews 1:5 – I will be to **Him** a **Father** and **He** shall be to **Me** a **Son**.

1 John 1:3 – Have fellowship with the **Father** and with **His Son Jesus Christ**.

2 John 3 – Grace from God the **Father** and from **Jesus Christ the Son of the Father**.

2 John 9 – Abide in the teaching and have **both the Father and the Son**.

A father and his son are necessarily two separate and distinct individuals. A single individual can be both a father and a son at the same time – a father to one person and a son to another person. But no one can be the same person as **his own** son, and no person can be the same individual as **his own** father!

If Jesus and His Father are the same individual, as some claim, then Jesus is both **his own father and his own son**!

Further, the passages describe both an "I" and a "He" (or "me" and "him"). Use of both these terms also necessarily implies plurality of individuals.

And further note that 2 John 9 expressly mentions "**both**" the **Father and the Son**. The Father and the Son are a "**both**" – **two** individuals.

Further, 1 John 1:3 and 2 John 3 refer to "**Jesus**" by name as the **Son** and distinguish Him from the **Father**. The Father is never called "Jesus" in the Bible.

(Note also Romans 15:6; 2 Corinthians 1:3; 1 Thessalonians 3:11; 2 Corinthians 1:3; 11:31; 1 Peter 1:3; and many other passages below that mention both the Father and the Son.)

The Father prepared a body for the Son – Hebrews 10:5

When Jesus came into the world, He said, "a **body You** have prepared for **Me**." "You" is God the Father (verse 7). "Me" is Jesus the Son (verse 10). The "body" is the body in which Jesus came into the world (verses 5,10).

Again, "you" and "me" necessarily refer to a plurality of individuals. Jesus was the "me," not the "you" (the Father).

And Jesus is not just the "body." The body was **prepared** for the "Me" (Jesus). Here are two separate and distinct spirit beings discussing the body. Did the Spirit that inhabited the body prepare the body for Himself? Is Jesus talking to Himself, saying You (Jesus) prepared this body for Me (Jesus)?

Judgment given by the Father to the Son – John 5:22

The **Father** does not judge any man, but has given all judgment to the **Son**. If the Father and Son are the same individual, then when Jesus judges someone, the Father **is** judging him. But the Son judges and the Father does not judge. Therefore, they must be separate individuals.

Jesus prayed to the Father – John 17:1-5 (Matthew 26:39; John 11:41)

Jesus lifted His eyes to Heaven and prayed to the Father (verse 1). He said, "I have glorified **You** … **I** have finished the work **You** have given **Me** to do" (verse 4). **I** and **you** make plural individuals. But if the Father and Son are the same individual, then Jesus prayed to Himself!

Jesus was WITH the Father before the world began – John 1:1-3,14; 17:5,24

The "Word" (1:1) is the only begotten Son of the Father (1:14,18). He was in the beginning **with** God and **was** God (verse 1).

He (Jesus) said "**Father**, glorify **Me** together with **Yourself** with the glory which **I** had **with You before the world was**" (17:5). Further, the **Father loved the Son before the foundation of the world** (17:24).

Even before Jesus had a fleshly body on earth, there was a Father (**You**) who was His own **self ("yourself")** – one individual. Sharing glory **with Him** was **Me** or **I** (Jesus) – a second individual who was **with** the Father and was loved by the Father before the world began.

You and **Me** implies separate individuals. The Father was one "**self**," but Jesus was **with Him**. All this was before there ever was any fleshly body. Was Jesus **with Himself** before the world began? Did He **love** Himself and share glory with **Himself**?

God of the Bible

The Son is on the Father's right hand – Ephesians 1:17,20

The **Father** raised **Jesus** from the dead and made Him sit at **His right hand**. Clearly this describes a relationship between two separate individuals. If Jesus and the Father are the same individual, then Jesus is sitting at His own right hand! (See also Acts 2:33; 7:55,56; Romans 8:34; Colossians 3:1; 1 Peter 3:22.)

Jesus and the Father had independent wills – Matthew 26:39

Jesus prayed, "**Not as I will but as you will**." **My will and your will** make two distinct minds each capable of making its own decisions. The Father's will and the Son's will agree and are united, but each has individual power to choose and to will. Each has His own mind and intelligence separate from the other.

Two distinct wills necessarily imply two distinct intelligent beings.

(See also John 6:38-40; 8:28,42; 5:30; 7:16; 12:49; 14:10,24. Note that the Father knew something the Son did not know – Mark 13:32).

The Father and the Son make TWO witnesses – John 8:13,16-18,29

Jews accused Jesus of testifying of Him **self** (verse 13). Jesus said the law required **two** witnesses (verse 17; compare Deuteronomy 19:15). He claimed He was **not alone** because "**I am with the Father** who sent me" (verse 16). Further, **I am One** that bears witness of **Myself,** and the **Father** bears witness of **Me** (verse 18). That fulfills the requirements for **two** witnesses (verse 17). So, **He** who sent me is **with Me**; **He** has not left **Me alone** (verse 29).

Again, **I and My Father** make a plurality of individuals. If Jesus and the Father were the same individual, then Jesus would be **alone** and would have only **one** witness. But Jesus said He was **not alone** and He and His Father fulfilled the requirement of **two** witnesses. This can only be true if they constitute two separate and distinct individuals.

Jesus and His Father are "WE" – John 14:23; 17:20-23

Jesus ("me") and "my Father" love those who obey. "**We**" will come and dwell with them (14:23). The Father and Son are an "**Us**" and a "**We**" (17:21,22). How can "we" and "us" be one individual?

I am not alone, but the Father is with me – John 16:32

But if Jesus and His Father are the same individual, He would have been alone. He was not alone because the Father (a separate individual) was with Him.

Jesus had a spirit separate & distinct from that of His Father – Matthew 27:46,50; Luke 23:46

When Jesus was on the cross, the Father **forsook** Him (Matthew 27:46). Clearly the Father's spirit was no longer with Jesus. Yet Jesus continued to live awhile, having **His own spirit,** which then departed when He died (verse 50). When He died, He commended **His spirit** into **His Father's** hands (Luke 23:46). Did Jesus commend His own Spirit into the hands of His own Spirit, and then give up His spirit? No, Jesus had His own Spirit separate from His Father's spirit.

In death the spirit of a person leaves his body and returns to God (James 2:26; Ecclesiastes 12:7; Acts 7:59). Just like any man, Jesus had His own spirit separate from the spirit of His Father. Jesus' spirit remained in His body even after the Father forsook Him, then it left when Jesus died.

The fact a man has his own spirit, separate from the spirit of other beings, is what makes him a separate individual. But Jesus had his own spirit separate from the Father's spirit, therefore He must have been a separate and distinct individual from His Father.

Note again that there is a **You** and a **Me**, each of whom had his own spirit. Clearly this makes two separate individuals.

Jesus & His Father are one as His disciples are one – John 17:20-23

Again, the Father and Son are described as **You** and **Me**, **I** and **You**, clearly identifying separate individuals. They are also called **we** (verse 22) – **plural** individuals.

Further, Jesus and His Father are one **even as** His disciples should be one. How should disciples be "one"? Do we all become **one and the same individual** – one living being? No, we remain separate individuals, but we are one in purpose, faith, goals, character, doctrine, practice, etc. (1 Corinthians 1:10-13; 12:12-20, 25-27; Ephesians 4:1-4; etc.)

If the Father and Son are one individual, then this passage says all His disciples must become one individual – an impossibility! But if we are not all one individual, but the Father and Son are one **even as** we are one, then the Father and Son cannot be one individual.

Other miscellaneous points

John 17:18; 20:20,21 – As the Father sent Jesus, **even so** Jesus sent His disciples. Does a person send himself elsewhere? When Jesus sent His disciples, He was one individual sending other separate individuals to do a job for Him (compare John 1:6). Even so, when the Father sent the Son, the Father was one individual sending another individual to do a job. And note again that a Father and His Son are two distinct individuals. And You and Me are separate individuals.

(Note the Bible pictures Jesus as leaving the Father in heaven to come to earth. Then when He ascended to heaven, He went back to the Father. John 5:30,36-38; 3:16,17; 7:33; 14:12; 8:42; 6:38,57,62; 16:27,28; 17:8; 13:3; 20:17; 1 John 4:9,14; compare Matthew 6:9; 7:21; 18:19; 12:50).

John 15:24 – **Both Me and My Father**. The Father and Son together constitute **both** – **two** individuals, not just one individual. (Compare 2 John 9)

John 14:28 – My Father is greater than I. How could Jesus be greater than Himself?

1 Corinthians 11:3 – The Father is head of the Son as the Son is head of man and man is head of woman. Headship implies a relation between separate individuals. Are man and woman the same individual or different individuals? Are Jesus and man the same or different individuals? Then likewise Father and Son are different individuals. Is Jesus His own head?

1 Timothy 2:5 (compare 1 John 2:1) – Jesus is mediator (go between) *between* God and man. If God is Jesus, then who is Jesus *between*? Is He between Himself and man?

John 6:46 – No man has seen the Father. But they have seen Jesus. How then could Jesus be the Father? (Compare John 5:37.)

Philippians 2:5,6 – Jesus was on an equality with God. Was He on an equality with Himself? Note that this was even before Jesus came to earth as a man.

1 Corinthians 15:23,24 – When Jesus delivers the kingdom back to the Father, whom will He deliver it to – Himself?

Hebrews 9:14,24 – Jesus offered Himself to God and went into Heaven to appear in the presence of God for us. Did He offer Himself to Himself? Did He go into Heaven into His own presence?

(See also most of the Scriptures in the next section).

Passages that Demonstrate 3 Beings (or a Plurality of Beings) in the Godhead

We have now proved Jesus and His Father to be two separate individual beings. Consider now general evidence for plural beings in the Godhead (not necessarily specifying who they are) and other evidence that the Father, Son, and Holy Spirit are three separate beings.

Plural pronouns used for God at creation – Genesis 1:26; (3:22).

God said let *Us* make man in *Our* image after *Our* likeness. Man was created in *God's* image, not the image of angels or animals (compare verse 27). Yet God is referred to as *Us* and *Our* – terms implying plural individuals. (Similar instances exist in Genesis 3:22; 11:6,7; Isaiah 6:8. In fact ELOHIM, the most common Hebrew word for God, is plural in form.)

Other verses show that Father, Son, and Holy Spirit were all three present at creation. The Father was present (Hebrews 1:2; John 1:1-3; 17:5,24), the Son was present (Hebrews 1:2; John 1:1-3; 17:5,24; Colossians 1:16,17), and the Holy Spirit was present (Genesis 1:2; Job 33:4).

We have already shown that the Father and Son are a **We** or **Us** (John 14:23; 17:22). Clearly the one God includes a plurality of individuals.

All three were present at Jesus' baptism – Luke 3:21,22

Jesus was on earth, having been baptized, and He was praying. The **Holy Spirit** descended in a bodily form like a dove (He is not a dove but took a bodily form **like** a dove). A voice from heaven said, "**You** are **My** beloved **Son**."

The voice was clearly the Heavenly Father (compare to the transfiguration where a similar thing happened, and Peter said the voice was God the Father – Matthew 17:5; 2 Peter 1:16-18). The voice of God demonstrates the presence of God (Genesis 3:8). The very words spoken prove the speaker is not Jesus, because **You** and **I** refer to separate individuals. And a **son** cannot be the same person as his father.

And note that the Son and the Holy Spirit each had a bodily form, clearly showing them to be separate beings.

So in this story all three are present and are presented as being three separate individuals.

The Father and Son sent the Holy Spirit – John 14:16,26; 15:26; 16:7,13-15

When Jesus left the earth, He requested that the Father send the Holy Spirit to guide the apostles, etc. The pronouns used – **I** and **He** – implies these are different individuals, just as surely as Jesus and His apostles were different individuals when He referred to them as **I** and **You** (compare notes on John 17:18; 20:20,21).

The Father and Son acted together in sending the Spirit (i.e., the Son requested the Father to do it and He did do it – 14:16,26; 15:26; 16:7). When Jesus sent His apostles, He was not sending Himself. So in sending the Holy Spirit, Jesus did not send Himself, and the Father did not send Himself. The Holy Spirit was a separate individual.

And the Holy Spirit would be **another** comforter (Greek for "another" is αλλος meaning another one of the same sort). Jesus had been a source of strength & comfort, an advocate on behalf of the disciples. Now He was leaving, but did not want the disciples left alone. So He sent **another** comforter (14:26; 16:13-15). If the Spirit is the same person as Jesus, then Jesus did not send **another** comforter, but the **same** one.

The Holy Spirit would not speak from **Himself** (His own initiative), but would speak what the Father and Son provided for Him to declare (16:13-15). This distinguishes both the Father and Son from the Spirit – they must be different "selves." If the Father or the Son are the same "self" as the Spirit, then He would have been speaking from Himself.

All three are listed in Ephesians 4:4-6

This passage mentions seven things of which there is only one each in God's plan for unity: one body (the church – 1:22,23); one Spirit (the Holy Spirit – Acts 2:4; 1 Corinthians 12:3-13; Luke 4:1); one hope; one Lord (Jesus – 1 Corinthians 8:6); one faith; one baptism; one God and Father.

Note that each item listed is separate and distinct from each other item. The body is not the hope. The baptism is not the Lord. The faith is not the Father, etc. Likewise, the Father is not the Spirit, the Spirit is not the Lord, and the Lord is not the Father.

It follows that this passage is distinguishing the Father, Son, and Holy Spirit as three separate and distinct individuals.

Baptism in the name of the three – Matthew 28:19

The apostles were commanded to baptize in the name of the Father, Son, and Holy Spirit. It is clear from our studies that the Father and Son are two separate individuals. Surely then the "Holy Spirit" must also be a living individual separate from the other two. Why list two separate beings and then list a third term, which is just a part of the others or just another title for one of the others?

Other verses that mention Father, Son, and Holy Spirit, all three

2 Corinthians 13:14 – The grace of the **Lord Jesus Christ,** and the love of **God**, and the communion of the **Holy Spirit.**

Ephesians 2:18 – Through **Him (Christ)** we have access by one **Spirit** unto the **Father**.

1 Peter 1:2 – Elect according to the foreknowledge of **God the Father**, through sanctification of **the Spirit**, unto obedience and sprinkling of the blood of **Jesus Christ**.

1 Corinthians 6:11 – Justified in the name of our **Lord Jesus and** by the **Spirit** of our **God**.

(See also Acts 1:4,5; 2:32,33; 10:38; John 20:21,22; 3:34; 1 Corinthians 12:4-6; 2 Corinthians 1:21,22; Hebrews 9:14; 10:29; Romans 8:16,17; 2 Thessalonians 2:13,14; Jude 20,21.)

Other verses that distinguish Jesus from the Holy Spirit

Matthew 12:31,32 – Blasphemy against the Son would be forgiven, but blasphemy against the Holy Spirit would not be. So, the Son is not the Holy Spirit, for if He were, then blasphemy against the Spirit would be the same as blasphemy against the Son.

John 14:17,19 – The world did not behold the Spirit, but it did behold the Son. So, Jesus is not the Spirit.

Matthew 1:18 – The Holy Spirit conceived Jesus in the womb of Mary. Did the Spirit conceive Himself, or did He conceive a separate individual?

Conclusion

The Bible definitely teaches that there is only one true God. But the Bible also teaches that there are three separate and distinct individuals or living personal beings that possess Deity and are therefore in the Godhead. If the passages we have studied do not establish the plurality of individuals in the Godhead, then what is the point of these statements? Why would God make such statements if in fact there is only one individual in God?

John 17:20-23 explains the sense in which these three individuals are *one* (see previous notes). They are one even as all true believers should be one – not one individual, but united and harmonious in faith, doctrine, character, purpose, etc.

Evidence Offered to Show There Is One Individual in the Godhead

People, who believe that there is only one individual or living personal being in the Godhead ("Jesus only"), also offer evidence for their view. Let us examine this evidence.

Jesus Is Called God; There Is One God; Jesus & the Father Are One

Scriptures are cited showing terms for God are used to refer to Jesus – John 20:28; Colossians 1:16 (creator); Matthew 1:23 (God with us); Acts 20:28 (God's blood); Revelation 1:8,17; 2:8; 22:13 & 21:5-7 (Almighty and First and Last); John 8:58 (I Am); 1 Timothy 3:16; Micah 5:2 (everlasting); Titus 2:13; etc.

References are cited to show there is *one* God, and singular pronouns are used to refer to God – Deuteronomy 6:4; Isaiah 43:10-13; 44:6,8,24 (God is "alone, and formed the earth "by myself"); 45:5,22; 52:6; Zechariah 14:9; Matthew 4:10; Mark 12:29; Ephesians 4:4 compare Romans 8:9 (one Spirit must be Jesus' spirit); James 2:19.

John 10:30 – I and the Father are one. 1 John 5:7 – Father, Word, and Spirit are one (KJV). So, it is concluded that there can only be one individual in the Godhead, and that individual is Jesus. The Father and the Spirit are just different titles or different parts of that individual, etc. However:

We agree there is one God, and we agree Jesus is called God because He possesses Deity.

But we have seen that the Father and Holy Spirit are also called God because they possess Deity. **The question is: how is God**

"one" – in what sense? Is it one individual, or is there some other sense in which three individuals could be "one"?

The word "God" does not inherently mean an individual, such that "one God" is equivalent to one individual.

"God" refers to whoever created and rules the universe, Deity, whatever deserves our worship. God is one, but not necessarily one individual.

We have shown evidence that the Father, Son, and Spirit are separate individuals, yet one God.

To say there is one God does not disprove our position because it does not prove God is only one individual living Being.

John 17:20-23 explains HOW the Father and Son are one – even as believers should be one.

We are not one individual, but many different individuals. We are united as one body, one church, united in faith, practice, goals, character, etc. The inspired comparison is that there is **one God** or Godhead that consists of plural members, just as there is **one** church that consists of many members (Acts 4:32; Romans 12:4,5; 1 Corinthians 1:10-13; 12:12-27; Galatians 3:28; Ephesians 1:22,23; 2:14,16; 4:1-6,16; Philippians 1:27; 2:2; etc.)

Another illustration is Genesis 2:24 – the two become one.

A man and his wife are two separate individuals, but in marriage they are united. Yet they remain separate individuals. So God can be so united as to be called "one," yet three separate individuals.

Ten curtains joined together become "one" – Exodus 36:13,18.

They are still separate individual curtains, but when joined they are viewed as one. So the Father, Son, and Holy Spirit are separate individuals, but are so united that they are one God.

We have cited many examples where the pronouns imply plural individuals ("we," "us," "I and Thou," "I am not alone," etc.).

Plural individuals are implied in the very passages people use to make this argument: "I and my Father" (an individual and his father make two individuals); "these **three** are one."

Jesus' inspired illustration of oneness (plural individuals in the one church – John 17:20ff) shows why plural and singular pronouns are both appropriate. Sometimes believers are referred to by plural terms that emphasize the plurality of individuals – 1 Corinthians 12:12,14,18,20; Romans 12:4,5; etc. But sometimes singular terms are used to emphasize the oneness or unity of the church – Ephesians 5:25*,26*,27 ("it" is translated "her" in NASB & NIV); Ephesians 4:16

("itself"); Galatians 1:13*; 1 Timothy 5:16; compare 1 Corinthians 12:12,14,18,20,24,27,28; Galatians 3:28; Romans 12:4,5 (* asterisks indicate the Greek pronoun is feminine).

So with God, instances of singular pronouns simply emphasize the oneness of God, while the plural pronouns point out the plural individuals in that one God. This is completely legitimate grammatically. Our position can explain both the singular pronouns and the plural pronouns. But the "Jesus only" view cannot explain the plural pronouns.

Statements about the one God are intended, not to deny the plurality of individuals in God, but rather to contrast the unity of God to the plural gods of heathen idolatry.

In context those passages do not discuss the relationship of Father and Son, but contrast the true God to the various gods worshiped in heathen idolatry. Those gods have different character, authority in different areas of life or different areas of the earth, and often disagree or even war among themselves in their beliefs, purposes, teachings, and will for men. We worship, not such gods as these, but a united, harmonious God with one will and plan for us.

(To demonstrate this point, note the context of virtually all passages we have listed about the one God – Deuteronomy 4:15-40; 6:4,14; 32:15-21,35-39; Psalm 86:8-10; Isaiah 41:21-23,29; 42:5-8,17; 43:9-13; 44:6-19,24; 45:5,16-23; 46:5-10; Matthew 4:9,10.)

Finally, it is interesting that the same groups that so strongly emphasize one **God**, often at the same time practice **two** separate and distinct baptisms, despite Ephesians 4:4-6.

Father Is in the Son and Vice-Versa - John 10:38; 14:10,11; 2 Corinthians 5:19

It is affirmed that, in saying the Father is in the Son, the Bible explains how they are the same individual: the "Father" is the Spirit that dwells in the Son's body.

However:

Many other passages speak of separate persons being "IN" one another.

To say one is "in" the other does not prove they are the same individual. For example, Christians are "in Christ" and "in the Father"; and Father and Son abide "in" us – John 14:20,23; 15:4-7; 3:21; 6:56; Romans 8:1; 2 Corinthians 6:16; Galatians 2:20; 3:26-38; Ephesians 3:17; Philippians 1:1; 3:8,9; Colossians 1:27; 1 Peter 5:14; 1 John 2:6,24; 3:24; 4:12-16. Do these verses prove that we are the same individual or personal being as the Son or the Father?

(Note also that the Holy Spirit dwells in Christians – 2 Timothy 1:14; Romans 8:9; 1 Corinthians 3:16; 6:19).

God of the Bible

Again, John 17:20-23 explains the real meaning of the expression.

For Jesus to be "in the Father," and vice-versa, is here explained to mean simply that they are "one." "That they all may be **one**; as You, Father, are **in Me**, and I **in You**, that they also may be **one in Us**...; that they may be **one** just as **We are one**; I **in them, and You in Me**, that they may be made perfect in **one**..."

To say that one person is "in" another simply means that they have fellowship and unity – a harmonious, united relationship. It does not mean they are one individual.

(Compare John 1:18 – in the bosom of the Father.)

To Know Jesus is to Know the Father; to See Jesus is to See the Father (John 14:7,9; 12:45; 8:19); to Have the Son is to Have the Father (1 John 2:23); When the Spirit Came, Jesus Came (John 14:16,28.

It is argued that these expressions prove the Father, Son, and Spirit are the same individual. However:

We have already seen that the expressions used in the very context of these passages show a plurality of individuals.

They use the terms "Father" and "Son" which must refer to separate individuals. The Father and Son sent the Spirit, etc. (See previous discussion.)

Other passages use this kind of representative language.

In such expressions, separate individuals are involved, but one is viewed as a representative of the other. So if we do something to one person, it is taken to be the same as if we had done it to the other person. Note:

Mark 9:37

Whoever receives a child in Jesus' name, receives **Jesus**. Likewise, whoever receives **Jesus** receives the **One who sent** Him. This explains the languages perfectly. Is Jesus the same individual as the child? No, but the way we treat the child is taken as the way we treat Jesus. So the way we treat Jesus is the way we treat the Father.

So, Jesus' own illustration here proves that Jesus is not the same individual as the Father any more than the child is the same individual as Jesus. If Jesus is the same individual as the Father, then the child is also the same individual as Jesus!

Luke 10:16

He who hears **Jesus' messengers**, hears **Jesus**; he who despises the messengers, despises Jesus; and he who despises **Jesus**, despises the **One who sent Jesus**. Again, by Jesus' own authority, the language is exactly parallel to the verses we are studying. How we treat the messengers is how we treat Jesus, just the same as how we treat Jesus is how we treat the Father.

But are the messengers the same individual as Jesus? No, and neither is Jesus the same individual as the Father. When "Jesus' only" advocates make this argument, by taking other passages using similar language we have proved that the language actually proves Jesus is **not** the same individual as the Father. The language actually means the very opposite of what they claim! (Compare John 13:20.)

Other examples are:

Matthew 25:40,45 – Doing good to others is the same as doing good to Jesus.

Acts 9:1,4,5 – Persecuting the church is the same as persecuting Jesus.

John 3:22; 4:1,2 – When the apostles baptized, it is said that Jesus' baptized, because they acted as His representatives.

1 John 2:23 is similar, but note that the Father and Son are so united that you cannot be in fellowship with one without having fellowship with the other, nor can you be out of fellowship with the one and still be in fellowship with the other (compare 1 John 1:3 – fellowship with Father and Son = two individuals). If you reject the one, the other will not fellowship you. You cannot serve one while refusing to serve the other.

No man has literally seen the Father – John 6:46; 1:18; 5:37; 1 John 4:12.

So Jesus' expressions about seeing the Father must be taken symbolically, not literally. What is the meaning of the expression then?

John 14:10,11 explains the meaning of 14:7,9 (and the other expressions likewise).

The disciples "saw the Father" when they saw Jesus because Jesus was "in the Father and the Father in" Jesus. The Father abiding in Jesus did His works.

But we just studied this phrase above. We showed that the meaning of the expression is, not that they are the same individual, but that they are in fellowship, unity, harmony. So harmonious were their character and wills that, when Jesus worked, the work He did was the Father's work.

John 1:18 also explains.

No one has literally seen the Father, but the Son **declared** Him. The Son is not the same individual as the Father, but He is so like the Father and knows the Father so well that He is the one best qualified to reveal what the Father is like. In fact, the Father and Son are so alike

God of the Bible

that, when we know what Jesus is like, we know exactly what the Father is like.

Hebrews 1:3 – Jesus is the "express image" of God's person.

Colossians 1:15 – He is the **image** of the **invisible** God. An image is not the same thing as that which it is a likeness of (compare Genesis 1:26,27). We cannot literally see the Father when we see Jesus. But they are so alike that, when you see Jesus, you have seen what the Father is like. When you know Jesus, you know what the Father is like.

Compare this to our expressions: "Like father, like son." "He's the exact image of his father." "When you've seen one, you've seen 'em all."

"In the Name of"

It is argued that God has one name (Zechariah 14:9; compare Isaiah 52:6). Jesus came in the Father's name (John 5:43; 10:25), and the Spirit came in Jesus' name (John 14:26). So it is argued they must all have the same name ("Jesus") and must therefore all be the same individual. ("Father," "Son," and "Holy Spirit" are said to be "titles," not names.) Other verses are added to show how important God's name is.

Further, we are told we must baptize in the name of Jesus (Acts 2:38; 8:16; 10:48; 19:5; compare 4:12; 2:21 – salvation in no other name), and this is what must be **said**. Matthew 28:19 is baptism in **the name** (one name) of the Father, Son, and Holy Spirit. They all have the same name, and that name is "Jesus." So we must baptize in the name of Jesus only.

However:

Even if Father, Son, and Holy Spirit all did have the same name, that would not prove they are the same individual.

Often different individuals have the same name. A father and son share a common name, but they are not the same individual. In marriage, a woman takes her husband's name, but she is still a separate individual.

In fact, however, these expressions do not mean the three do have the same name, as we will see.

One individual can act "in the name of" another individual, yet they are still two distinct individuals.

To say that one acts "in the name of" another does not prove they have the same name, still less does it prove they **are** the same individual.

Those who baptize "in Jesus' name" (only) should be asked: If you baptize a person "in Jesus' name," does that make **you** and Jesus the same individual?!

Bible examples:

    * Inspired men gave commands in the name of the Lord – Acts 9:27,29; 2 Thessalonians 3:6; James 5:10.

    * Christians should assemble in Jesus' name – Matthew 18:20.

    * We can receive a child in Jesus' name – Mark 9:37.

    * Apostles did miracles in Jesus' name – Acts 3:6; 16:18.

    * The name of God would be called upon the Gentiles – Acts 15:17.

    * Everything we do, in word or deed, should be done in Jesus' name – Colossians 3:17. (Study also John 17:11,12; 1 Corinthians 6:11; 5:4; Matthew 18:5; Revelation 3:12.)

When a person acts "in the name of" another person, that does not mean they both have the same name, and even less does it prove they are the same individual. In fact, the expression does not even mean we must **say** "in Jesus' name" every time we so act.

The expression "in the name of" actually means "by the authority of," "on behalf of," etc. (Random House College Dictionary).

It is an expression showing that one individual is acting as the **representative** of another, acting in accordance with his will and instructions, by his authority. So we still have two separate individuals, but one represents or acts on behalf of the other, just as in the above Bible examples.

Note carefully Acts 4:7-10.

"By what **name**" (verses 7,10) = "by what **power**" (verse 7) = "by what **means**" (verse 9) = "by **Him**" (verse 10). (Compare Ephesians 1:21.)

Other examples:

"Stop, in the name of the law," means one person issues a command acting as a representative by authority of the law.

An ambassador acts "in the name of" a country – by the authority of that country, empowered by its laws, as its official representative, acting on its behalf.

When you sign a check, your name authorizes your bank to transfer funds on your behalf and pay your money, acting in your name.

So, Jesus came in His Father's name because the Father sent Him, He was the Father's representative, acting on His behalf, to do the Fathers' will. Likewise, the Spirit came in Jesus' name in the same way.

This shows how Matthew 28:19 (in the name of the Father, Son, and Holy Spirit) harmonizes with Acts 2:38, etc. (in the name of Jesus).

The Father, Son, and Holy Spirit are three separate Beings; but they all have exactly the same will or authority, for they are completely in harmony and united in will. What one authorizes is what the others authorize. What one says to do is what the others say to do. **To act by the authority (in the name of) one, then, is to act by the authority (in the name of) all three, for it is the same authority.** The three are the same, not in the sense that they are the same individual, nor that they all wear the name "Jesus," but in that they all have the same **will or authority**.

(Note, for example, that an ambassador might say he acts "in the name of the President of the USA," or he might say he acts "in the name of the President, the Congress, and the people of the USA" The statements are both correct, but they do not mean that the President, Congress, and people are all the same individual. The statements simply mean that he acts by the authority of all three, but all three share the same will or authority in acting through him.)

In Jesus Dwells All Fullness of the Godhead Bodily - Colossians 2:9

Some claim this means that all the Godhead is fully embodied in Jesus – Father, Son, and Holy Spirit. So, Jesus is all there is. However:

We must understand the term "Godhead" (KJV).

Other translations say "all the fullness of **Deity**" (NASB, RSV, NIV, etc.). "Godhead" means Deity, Godhood, the essence or substance of God, the state or condition of being God (see Vine, Thayer, etc.).

Fullness means a full measure – that which completely fills a thing.

But it does not mean that no one else can possess the fullness of that quality also. (Compare Ephesians 3:19.)

If I say, "In my wife dwells all the fullness of womanhood or femininity," I would not mean that she is the **one and only person** who possesses womanhood or femininity, and no one else is feminine. I would mean that she is totally and completely feminine, but that would not prove that she is the only individual in existence who is feminine.

So, Colossians 2:9 means that Jesus fully and completely possesses Deity or Godhood: He is filled with the essence and nature of God. But that does not prove Deity is a single person, nor does it prove no other individual can possess that Deity.

Jesus Is Called the "Everlasting Father" - Isaiah 9:6

Some teach that this proves Jesus is the same individual being as His Heavenly Father.

However:

The word "father" is used in different ways.

Genesis 45:8 – Joseph was a father to Pharaoh.
Job 29:16 – Job was a father to the poor.
Romans 4:11,12,16 – Abraham is father of all believers.

John 8:38,41,44 – The Devil is father of all wicked people.

Clearly people can be called "father" in different senses of the word, or in different relationships. Just because two people are referred to as "father," does not prove they are the same individual.

In particular, separate individuals can be called "father" in different relationships, but no one can be a father or son to Himself.

Enos Pratte is a father to me, and I in turn am a father to my son Timothy. My father and I are both fathers, but we are not the same individual. No one can be his own father or his own son.

So the Heavenly Father and Jesus are both "fathers." Jesus is a "father" to every one of us in that He created the universe (compare John 1:3; Colossians 1:15; Hebrews 1:2). But no Scripture says that Jesus is "Father" in relationship to **Himself,** but that must be true in order for Him to be the same person as the Heavenly Father.

The Holy Spirit Is Just a Force or Power, not a Personal Being

Some say the Holy Spirit cannot be a separate individual, because it is not a personal being but just a force. However:

Consider the following personal characteristics of the Spirit.

How can a non-personal force possess these qualities?

John 16:13 – The Spirit **hears**.

1 Corinthians 12:8 – The Spirit **gives** gifts.

Acts 15:28 – He **decides** or determines whether or not an act is good.

1 Corinthians 6:11 – He **justifies**.

Romans 15:30 – He **loves**.

Acts 5:9 – He can be **tried** or tested.

1 Corinthians 12:11 – He **wills** (power to choose).

Romans 8:27 – He has a **mind**.

1 Corinthians 2:11 – He **knows**.

Acts 5:3 – He can be **lied** to.

Ephesians 4:30; Isaiah 63:10 – He can be **grieved**.

In addition, many Scriptures we have cited list the Holy Spirit right along with the Father and the Son.

He is indicated as acting with them. If the Father and Son are living beings, surely the Spirit is just as much so. Why list two personal beings, and then right along side list an impersonal force?

The Word "Trinity" Is not in the Bible.

"Trinity" is a word for three persons in the one Godhead. It is argued that, if this is a true doctrine, the word would surely be used in the Bible.

God of the Bible

But we have clearly established from the Bible the truth that there is one God, but three separate and distinct individuals in that God.

The fact that a particular word is not found, does not prove the doctrine is not found.

In the present study we have defended our view at length, but up till now have never used the word "Trinity." We use the word now only to answer an objection raised by those who disagree. The word "Trinity" is in no way essential to our belief. The Bible can and does establish the doctrine without ever using the word "Trinity," and we have done the same.

People who believe "Jesus only" generally hold ideas for which neither the word nor the concept is found in the Bible.

Many, for example, are members of groups called "United Pentecostal Church" or similar names. Neither this name nor the concept can be found in the Bible. Yet they criticize us because a certain word is not found in the Bible, even though the doctrine itself is clearly taught there.

Miscellaneous Arguments

1 John 5:7

This passage says, in the King James Version, "these three are one" (referring to the Father, Son, and Holy Spirit). But many translations do not contain the verse, because it is missing from some ancient Bible manuscripts. It is argued that people who believe in the "Trinity" added this verse to the Bible so they could defend their belief.

However, without making one single reference to 1 John 5:7, we have abundantly established our belief in one God who consists of three distinct individuals. Regardless of whether or not this verse is inspired, we can easily establish our position by other verses that are unquestionably authentic.

Many of the same people, who make this argument on 1 John 5:7, will defend their view of miracles using arguments that depend on Mark 16:17,18, even though that passage also is not found in some ancient manuscripts. This is self-contradictory.

John 3:13

Jesus came down from heaven, yet He said He is *in* heaven. So it is argued He is both the Son on earth and the Father in heaven at the same time.

This phrase is equivalent to John 1:18 – the Son *is* in the bosom of the Father, even though He was on earth at the time. Note that, for Jesus to say He was "in" heaven or "in the bosom of the Father" did not mean that He was the same individual as the Father.

While He was physically on earth, He continued a unique spiritual relationship with the Father. He was in the bosom of the Father, but He was not His own Father. Nothing here disproves our evidence for three individuals in God.

1 Timothy 3:16

Jesus was God **manifest** in the flesh. So it is argued He is not really a separate individual from His Father, but is just a **manifestation** of the Father.

But to manifest means to reveal or make known. A person can manifest or reveal the character or will of another person – 2 Corinthians 4:10. Compare John 1:18 – since no one can see the Father, Jesus revealed Him for men. Nothing here proves the Father and Son were not separate individuals.

Isaiah 43:10; 44:6,8; compare Revelation 1:8,17; 2:8; 21:5-7; 22:13

No god was formed before or after God. He is "first and last." But it is argued that, if another person is also God, then that person must have been formed before or after God. One or the other must have come "first."

However, the answer is that all three Beings are eternal (compare Micah 5:2). So, none was formed before or after the other. All three have existed eternally. We have already shown that the Son was with the Father before the world began. So any "god" formed later surely would not be the true God. But all three Beings of the Godhead are separate individuals, none of whom were formed later than the others.

"First and last" simply refers to eternal existence. All three are eternal and together they form one God, besides whom there is no God. Nothing here contradicts anything we have said.

Matthew 28:18

Jesus has all power in heaven and on earth. John 3:31 – He is above all. Philippians 2:9; Ephesians 1:21 – His name is exalted above all names. We are asked to explain how all three could be Deity if Jesus has **all** power and is **above** all, etc. What power can the Father and Spirit have? (Compare 1 Timothy 6:15,16).

The very passages cited mention both the Father and the Son who, as we have seen, must be separate individuals (Ephesians 1:17). If Jesus was "equal" with the Father, then He must not be the same individual – what would it mean to say someone is equal with Himself?

The passages are simply saying that, when Jesus came to earth, He humbled Himself to act as a servant like men are (Philippians 2:7,8). When He had perfectly accomplished His mission, God exalted Him again to a position of supreme authority, higher than any other authority (Philippians 2:9-11; Ephesians 1:17-21).

God of the Bible

But in doing this, did God exalt Jesus above the very One who was exalting Him? We must take all the Bible says on a subject, and the Bible expressly states that the Father is an exception. He is not subject to Jesus' authority (1 Corinthians 15:24,27,28).

Jesus' exaltation gives glory to God (Philippians 2:11). Clearly the implication is that Jesus has authority over all created things, in heaven and on earth. But this does not mean he has authority over the Father. Nothing here is intended to say that the Father and the Holy Spirit do not possess authority of Deity as surely as the Son does. (Compare 1 Corinthians 11:3).

Matthew 1:18

The Holy Spirit conceived Jesus in Mary's womb. But if the Holy Spirit and the Father are two separate beings, how can the Father be called Jesus' Father if the Holy Spirit conceived Jesus?

Regardless of the Holy Spirit, this passage clearly proves the **Son** is a separate Being from the Father. Surely God did not conceive Himself! A Father and His Son are two separate individuals.

But Jesus' conception was not a normal conception – no one had physical intercourse with Mary. Miraculous intervention was involved. Probably the point is that this was done by the Father by means of the Holy Spirit, just as God does other miracles through the Spirit and like God created the worlds through Jesus (Hebrews 1:2; compare Luke 1:35). The one is said to act, but the act is done by another individual as His representative (see previous notes).

In any case the terms "Father and Son" primarily refer to a **relationship** that exists between two individuals, which is similar to that between fathers and sons (as Abraham is the father of believers, etc.). Jesus is eternal as the Father is, so there was no real procreation as earthly fathers do.

Acts 8:16

"**Only** they were baptized in the name of Jesus" – it is said this means baptism is in the name of Jesus only – one individual not three!

Read the context! Nothing is said about Jesus in contrast to Father and Holy Spirit, or regarding number of Beings in God. They were **only** baptized in Jesus' name, in contrast to receiving miraculous powers by the Spirit (verses 14-16). They had not received the Holy Spirit; they had only been baptized!

Revelation 22:16

Jesus is both root (ancestor) and offspring of David. So one person can be both his own ancestor and his own descendant.

But this passage proves **our** point. Jesus and David are two separate individuals, not the same individual. Jesus cannot be both root and offspring to **Himself**, especially not while His Father still exists, and He prays to Him, etc. A father and his son are still two individuals.

Is God a "person"?

Some argue that the Bible never calls God a "person" at all, so how can there be **three** persons in God? A person must have flesh and bones (Luke 24:39). However:

Hebrews 1:3 says Jesus is the express image of God's "**person**" (KJV). So God is a person and Jesus is His express image, so He is another person.

Luke 24:39 does not say a "person" must have flesh and bones. It just says a "spirit" does not have flesh and bones.

We have defined what we mean by three individuals in God, and that definition has nothing to do with flesh and bones.

Conclusion

The Bible does not teach the doctrine that God consists of just one individual. Where then did the idea come from? Here is the explanation given by the United Pentecostal Church:

> "In the year 1914 came the revelation on the name of the Lord Jesus Christ. The pivotal doctrines of the absolute deity of Jesus Christ and the baptism in His name became tenets of faith." (Foreword, *United Pentecostal Church Manual*, via *The Oneness Doctrine of Pentecostalism*, G. Frost, page 3; compare Wallace-Vaughn Debate, page 86)

This explains why we did not find the doctrine in the Bible: it was not revealed until nearly 1900 years later! The Scriptures provide us to all good works (2 Timothy 3:16,17), but this doctrine was not revealed till nearly 1900 years later. To preach and believe it, therefore, must not be a good work.

The doctrine was revealed nearly 1900 years too late to be part of the gospel preached by the original apostles and prophets. Therefore, it must not be true, for they received all truth (John 16:13). Further it must be a different gospel, and those who preach it are accursed (Galatians 1:8,9). Those who teach it have neither the Father nor the Son and we must not bid them Godspeed (2 John 9-11).

God of the Bible

The Deity of Jesus

Introduction:

The purpose of this study is to examine Bible claims regarding the Deity of Jesus.

Did Jesus and the inspired Bible writers claim that Jesus possessed Deity? Was He God in the flesh? Did He possess the characteristics of Deity? Did He do the works and accept the honors and glory of Deity?

Some people, who claim to believe in Jesus, would yet deny that Jesus is God in the same sense that God the Father is God. Others believe that Jesus did not possess the characteristics and power of Deity, or that He did not possess these characteristics while on earth.

It is not the purpose of this study to deny or in any way belittle the humanity of Jesus on earth. He was both God and man, God in the flesh. Several verses we will study will confirm this. However, the purpose of this study is to focus on Jesus' Deity, not on His humanity.

Limited humans are unable to fully understand God's nature and character.

God is infinite; we are finite. Our human limitations make it impossible for us to fully comprehend God (Romans 11:33-36; Job 26:14; 11;7; 36:26; 37:5,23; Isaiah 40:28; 55:8,9; Deuteronomy 29:29). Therefore, neither this nor any other study will answer all questions about God.

However, by faith we can accept as true whatever the Bible says about God and specifically about the Deity of Jesus. We can believe revealed truths even when we cannot fully explain how they can be so or answer all questions about them. (Compare 1 Corinthians 2:9-11; 2 Timothy 3:16,17).

For example, we can believe that God is eternal and that He answers prayer. But who can fully grasp the concept of eternity or explain in detail **how** God can hear and answer the prayers of so many people? Likewise, we cannot explain how Jesus could be both God and man at the same time, yet we must still believe and not deny the Bible teaching.

Consider some definitions:

The following definitions are my summary of Bible teaching. I will not cite specific Scriptures at this point, but our study will show that these definitions fit Bible teaching.

"God" – The eternal, independent, self-existent Supreme Monarch or Ruler who created the universe, sustains its existence, and who therefore possesses absolute power and sovereignty over all created things. God alone is infinite in knowledge, power, and holiness. So, only God is worthy to be worshiped as Deity by man.

"Godhead" – same as God

"Deity" – The essence or substance of God; the state or quality or condition of being God

"Godhood" – same as Deity

"Divine" – possessing Deity; having qualities or characteristics possessed by God

"Creation" – Everything that has been created or brought into existence by the supernatural power of God. The creation includes the earth, the heavenly bodies, and everything in or on them, including plants, animals, and men.

The character of God is unchangeable.

Hebrews 13:8 – Jesus is the same yesterday, today, and forever. This refers to the characteristics of Deity. God's laws have changed from Old Testament to New Testament in harmony with God's eternal plan. His works also change (He is not, for example, still dying on the cross). Jesus also took on the characteristics of man, but He could never lose the qualities of Deity.

God's nature cannot change. If the Father, Son, and Holy Spirit ever possessed the characteristics of Deity, then they always possessed them and always will possess them. They may choose at times not to exercise certain powers, but they must always possess those powers.

To say that Jesus (or the Father or the Spirit) ever at any time failed to possess any characteristic of Deity is to (perhaps unknowingly) deny His Deity. God could not lose the characteristics of Deity without ceasing to be Deity. That is impossible. God cannot cease to be God.

The Bible teaches the existence of only one true God.

Some people claim that Jesus could not possess Deity, because they say that would make two gods (the Father and the Son); whereas the Bible says there is only one God.

God of the Bible

We agree the Bible teaches there is **one** God and that singular pronouns are used to refer to God – Deuteronomy 4:35,39; 6:4; Isaiah 43:10-13; 44:6-8,24; 45:5,6,14,18,21-23; 52:6; Matthew 4:10. (See also 2 Samuel 7:22; 1 Chronicles 17:20; Exodus 20:3-6; 34:14; Deuteronomy 6:13-15; 32:39; Psalm 86:10; Zechariah 14:9; Mark 12:29; 1 Corinthians 8:4-6; James 2:19; 1 Timothy 2:5.)

The question is **how** is God "one" – in what sense? Is God one individual, or could several individual beings constitute one God?

The word "God" does not necessarily mean a single individual, such that "one God" is equivalent to one individual. God simply means Deity, the Creator and Ruler of the universe, whatever possesses the characteristics of Deity and therefore deserves to be worshiped. God is one, but not necessarily one individual.

John 17:20-23 explains *how* the Father and Son are *one* – even as believers should be one.

But believers are not one individual; they are many different individuals. We are united as one body, one church, united in faith, practice, goals, character, etc. (Acts 4:32; 1 Corinthians 1:10-13; Ephesians 1:22,23; 2:14,16; Philippians 1:27; 2:2; etc.)

Sometimes believers are referred to by plural terms that emphasize the plurality of individuals – 1 Corinthians 12:12,14,18,20; Romans 12:4,5; etc. But sometimes singular terms are used to emphasize the oneness or unity of the church – Ephesians 5:25,26 ("it" is translated "her" in NASB & NIV; the Greek pronoun is feminine); Ephesians 4:3-6,16 ("itself"); Galatians 1:13; 1 Timothy 5:16; compare 1 Corinthians 12:12-28; Galatians 3:28; Romans 12:4,5.

Likewise, Jesus said He and His Father are "one" (John 10:30; 17:20ff). But are they just one individual? The **one God** or Godhead consists of plural members just as the **one** church consists of many members

Another illustration: Genesis 2:24 says a man and his wife become one.

The man and wife are still two separate individuals, but in marriage they are united. So God can be so united as to be called "one," yet three separate individuals. (Note that "man" can refer to all humanity or to a particular individual who possesses humanity.)

The singular pronouns used for God emphasize God's oneness, while the plural pronouns point out the plural individuals in that one God. This is completely legitimate grammatically.

Statements affirming the oneness of God are intended, not to deny there are a plurality of individuals in God, but to contrast to the plural gods of heathen idol worship. The contexts are not discussing the relationship of the Father to the Son, but are contrasting the true God to the plurality of different gods such as heathen idol worshipers embrace. Heathen gods have different character, possess authority in different areas of life or different areas of the earth, and often disagree and even war among themselves. They differ in their beliefs, purposes, teachings, and their wills for men. In contrast, the Bible teaches that we worship a united, harmonious God with one will and plan for us.

So to affirm that Jesus possesses Deity is not to deny the concept of one God. We can believe in one God and still believe that the Father and the Son and the Holy Spirit all possess Deity.

(Note, for example, the context of virtually all the passages above – Deuteronomy 4:15-40; 6:4,14; 32:15-21,35-39; Psalm 86:8-10; Isaiah 41:21-23,29; 42:5-8,17; 43:9-13; 44:6-19,24; 45:5,16-23; 46:5-10; Matthew 4:9,10.)

General Passages Affirming Jesus' Deity

John 1:1

"In the beginning was the Word, and the Word was with God, and the Word was God." The "Word" refers to Jesus (verses 14-17), the only begotten of the Father who became flesh and dwelt among us (verse 14). This affirms that Jesus is a separate individual from the Father (He was **with** God), and yet He Himself possesses Deity (He **was** God). Note that the context affirms both Jesus' Deity and His humanity: God became flesh and dwelt among us.

Some argue that the Greek "was God" has no definite article before "God," whereas there is a definite article in "with God." So, it is claimed that Jesus is god is a lesser sense, different from the Father. So, the "New World Translation" says, "the word was a god." However,

(1) **All major standard translations say, "the Word was God."** None say "a god." So they contradict the NWT. (See NKJV, KJV, ASV, NASB, RSV, NIV, etc.).

(2) **If Jesus is "god" in a lesser sense than the Father, then we would have *two* different true gods!** Clearly Jesus is not a false god; so He is true God. But if He is "god" in a different sense than the Father, that would violate the passages saying there is one true God!

(3) **Many Scriptures use "God" (Gk. θεος) *without* an article to refer to the true God.** See Matthew 5:9; 6:24; Luke 1:35,78; John 1:6,12,13,18; Romans 17:17; and many others.

(4) **Many Scriptures use "God" both with and without an article in the same context, yet both uses clearly refer to the true God.** See Matthew 4:3,4; 12:28; Luke 20:37,38; John 3:2; 13:3; Acts 5:29,30; Romans 1:7,8,17-19; 2:16,17; 3:5,22,23; 4:2,3; etc.

God of the Bible

(5) **The context of John 1:1-3 shows that Jesus is eternal and created all things.** (See our later discussion on the character and works of Jesus). To call Him "God" in such a context must surely mean He is God in the same exalted sense as the Father.

(6) **We will soon see other passages referring to Jesus as "God" using the definite article.** If the NWT distinction is valid, then these passages must prove conclusively that Jesus is God in the same sense as the Father.

So, John 1:1 refers to both Jesus and the Father as "God" in a context that affirms the eternal existence of Jesus and that He is the Creator of all (verses 1-3). This would be blasphemy if He does not possess Deity as the Father does.

(Marshall, Vine, Vincent, Lenski, Robertson, and other Greek scholars contend that the article is absent from "was God" in John 1:1, not to imply that Jesus was a "lesser god," but simply to identify "God" as the predicate nominative despite the fact it precedes the verb for emphasis – Colwell's Rule. If it had the definite article, that would imply that "the Word" and the Father are the same person. In any case, the Scriptures listed above clearly show that the lack of the article does not prove Jesus is God in a lesser sense than the Father.)

Colossians 2:9

"For in Him dwells all the fullness of the Godhead bodily" (NKJV, KJV, ASV). Or: "For in Him all the fulness of Deity dwells in bodily form" (NASB, RSV, NIV is similar).

"Fulness" (πληροωμα) means "...that which is brought to fulness or completion ... sum total, fulness, even (super) abundance ... of something ... the full measure of deity ... Colossians 2:9" – Bauer-Arndt-Gingrich.

"Godhead" or "Deity" (θεοτης) means: "...the state of being God, Godhead ..." – Grimm-Wilke-Thayer. Trench says the language here means Jesus "was, and is, absolute and perfect God" (quoted in Vine, Vol. I, pages 328,329).

So the passage says that, in Jesus dwelt bodily "the full measure of" "the state of being God."

(Some claim that Jesus possesses only the *characteristics* of God, not His essence or substance. This confuses the language. The word used here for "Deity" (θεοτης) means the essence or state of being God. A different word (θειοτης) means "divinity" or the characteristics of God. See the definitions. Nevertheless, how could Jesus possess "all the full measure of the characteristics of God in a bodily form" without being God? Even if the mistaken definition were accurate, the passage would still prove Jesus is God.)

Hebrews 1:3

Jesus was "the express image of His [the Father's] person" (NKJV, KJV) or "the very image of his substance" (ASV), "the exact representation of His nature" (NASB), "the exact representation of his being" (NIV). The context describes Jesus as the Creator, far above the angels so that He deserves to be worshiped (as will be considered in more detail later.)

"Express image" (χαραχτηρ) means "the exact expression ... of any person or thing, marked likeness, precise reproduction in every respect (compare facsimile) ..." – Grimm-Wilke-Thayer (compare Bauer-Arndt-Gingrich).

"Person" (υποστασις) means "the substantial quality, nature, of any person or thing ..." – Grimm-Wilke-Thayer. Or "...substantial nature, essence, actual being, reality ... a(n exact) representation of his (= God's) real being Hebrews 1:3..." – Bauer-Arndt-Gingrich.

So, Jesus is "the precise reproduction in every respect" of the "essence, actual being, reality" of God. How can Jesus be an exact expression of the real being of the Father without Himself possessing true Deity?

We will see that God possesses certain characteristics that are so unique that no one but God can possess them (eternal, all-powerful, etc.). If no one but God possesses these, yet Jesus is the exact reproduction of the essence of God's nature, then He must possess these qualities. But if Jesus possesses all qualities that are unique to God, He must be God, He must possess Deity.

Philippians 2:6-8

Christ existed in the form of God, but did not consider it robbery (a thing to be grasped – ASV) to be equal with God. He made Himself of no reputation (emptied himself – ASV), took the form of a servant and came in likeness of a man, He was found in appearance as a man, and humbled Himself even to the death on the cross. The teaches the following:

Before coming to earth, Jesus existed in the form of God (verse 6).

This is so translated in KJV, NKJV, ASV, NASB, RSV. NIV says: "being in very nature God."

"Form" (μορφη) – "the special or characteristic form or feature of a person or thing..." – Vine.

This must mean that Jesus truly possessed Deity before He came to earth. Verse 7 uses the same word to say that He took the form (μορφη) of a servant. Was Jesus really a servant on earth? Of course, He was (Matthew 20:28; John 13:1-6; 2 Corinthians 8:9; Acts 4:27,30 ASV). It follows that, before He came to earth, He really possessed the nature of God.

We have already learned that God cannot lose the characteristics of God. So, if Jesus ever possessed those characteristics, then He always possessed them, including while He was on earth. He could never exist without possessing those qualities, and nothing here or elsewhere says otherwise.

God of the Bible

He did not consider it robbery to be equal with God (verse 6).

KJV & NKJV so translate. Others say he did not count the being on equality with God a thing to be grasped (ASV, NASB, RSV, NIV). Some claim these latter translations mean He was not equal with God and did not exalt Himself to try to become equal with God. Such a view would contradict the context and all other passages we will study.

As already shown, verse 6 and many other passages say that Jesus really existed in the form of God. So, Paul has already said Jesus was equal with God.

Verse 7 shows that Jesus made Himself of no reputation or emptied Himself by becoming a man. The context is not discussing whether or not Jesus wanted to **exalt** Himself to become **greater** than He had been. It is showing that He already **had** an exalted position but was willing to humble Himself and take a lower status and reputation than what He had. So, verse 6 is discussing a position Jesus already possessed (Deity) but was willing to also accept a lower position (humanity). It is not discussing whether He sought to achieve some higher position.

The meaning then is that Jesus **was** equal to God, but He did not consider that as something He had to jealously hold to or retain (a thing to be grasped). He was not like a robber, taking something that did not belong to Him and then clinging to it with determination. He "did not look upon equality with God as above all things to be clung to" (TCNT). He was by right equal with God from the beginning, then willingly humbled Himself to the position of a servant.

He made Himself of no reputation or emptied Himself (verse 7).

KJV & NKJV say He made Himself of no reputation. Others say He emptied Himself (ASV, NASB, RSV), or made himself nothing (NIV). What does this mean?

"Empty" (κενοω) – "...1. to empty, make empty ... Philippians 2:7 ... 2. to make void i.e. deprive of force, render vain, useless, of no effect ... 3. to make void i.e. cause a thing to be seen to be empty, hollow, false ..." – Grimm-Wilke-Thayer.

In what sense did Jesus make Himself empty? Some say He gave up, lost, and no longer possessed some characteristics of Deity. But that is impossible, as already discussed. God cannot lose the qualities of God (Hebrews 13:8). Where does the verse say He emptied Himself of the characteristics of God? Neither this nor any other passage so states.

Just keep reading! The context proceeds to explain that He emptied himself by "taking the form of a servant," and coming as a man He "humbled himself becoming obedient" even to die on the cross (verses 7,8). He emptied Himself by humbling himself as an obedient human servant. That is the explanation the passage gives. To argue anything else is to argue against the passage!

Jesus did not lose the characteristics of Deity but added the characteristics of a servant, a man. He lived a life of obedience and service. In so doing, He humbled Himself. What He sacrificed was His reputation, privileges, glory, honor, and status in the eyes of men. He did not "appear" on earth before men in the glory He had in heaven, but He "appeared" as a man, a servant.

So He "emptied Himself of His privileges" (NKJV footnote). He "laid aside His privileges" (NASB). So, the KJV & NKJV are right: He "made Himself of no reputation." It was His reputation and glory He lost, not His Divine powers and characteristics.

Jesus came here to experience first-hand what it means to be a servant, so He could leave us a perfect example of how we should obey the Father. Then He died as the sacrifice for our sins (Hebrews 5:8,9; 4:15,16; John 5:30,43; 12:49,50; 8:28,29,42; 14:10; 6:38; 4:34; 7:16). To accomplish His purposes as a man, He served and obeyed His Father as other men must. This required Him at times to not exercise His Divine powers. He voluntarily limited Himself so as not to use His powers in ways that would contradict His purposes as a man. But nothing here or elsewhere says He ever lost, gave up, or failed to possess those powers.

After His perfect service on earth, God again exalted Him to that place of honor and glory He previously enjoyed (verses 10,11; see notes below on John 17:5; etc.). This again shows that what He gave up was honor, exaltation, etc., on earth, but He received it back afterward.

For more passages stating Jesus is God (John 20:28 and others), see the next section.

(Note: Verse 5 shows that Paul discusses all this primarily to teach us to have the mind of Christ. We should be willing to have the kind of attitude He had. But if the passage teaches that Jesus divested Himself of Deity, how could we have that attitude? We could not do so if we wished. But we can "humble" ourselves and make ourselves servants to others to the point of obeying God's will for us. That is what Jesus did, and that is the lesson. To claim that Jesus lost His fundamental nature would defeat the purpose of Paul's writing, since we cannot do that anyway.)

Jesus Wears the Unique Names of God.

The Bible uses certain terms that refer only to the true God or are used in ways that show they refer to the true God. We will see that inspired men used these unique terms to refer to Jesus. This would be blasphemy if Jesus did not possess Deity.

"God"

The Old Testament word for "God" is ELOHIM (and the variations EL, ELAH, ELOAH). It comes from a root meaning "to fear and reverence," emphasizing the respect that is due God because of His power and authority. The corresponding New Testament word is THEOS (θεος).

Since the Bible teaches there is only one true God, if the word is used for Jesus then He must possess true Deity (unless something in context shows He is a false god or that an exceptional meaning is being employed).

We have already studied some general passages where forms of this word are used for Jesus: John 1:1; Colossians 2:9; and Philippians 2:6. Consider these other cases:

John 20:28,29

After he saw proof of Jesus' resurrection, Thomas addressed Jesus as "my Lord and my God" (KJV, NKJV, ASV, NASB, RSV, NEB, NIV). Clearly Thomas is here calling Jesus "God." Consider:

This statement is clearly addressed to Jesus. Some claim Thomas spoke to the Father, but the passage clearly shows "Thomas answered and said *to Him*," i.e., to Jesus.

The word for God is θεος *with the definite article*. According to their argument on John 1:1, even Jehovah's Witnesses must admit that this means the one *true* God, in the same sense as the Father.

If Jesus did not possess Deity, Thomas' statement would have been blasphemy, and Jesus should have rebuked Him. Instead, Jesus praised Thomas and pronounced a blessing on everyone who believes the same (verse 29)!

Note further that Thomas combined the terms "Lord" and "God" in a phrase of address to Jesus. These terms, when so combined in the Scriptures, are always a term of address for the True God.

Hebrews 1:8

The Father said to Son, "Your throne, O God, is forever and ever" (KJV, NKJV, ASV, NASB, RSV, NEB, NIV). This is a quotation from Psalm 45:6,7, which is translated exactly the same (KJV, NKJV, ASV, NASB, NIV).

Note that God the Father Himself is here addressing Jesus as "God" (compare verses 1-9).

Further "God" here has the definite article so even Witnesses must admit it refers to the one True God.

To try to avoid the force of the argument, the Witnesses' "New World Translation" says, "God is thy throne for ever

and ever." This makes "God" the subject of the sentence, not a noun of address. However:

    * *The translation "God is thy throne..." is meaningless and absurd.* How could God be Jesus' throne? God is not a throne, but a person. No Scripture elsewhere ever uses such language.

    * *No other standard translation so translates Hebrews* 1:8. All translate "Thy throne, O God, ..." (see above). (The ASV places in the footnote "Thy throne is God...," and the RSV and NEB have "God is thy throne" as footnotes, but none of them accept it as being the best translation here. The others do not even list it as a possibility.)

    * *On Psalm 45:6,7 no standard translation gives "Your throne is God" as even a possibility in the footnote!* Keil & Delitzsch say, regarding such translation, that it "cannot possibly be supported in Hebrew by any syntax." So, even if it could be grammatically possible in the Greek of Hebrews 1:8, it is **not** possible in the Hebrew passage from which Hebrews 1:8 is quoted! (ASV footnote on Psalm 45:6 has "Thy throne is *the throne of* God...," adding the italicized words." But this is not possible in Hebrews 1:8!)

(Virtually all recognized Greek scholars agree that "God" in Hebrews 1:8 is a noun of address, not the subject nor a predicate nominative. This includes all the standard translations (as above) plus Arndt & Gingrich, Vine, Vincent, Marshall, and Keil. Lenski adds: "...only the unwillingness of commentators to have the Son addressed so directly as ... 'God' causes the search for a different construction." So, it is not the original language that motivates the translation but the preconceived beliefs of the translators!)

So, the **only** possible translation that fits **both** the Greek of Hebrews 1:8 **and** the Hebrew of Psalm 45:6 is "Your throne, O God, is for ever and ever." God the Father Himself called Jesus "God" (with the definite article).

Psalm 102:24

"I said, O my God, Do not take me away..." Hebrews 1:10-12 directly quotes Psalm 102:25-27 and says that it was spoken "to the Son" (verse 8). The context of Psalm 102:24 shows it is clearly addressed to the same person addressed in verses 25-27.

So, in verse 24 Jesus is addressed as "O my God."

Isaiah 9:6

Jesus' name would be called "Wonderful, Counselor, Mighty God..." This is clearly a prophecy of the Son, as seen in the beginning of the verse. So, Jesus is called "Mighty God."

Some respond that there is no definite article, but this position has been answered on John 1:1 (see notes there). Note also Isaiah 10:21 where identical language (EL-GIBBOR), without the article, clearly refers to the one true God (even in the NWT). Compare Jeremiah 32:18; Deuteronomy 10:17; Nehemiah 9:32.

Titus 2:13

"...looking for the blessed hope and glorious appearing of our great God and Savior Jesus Christ" (NKJV, NASB, RSV, NEB, NIV, ASV footnote). Older translations say "the great God and our Savior" (KJV, ASV), which some argue implies two separate persons. Consider:

* **Newer translations listed above all make clear that one person (Jesus) is being referred to both as "God" and "Savior."**

* **We are looking for the glorious appearing of this "great God."** But whose appearing are we expecting? Other similar passages refer to the coming of Jesus: 1 Timothy 6:14 (1 Corinthians 1:7; Colossians 3:4; Philippians 3:20; Acts 1:11; 2 Timothy 4:1,8).

* **In the Greek, one article here precedes two descriptive terms ("God" and "Savior") connected by "and."** Whenever this is done, both terms describe the same person. In order for two people to be meant, two articles would be needed.

Here are other similar examples (in each case, one Greek article precedes two descriptive terms, both terms therefore describing one person.):

2 Peter 1:11 – "the everlasting kingdom of our Lord and Savior Jesus Christ"

2 Peter 2:20 – "the knowledge of the Lord and Savior Jesus Christ" (compare 3:18)

2 Peter 3:2 – "the apostles of the Lord and Savior"

(This is called Sharp's rule. Arndt & Gingrich say, "θεος certainly refers to Christ in ... Titus 2:13..." See Vine, Vol. II, pages 160,161; also the grammars of Schmiedel, Moulton, Robertson, and Blass-Debrunner – quoted by Metzger; also Dana & Mantey, and Blackwelder – quoted by Barnett.)

So, here is another passage referring to Jesus as "our great God," using a definite article in Greek. This expression is used often in the Old Testament referring to the true God (Daniel 2:45; Deuteronomy 10:17; Jeremiah 32:18; Ezra 5:8).

2 Peter 1:1

"...the righteousness of our God and Savior Jesus Christ" (NKJV, NASB, RSV, NEB, NIV, ASV footnote). The point here is the same as on Titus 2:13. The Greek has one article then two descriptive terms separated by "and." The rule described above means both terms refer to the same person. So, Jesus is here called "our God" with the definite article.

(KJV translates "of God and our Savior Jesus Christ." ASV has "our God and the Savior Jesus Christ." But the evidence above shows one person is meant.)

(Lenski says: "The use of the one article would say that but ONE person is referred to ... The effort to find a reference to two persons, God and Christ, is nullified linguistically by the use of but one article in the Greek. There is nothing more to say." Vine agrees. Clarke says: "...it is an absolute proof that Peter calls Christ 'God' even in the properest sense of the word, with the article affixed.")

(Another less obvious example is Revelation 22:6 – The "Lord God" sent his angel to reveal these things. But He said, "I am coming quickly" (verse 7), clearly referring to Jesus (3:11; 22:20). See also Romans 9:5; Acts 20:28.)

Conclusion regarding the term "God."

So, the Scriptures repeatedly call Jesus "God." But there is only one true God. Jesus is not a false God. So, He must be referred to as the one true God. He possesses Deity and is part of the Godhead along with the Father (and the Holy Spirit, as other passages show).

Note Acts 12:20-23 where Herod was killed for allowing people to call him a god. If Jesus were not Deity, the references to him as "God" in all these passages would be blasphemous. Yet they were spoken by inspired men and were praised by Jesus.

"The First and the Last," "Alpha and Omega"

These terms are used for the Almighty Jehovah God.

Isaiah 44:6 – "Thus saith Jehovah ... Jehovah of hosts: I am the first, and I am the last; and besides me there is no God" (ASV). Clearly "the first and the last" refers to the one true God. Like the terms "I am" and "Jehovah," this expression emphasizes God's eternal self-existence (compare Isaiah 43:10). See also Isaiah 41:4; 48:12.

Revelation 1:8 – "I am the Alpha and the Omega, the Beginning and the End ... who is and who was and who is to come, the Almighty." So, the Almighty, who is eternally existent, calls Himself "the Alpha and the Omega" (the first and last letters of the Greek alphabet), "the Beginning and the End." The meaning is the same as "the first and the last."

Revelation 21:6,7 also shows that "Alpha and Omega" means the same as "Beginning and End" and refers to God.

These terms are also used for Jesus.

Revelation 1:17 – "I am the First and the Last." The context (verses 10-20) shows Jesus is speaking. He was like the Son of Man (verse 13), who lives, was dead, and is alive forever (verse 18). (1:11 uses these same expressions in NKJV, but they are not in ASV.)

Revelation 2:8 – "These things says the First and the Last, who was dead, and came to life." Clearly this is Jesus again speaking. Some quibble saying this means He was the first and last to be raised by the Father. But no such dodge is available on the next verse.

Revelation 22:13 – "I am the Alpha and the Omega, the Beginning and the End, the First and the Last." All three expressions are used together, showing they mean the same thing. The identical use in Revelation 1:8 proves they refer to the Almighty. But who is speaking here?

* The "I" of verse 13 is identified in verse 12 as the "I" who comes quickly to reward everyone according to His work. Throughout Revelation this refers to Jesus (Revelation 1:1,2,7; 3:3,11; 2:23; 22:20;

God of the Bible

compare Matthew 16:27; 2 Corinthians 5:10). The Father has given all judgment to the Son (John 5:22,23).

* The "I" of verse 13 is identified in verse 16 as "Jesus" who sent His angel to testify these things to the churches. He is the offspring of David.

* The "I" of verse 13, who comes quickly (verse 12) and who testified these things (verse 16), is identified in verse 20 as the "Lord Jesus."

So, Jesus is the "First and Last," the "Alpha and Omega," "Beginning and End." These are terms for Deity in Isaiah 44:6 and Revelation 1:8, yet are used in exactly the same way for Jesus.

"Lord of Lords"

This expression is used for the true God.

Scripture sometimes uses "lord" to refer to people who exercise authority over others (masters or civil rulers). When used religiously, however, it is a term for Deity (Hebrew ADONAI, Gk. KURIOS or κυριος).

Deuteronomy 10:17; Psalm 136:3; Daniel 2:47 – The true God is called "Lord of lords" and "Lord of kings." This shows He has supreme authority over all rulers. Others may rule over men, but God rules over all rulers. Hence, "Lord of lords."

Psalm 97:5; Joshua 3:11,13 – God is Lord of the whole earth. (Psalm 95:3)

This expression is also used for Jesus

Revelation 17:14; 19:16 – Jesus (the Lamb) is "King of kings" and "Lord of lords."

Acts 10:36; Romans 10:12 – He is Lord of all (compare Lord of the whole earth).

Here is another term used in the Bible to show the supreme authority of God, yet it is used for Jesus.

"I Am"

The expression is a unique name for God

Exodus 3:13-15 – When God called Moses to lead Israel from captivity, Moses asked God's name. God replied, "I AM WHO I AM." Moses was to tell Israel that "I AM" (Hebrew EHYEH) had sent him.

This expression is related in form to "Jehovah" (ASV footnote). It describes the eternal, self-existing, unchanging nature of God.

"I am" is also used with no modifying words (substantively or absolutely) to describe God in Deuteronomy 32:39; Isaiah 41:4; 43:10,13; 46:4; 48:12. The meaning is the same as Exodus 3:14 (see Keil and others).

The expression is used for Jesus.

John 8:58 – Jesus said, "...before Abraham was, I AM" (capitals in the original – NKJV; NASB). Other translations say "I am" (no capitals – KJV, ASV, RSV, NEB, NIV). There are several reasons for believing Jesus intended the meaning to be the same as the name for God in Exodus 3:14.

* **"I am" (Gk. EGO EIMI or εγο ειμι) has no modifiers** (substantive or absolute use) just as in Exodus 3:14. There is no predicate nominative (as "I am tired," "I am a Jew," etc.). (See Thayer and Arndt & Gingrich on ειμι.)

* **Jesus' statement is clearly intended to claim He has existed eternally.** When questioned about how He could be old enough to have seen Abraham (verses 56,57), He said Abraham existed (had a birth and death), but before that, "I am." He did not say, "I was," meaning just that He was older than Abraham. "I am" implies no beginning but just continual existence even prior to Abraham. This is the very significance of the term "I am" as used by God in Exodus 3:14. (See Vincent and Lenski, also Blackwelder and Robertson as quoted by Barnett.)

* **The Jews tried to stone Jesus for this statement (verse 59).** The only possible reason for this reaction is that, knowing the Old Testament and the verb tense Jesus used, they recognized the expression "I am" to be a claim to Deity. Since they did not believe Jesus to be God, they viewed His use of the term to be blasphemy.

So, here is another unique name of God which is used by Jesus to refer to Himself. He is the eternally existent "I am."

Additional notes

Jesus used similar "I am" expressions in John 8:24,28; 13:19; 18:5-8. However, the context is not discussing His eternal existence, so it is not so clear He intended to be using the name of God. These verses are often translated "I am *he*," but note that "he" is added by the translators, as is done when referring to God in Isaiah 43:10,13; 46:4; etc.

Witnesses respond to the above evidence by claiming that the wording of Exodus 3:14 is different from John 8:58. They claim that Exodus 3:14 in the Septuagint uses HO ON where John 8:58 used EGO EIMI.

The Septuagint is not the original Scripture, but simply a translation of the original into Greek. Nevertheless, the argument is deceptive. In fact EGO EIMI is found in Exodus 3:14. The Septuagint says "EGO EIMI HO ON" ("I am who I am").

The argument is also deceptive because it leaves the impression HO ON is different from EGO EIMI, but in fact they are just different

God of the Bible

forms of the word for being (like our words "am" and "being"). ON is simply the present participle of EIMI (Analytical Greek Lexicon).

Witnesses also try to argue that John 8:58 is simply "historical present" tense. But that tense is used only in narration, not in argumentation such as in John 8:58. Further, this view ignores the contextual evidence we have discussed showing that Jesus was referring to His eternal existence and that the Jews attempted to stone Him for blasphemy.

"Jehovah"

Exodus 6:3; Psalm 83:18; Isaiah 12:2; 26:4 are a few passages where the true God is called "Jehovah" (KJV). However, this is actually the most frequently used Old Testament name for God. Most translations translate it "Lord," but the best way to observe the word is in the ASV which uses "Jehovah." It is never used in the New Testament, (though the "New World Translation" adds it without textual basis whenever it suits their doctrine).

The word means "He who is," and is a form of the word for being (related to "I am"). It emphasizes God's eternal, changeless, self-existence.

Since it is strictly an Old Testament word, and Jesus is described mostly in the New Testament, the only way to determine whether or not Jesus is called "Jehovah" is to look at Old Testament passages that are proved by the New Testament to refer to Jesus.

We have earlier learned that Jesus possesses Deity and is repeatedly called by other unique names of God, so we should not be surprised to learn that Jesus is also called "Jehovah."

Isaiah 44:6 compared to Revelation 22:13 (1:17; 2:10)

In Isaiah 44:6 **Jehovah** says that He is **the first and the last**, and there is no other God.

But we earlier showed that Jesus calls Himself "the first and the last" in Revelation 22:13, etc.

So, there is no God but Jehovah and He is the first and the last. But Jesus is the first and the last, therefore the term Jehovah must include Jesus!

Psalm 102 compared to Hebrews 1:10-12

We earlier showed that Psalm 102:25-27 is quoted in Hebrews 1:10-12, where verse 8 shows it is spoken "to the Son." But the context of Psalm 102 shows that the whole chapter is addressed to the same "God." And this God is repeatedly called "**Jehovah**" (verses 1,12,15,16,18,19,21,22).

Since the "God" addressed in Psalm 102 includes Jesus, and since that God is called "Jehovah," we must conclude that here is a passage in which Jesus is addressed as "Jehovah."

Isaiah 6:1-5,10 compared to John 12:36-43

In Isaiah 6, Isaiah saw the Lord sitting upon a throne (verse 1). He said that his eyes had seen **Jehovah** of hosts (verse 5; compare verse 3). He was then told to go tell the people that they would see but not understand because they would shut their eyes, etc. (verses 9,10).

In John 12, Jesus said He would be lifted up (die) to draw all people to Himself (verses 32-36). Nevertheless, though He (Jesus) did so many signs, yet the people did not believe in Him (verse 37). Their refusal to believe was a fulfillment of what Isaiah had prophesied – their hearts were hardened so they would not be converted (verses 39,40).

Then John adds that Isaiah said this "when he saw His glory and spoke of **Him**" (verse 41). Verses 42,43 then show clearly that it was **Jesus** that the people were not confessing. Clearly John is saying that the refusal of the people to believe in **Jesus** was the fulfillment of the prophecy Isaiah spoke when he saw **His** glory and spoke of Him (Jesus). But the original passage in Isaiah said He saw "Jehovah of hosts."

So, when Isaiah saw "Jehovah of hosts," he was seeing Jesus!

Isaiah 8:13-15 compared to 1 Peter 2:8

Isaiah 8:13-15 says "**Jehovah** of hosts" would be a stone of stumbling and a rock of offense.

1 Peter 2:8 quotes this very passage saying it was fulfilled when Israel rejected **Jesus** and killed Him (see 1 Peter 2:4-8; compare Acts 4:10,11).

So, when the Jews stumbled at Jesus, they were stumbling at Jehovah.

Joel 2:32 compared to Acts 2:16-21 & Romans 10:13

Joel 2:32 – Whosoever calls on the name of **Jehovah** shall be delivered. This is part of a lengthy prophecy regarding the Messiah's kingdom (verses 28-32).

Acts 2:16-21 quotes this very section from Joel, including that men must "call on the name of the Lord" to be saved. Romans 10:13 likewise quotes it, but the context shows throughout that the "Lord" refers to **Jesus** (verses 4,6,7,9,12,16). Specifically, calling on the Lord includes confessing the Lord **Jesus** (verses 9,10).

Acts 22:16 shows we call on the name of the Lord when we are baptized. 1 Corinthians 1:2 then shows that all Christians call on the name of Jesus Christ our Lord.

So, the prediction that, during the reign of the Messiah, men would call on the name of **Jehovah** is fulfilled in that men call on the name of **Jesus**.

Isaiah 45:21-23 compared to Philippians 2:10,11

In Isaiah 45:21-23 **Jehovah** claims "there is no God else besides me," "I am God, and there is none else." (Note: It follows that, if Jesus is not the true God, then He is not God at all.) This one true God swears that "unto **me** every knee shall bow, every tongue shall swear." So, the knees would be bowed, etc., to the true God, Jehovah.

Romans 14:10,11 – This passage quotes the Isaiah passage and says it will be fulfilled when we stand before the judgment seat of **Christ**. He will be the judge (John 5:22,23).

Philippians 2:10,11 – Then at the name of **Jesus** every knee will bow and every tongue confess. So, every knee will bow and confess to "**Me**" (Jehovah), the one true God. But that is done by men bowing to **Jesus** and confessing His name.

Note Philippians 2:9. This exaltation of Jesus occurs because God has given Him "the name which is above every name." How can this not include the name "Jehovah"? If Jesus has "the name which is above every name," how can the Father have a higher name? In any case, Jesus' must wear the names of Deity.

(Jehovah's Witnesses respond that this is done to the glory of the Father – Philippians 2:11. True, but no one disputes that the Father is glorified as God and called Jehovah. The issue is whether Jesus is also called Jehovah. Isaiah 45 said every knew would bow to "me" – Jehovah, the one true God – and that is fulfilled by every knew bowing at the name of Jesus.)

(Other examples can be cited where the name "Jehovah" is used in the Old Testament, but the New Testament shows the reference is to Jesus. See Malachi 3:1; 4:5,6; and Isaiah 40:3 compare to Matthew 3:3; 4:11; Mark 1:2,3,7,8; Luke 1:17,76; 3:4,16; John 1:23,26,27,33,34; 3:28. Also see Jeremiah 23:5,6 but compare Jeremiah 33:15,16. Compare Psalm 24:7-10 to 1 Corinthians 2:8 and James 2:1. Compare Psalm 97:9 to John 3:31; Romans 9:5. Compare Isaiah 60:19 to Luke 2:32 and Revelation 21:23. Compare Psalm 23 and Isaiah 40:10,11 to John 10 and Hebrews 13:20 and 1 Peter 5:4. Compare Psalm 34:8 to 1 Peter 2:3. See also verses below showing that Jesus has the characteristics of Jehovah and does the works of Jehovah.)

Conclusion

To appreciate the force of this evidence, try to find specific passages in which you can prove that the Heavenly Father is called "Jehovah." Do not assume anything (nor add "Jehovah" into New Testament passages without proof). How do you prove that the Father is called "Jehovah"? You can do it, of course, but the effort to do it will help you appreciate the evidence above to show Jesus is called Jehovah.

Jesus wears the unique names of Deity. This would be blasphemy if He did not possess Deity. Therefore, He does possess Deity even as the Father does. If He possesses Deity, then He has always possessed it and must always fully possess all the qualities of Deity. And He must be included in the one true God.

Jesus Possesses the Unique Characteristics of God.

Certain characteristics are unique to God. No one but God – surely no **created** being – can possess them. Our purpose is to consider whether or not Jesus possesses these qualities. If He possesses the character that only Deity can possess, then this confirms that He possesses Deity. To claim He possesses these qualities when He is not Deity would be blasphemy.

Note that some passages already studied make general claims which necessarily imply that Jesus possesses the qualities of Deity. He possesses all the fullness of Deity (Colossians 2:9). He is the very image of the Father (Hebrews 1:3), and had the form of God (Philippians 2:6). He also wears the unique names of God. It follows that He must possess the characteristics of God.

Let us consider these qualities individually to see whether or not the Bible affirms that Jesus did possess them. Remember that, if Jesus ever possessed these qualities, then He has always possessed them and always will possess them (Hebrews 13:8). Deity cannot cease to be Deity and cannot lose the characteristics of Deity.

Eternally Existent

Eternal existence is a unique characteristic of God.

Jehovah the true God has always existed and always will exist. He was not created. There was never a time when God did not exist. He is the everlasting Maker or Creator of all temporal, created things. The power of eternal existence is inherent in His nature (self-existence). He is the "living" God.

The names of God demonstrate this eternal nature. "Jehovah," "I am," and "First and Last" all imply eternal self-existence (see on the names of God). Note also the following:

Psalm 90:1-4 – Jehovah is "from everlasting to everlasting" (Hebrew OLAM). (Compare Genesis 21:33; Isaiah 40:28; Deuteronomy 32:40.)

Psalm 93:2 – His throne is "established from of old" (Hebrew ME-AZ). He is "from everlasting" (Hebrew OLAM).

Isaiah 57:15 – God "inhabits eternity" (Hebrew AD).

Habakkuk 1:12 – He is "from everlasting" (Hebrew QEDEM).

Psalm 55:19 – He "abides from of old" (Hebrew QEDEM).

(See also Deuteronomy 33:27; Jeremiah 10:10; Psalm 29:10; 9:7; Revelation 1:4; Exodus 15:18; Job 36:26; Romans 16:26; Isaiah 57:15; etc.)

Jesus possesses the characteristic of eternal existence.

Jesus is not a created being but existed eternally.

The names of God that imply eternal self-existence are used for Jesus (see the study of the names of Jesus: "First and Last," "I am," and "Jehovah").

Micah 5:2 – A ruler would come from Bethlehem, but his goings forth were actually "from of old" (Hebrew QEDEM), "from everlasting" (Hebrew OLAM). That this is a prophecy of Jesus is confirmed by Matthew 2:4-6.

Isaiah 9:6 – He is called "Everlasting" Father (Hebrew AD).

Psalm 102:24-27 – His "years are throughout all generations." The heavens and the earth are temporary so they will perish, but His "years will have no end." Hebrews 1:8,10-12 proves this was spoken to Jesus.

Isaiah 43:10,11 – No God was formed before Jehovah (the true God), nor will any be formed after. So, either Jesus is a false "god" (which surely contradicts the Bible), or else He is eternal like the Father.

Many passages show that Jesus was not created but is the Creator of all created things.

In another study we will consider in more detail regarding Jesus' role in creation. But consider briefly these passages:

John 1:3 – All things were made by Him, and without Him was not anything made that was made. Either He created Himself (which is absurd), or else He is eternal.

Colossians 1:16 – In Jesus were all things made, whether in heaven or on earth. Surely He did not make Himself, so, He is not created.

Revelation 5:13 – Every created thing gave praise to the Father and the Lamb. Jesus is classed with the Father, not with the created things.

Romans 1:25 – Created things should not be worshiped, but we will see that Jesus accepted worship. So, He is not a created thing, but is the Eternal Creator.

Jesus is not a created being (as some claim). He is the eternal Creator. Eternal existence is a characteristic that only God can possess, and He surely cannot lose it. Yet Jesus possesses this characteristic.

All-powerful (Omnipotent)

Unlimited power over all created things is a unique characteristic of the true God.

Men and created beings may have some power over some other created things, but this power is limited. Only God's power is unlimited such that He has all power over all created things. Nothing is impossible for God. He has the power to do anything with His creatures that He chooses to do.

Matthew 19:26 – There are things men cannot do, but with God all things are possible. So, this is a unique characteristic of Deity.

Job 42:2 – The Lord can do everything and no purpose of His can be withheld from Him.

Jeremiah 32:17 – God made heavens and earth. Nothing is too hard for God. (Mark 14:36; Genesis 18:14)

Acts 17:24 – God made the world and everything in it since He is Lord of heaven and earth.

1 Chronicles 29:11,12 – Everything in heaven and earth belongs to God. He reigns over all.

Psalm 50:10-12 – Everything in the earth belongs to God.

Psalm 24:1,2 – The earth and everything on it belongs to the Lord because He made it.

Deuteronomy 10:14 – Heaven, earth, and everything in it belongs to God.

Matthew 11:25 – God is Lord of heaven and earth.

Psalm 97:9; 83:18 – God is most high above all the earth.

Note the connection between creation and unlimited power. God possesses all authority over all that He created. Because He made it, it belongs to Him, and He has the right to do all whatever He chooses with it.

(Isaiah 33:22; 10: 21; 43:13; Psalm 146:10; 10:16; 115:3; 135:6; Genesis 28:3; 35:11; 43:14; 48:3; Daniel 4:35)

Jesus possesses unlimited power because He made and owns all things.

Matthew 28:18 – Jesus possesses all authority in heaven and on earth.

Philippians 3:20,21 – Jesus is able so subdue all things to Himself.

Colossians 1:16 – All things were created through Jesus and **for** Him. This is exactly the point we studied already regarding Deity. Jesus made everything, so all exists for His purposes and pleasure.

Revelation 17:14; 19:16 – Jesus is "King of kings and Lord of lords." He has authority above that of all the created things.

John 3:31; Romans 9:5 – Jesus is "above all" and "over all."

Acts 10:36; Romans 10:12 – Jesus is "Lord of all."

Philippians 2:9-11; Ephesians 1:21 – Jesus has the name which is above every name. His "name" includes His authority. So, every knee in heaven and on earth must bow to Him and every tongue confess that He is Lord.

John 16:15; 17:10 – Jesus possesses all things that the Father possesses. Jesus rules over all by right of ownership. He owns all by right of being Creator of all.

Isaiah 9:6 – Jesus is called "Mighty God." (Compare Revelation 1:8 and the discussion of "First and Last" above.)

God of the Bible

Note that unlimited power does not mean that God **does** everything He has power to do; rather, it means He has the power to do whatever He **wills or chooses** to do. For example, God still has power to destroy all men by means of a flood, but He voluntarily limits His power and does not exercise it because He has so chosen (Genesis 9:8-17).

Likewise, while on earth, Jesus still possessed all power because He was still God. But in order to fulfill His purpose here as a human servant (Philippians 2:6-8), He limited His use or exercise of His power, so He did not use it in any way that would conflict with His purpose as servant (Compare Matthew 26:53,54). He was often said to completely conform to the will of the Father even as all humans should. After His resurrection, all His glory and privileges were given back to Him by the Father, so He again fully exercises all power that was His by right from the beginning.

Some passages imply that Jesus is yet in some sense subject to the Father (1 Corinthians 15:24-28; 11:3). While we do not claim to understand all about the inner workings of Deity, these passages do not deny or belittle Jesus' Deity. Deity, as shown by the passages above, involves ownership, rulership, and unlimited power over the **created things**. Jesus possesses this in the same sense that the Father does.

All-Knowing (Omniscient)

Unlimited knowledge is a unique characteristic of Deity.

This characteristic is strongly tied to God's unlimited power. Because God has power to **do** everything He chooses to do, it follows that He has the power to **know** everything He chooses to know. God is unlimited in wisdom and knowledge in the same sense that He is unlimited in power. Unlimited power implies and results in unlimited knowledge.

Psalm 139:1-6 – God knows everything about us. Such knowledge is beyond our ability to attain unto. (Compare verse 7-18.)

Hebrews 4:13 – No creature is hidden from Him, but all things are open before His sight. (Psalm 33:13-15)

1 John 3:20 – God is greater than our hearts. He knows all things.

Psalm 147:4,5 – God counts and names the stars. He is mighty in power. His understanding is infinite. (Note the connection between His power and His knowledge.)

1 Kings 8:39 – Only God knows the hearts of all men. He will use this power in order to judge men (Jeremiah 17:10; 11:20; 1 Samuel 16:7; 1 Chronicles 28:9; Psalm 7:9). Man cannot know what is in the heart of a man unless the man somehow reveals it (1 Corinthians 2:11; 1 Samuel 16:7).

The ability to know everything He chooses to know and, in particular, to know what is in the hearts of men, is a unique characteristic of God.

Jesus possesses this unlimited wisdom and knowledge.

Colossians 2:2,3 – In Him are all the treasures of wisdom and knowledge hidden.

John 16:30; 21:17 – Jesus' disciples claimed that He knew all things. He never contradicted this claim nor rebuked them for it.

John 2:24,25 – Jesus had the ability to know what was in the hearts of all men without being told. Note that this was expressly stated to be a unique power of Deity, yet Jesus possessed this power and He exercised even while on earth. (Compare Mark 2:8; Matthew 9:4; 12:25; Luke 5:22; 6:8; 9:47; 11:17.)

Revelation 2:23 – Jesus searches the minds and hearts in order to reward men for their works.

Again, this unlimited knowledge rests on the Divine power to do whatever God wills. God knows because He chooses to know. But we learned previously that God's power is exercised or not exercised according to His will. He knows things only when it suits His purpose to exercise His power to know them (compare Genesis 11:5; 18:20,21). It follows that He may at times choose not to exercise this power to know certain future things, just as He may choose not to exercise His power to do certain things.

In this way, while He was on earth accomplishing His purposes as a servant, Jesus did not always exercise this unlimited power to know all things. Mark 13:32 lists one thing in particular that He did not know. We conclude, based on the above passages, that it did not serve His purposes on earth to exercise His power to know this matter.

Yet Jesus possesses the Divine power to know all things that He chooses to know, just as He possesses Divine power to do all things that He chooses to do.

Everywhere Present (Omnipresent)

The ability to be everywhere at once is a unique characteristic of God.

Man is limited by a physical body, so he can be only in one place at any one time. God, however, is spirit and can be everywhere in the universe at the same time. This power, however, is also related to His unlimited power to act and to know. God is present everywhere in the sense that everything everywhere is in His presence – He can see, know, and act in all places at once.

Psalm 139:7-12 – Wherever man is, God is there seeing him and knowing what man is doing.

Jeremiah 23:23,24 – God fills heaven and earth. He is at hand as well as afar off, so no one can hide that God cannot see Him.

God of the Bible

Acts 17:27 – Men everywhere can find God because He is not far from each of us.

It is because of this unique characteristic of God that He is able to know all things that men do, to read the hearts of all men, and to hear and answer the prayers of all of His people wherever they are. (1 Kings 8:26,27)

Jesus also possesses this unique characteristic of God.

Matthew 18:20 – Jesus is present in the midst wherever two or three are gathered together in His name.

Matthew 28:20 – He promised the apostles He would be with them always, even to the end of the age.

We have already seen that Jesus has all power and can know all things, including what is in the hearts of all men. This is the fundamental concept of being present everywhere.

While on the earth, Jesus limited His power by taking on a physical body, being physically present where that body was. Nevertheless, He possessed the power to be everywhere at once, a unique characteristic of God, in that He is able to see, know, and act upon events no matter where they are.

Unchanging (Immutable)

Immutability is also a unique characteristic of God.

Man's character is flawed, so we must continually be changing our character to make it what it ought to be. But God's character is perfect – without flaw – therefore it never needs to change and never does change. We have already studied certain characteristics unique to God. These characteristics He has always possessed and always will possess.

Malachi 3:6 – I am the Lord, I do not change.

James 1:17 – With God there is no variation or shadow of turning.

Numbers 23:19 – God is not a man who needs to repent. (1 Samuel 15:29)

To suit His eternal purpose, God has changed the laws and commands He has given to men, and He has at times changed what He does to suit His purposes. But His own **character** is what never changes. It follows that God can never lose His Divine characteristics. God cannot cease to be God and cannot cease to have the character of God.

Jesus possesses this characteristic of never changing.

Hebrews 1:12 – The earth and heavens will change (be destroyed), but you are the same. This is addressed to Jesus (verse 8). (This is a quote of Psalm 102:25-27 which says the same.)

Hebrews 13:8 – Jesus Christ is the same yesterday, today, and forever.

So, Jesus also possesses this unique characteristic of Deity. He is not like men who change but like the Father who does not change.

Note again that, since Jesus possesses this particular characteristic, it follows that Jesus always has and always will possess all the other characteristics of Deity. If He ever is (or was) Deity, and if He does not change, then He always is (and was) Deity. If He ever possessed the characteristics of Deity, then He always possesses those characteristics.

In order to accomplish His purposes, God may voluntarily choose at times not to exercise or use certain abilities. Jesus did this while on earth in order to fulfill His role as a human servant (Philippians 2:6-8). But He cannot lose or surrender the characteristics, else He would cease to be God and that is impossible.

Infinitely Holy & Righteous

Infinite holiness is a unique characteristic of God.

Man is not always holy (Romans 6:10-23; 1 John 1:8,10), but God is sinlessly perfect. He is always holy, just, and righteous. He never sins nor needs to repent of sins.

Leviticus 11:44; Psalm 99:5,9; Revelation 4:8; 16:5. He is the "Holy One of Israel" – Isaiah 41:14,16,20; 43:3,14,15; 47:4.

Only God is truly holy – Revelation 15:3,4; 1 Samuel 2:2.

Jesus also possesses this characteristic of holiness.

Acts 3:14; 4:27,30; 13:35; Hebrews 7:26; John 8:46; Hebrews 4:15; 1 Peter 2:20-23; Mark 1:24; Luke 1:35 (2 Corinthians 5:21; 1 John 3:5). Note John 14:30.

Some wonder how Jesus could be tempted as a human like we are if He was Deity all along (compare Hebrews 4:15 to James 1:13). We may not fully understand this, since we do not fully understand Deity. But the Bible affirms it to be true, so we must accept it by faith.

Remember that Jesus was Deity all along, but He **added** the characteristics of humanity. It was His human nature that was tempted, not His Divine nature. If God can limit the exercise of His other characteristics in order to suit His purposes (see notes above), we simply conclude that somehow Jesus was able to limit the exercise of His natural holiness in order that it not interfere with His ability to be tempted as a man. (It is also possible that, when the Bible says God is not tempted by evil, it does not mean it is impossible for Him to do evil but simply that He so controls Himself that He never chooses to do evil.)

Conclusion

Jesus possesses all the unique characteristics of God. But since **only** Deity possesses these characteristics, and since Jesus possesses them, it follows that Jesus must possess Deity. This confirms what we have learned in other studies of the passages that call Jesus God or other names for God. Jesus possesses true Deity even as does the Father and the Holy Spirit. These three together constitute the Godhead, the one true and living God we worship.

Jesus Accomplishes the Unique Works of God.

Just as there are names that only God has the right to wear and characteristics that only God possesses, so there are works that only the true God can accomplish. No mere man, angel, or other created being is capable of doing them. To say that Jesus does these works would be blasphemy unless He possesses Deity. On the other hand, if there is proof that He actually does these works, then that would constitute evidence that He is in fact God.

Consider these unique works of God and the evidence that Jesus does them:

Creating the Universe

Creation is a unique work that only God can perform.

Genesis 1 describes the creation and attributes it to the power of God (verses 1,3,26,27, etc.).

Isaiah 42:5 – Jehovah God created the heavens and spread forth the earth. He gives breath to the people on it.

Isaiah 45:18 – Jehovah created the heavens, formed the earth and created it.

Acts 17:24,25 – God is Lord of heaven and earth because He made the world and everything in it. He gives to all life, breath, and all things. (14:15)

Psalm 33:6-9 – The heavens and earth were made by the breath of Jehovah's mouth.

(See also Jeremiah 10:12; Exodus 20:11; Psalm 89:11; 90:2; 104:5-9,24-28; 19:1; 24:1,2; 95:5; 146:6; 136:5-9; 8:3,6-8; 148:5; Jeremiah 27:5; Isaiah 40:26; Hebrews 1:10; 11:3.)

Yet Jesus did this unique work of God.

We referred briefly to the following verses to prove the eternal existence of Jesus. Consider them now more closely to observe Jesus' involvement in creation.

John 1:1-3 – Jesus was in the beginning with God, was God, and all things were made through Him. Without Him nothing was made that was made.

Colossians 1:16,17 – By Him (Jesus – verses 13-15) were all things created, things in heaven and on earth, etc. He existed before them all. They all consist in Him, and were created through Him and for Him.

Hebrews 1:2 – The worlds were made through the Son.

Hebrews 1:10 – The Lord (Jesus – verse 8) laid the foundation of the earth. The heavens are the work of His hands. (Compare Psalm 102:25.)

Note that Jesus is not a created being through whom all "other" things were made. Rather, He created "all" things. Nothing that has been made was made without Him. Clearly, He did not create Himself, therefore He was not created at all.

This proves Jesus is eternal (see the characteristics of Jesus). But it also proves that He does work that only God can do. This work classifies Him with Deity, not with the created beings (see also Revelation 5:12-14; Romans 1:25).

Sustaining & Preserving the Universe

Sustaining the universe is a unique work of God.

Not only does God alone have the power to make the heavens and earth, including all forms of life, but only God has the power to maintain or continue the existence of what has been created.

Nehemiah 9:6 – Jehovah alone made heaven and earth and all things thereon. And He preserves them all.

Psalm 36:6 – Jehovah preserves man and beast.

Psalm 104:13,14 – He provides the rain and causes grass and herbs to grow to bring forth food for man and animals. (Deuteronomy 11:14,15)

Matthew 5:45 – The Father makes the sun rise and sends rain.

Acts 17:25,28 – God gives to all life, breath, and all things. In Him we live and move and have our being.

Acts 14:17 – God gives rain and fruitful seasons, filling our hearts with food and gladness.

Jehovah God provides all blessings necessary to sustain and maintain the earth and life on it. Were it not for His sustaining power, all things would immediately pass from existence.

Jesus does this unique work of God.

Colossians 1:17 – As in other passages above regarding God, having said that Jesus created all things, Paul adds that "in Him all things consist." It is by Jesus' power that all things continue to exist.

Hebrews 1:3 – The Son made the worlds (verse 2), and He upholds all things by the word of His power.

Hebrews 1:12 – Not only did the Son (verse 8) make the heavens and earth (verse 10), but they will cease to exist when He "folds them up."

What God has created, only He can sustain. All created things began to exist and continue to exist by His power. Created beings derive their life from God.

In contrast to the created things, God is the source of life – Creator and Sustainer. He has the power of life within Himself. No one ultimately gave Him His existence, and no one sustains His life.

Jesus is classed with God regarding both the creation and the continuation of that which is created. He was not created, but He created all things that were created, and He sustains their existence.

Ruling the Universe

We have already established that only God possesses unlimited power to rule over all created things (see under "Lord of lords" and "all-powerful" in our previous studies). This is both a characteristic of God and a work of God. Because He created all, God possesses right of ownership over all, and therefore rules over all.

We have also already established that Jesus is called "Lord of lords," and that He possesses unlimited authority over the creation because He created and owns all things. So, Jesus does this unique work along with the Father and the Holy Spirit: He rules the universe.

Redeeming Mankind from Sin.

Saving and redeeming men from sin is a unique work of God.

Since God possesses the highest authority in the universe, only He can make the ultimate laws of right and wrong. When men violate those laws, only God can grant forgiveness and declare the terms of forgiveness.

As humans we may grant forgiveness to those who sin against us, but we cannot grant forgiveness to those who sin against God's laws. Only God can offer or provide that redemption or salvation.

Psalm 3:8 – Salvation belongs to Jehovah.

Psalm 37:39 – Salvation of the righteous is of Jehovah.

Isaiah 43:1,14 – Jehovah who created is also the Redeemer. He says, "I have redeemed you."

Isaiah 43:11 – Besides Jehovah there is no savior.

Titus 3:4,5 – God our Savior saved us according to His mercy.

Isaiah 45:15,17 – Jehovah, God of Israel, is the Savior who provides everlasting salvation.

(Isaiah 62:11)

Jesus does this unique work of God.

John 4:42 – The Samaritans confessed Jesus to be the Savior of the world. (Luke 2:11)

Titus 1:3,4 – God is our Savior. The Lord Jesus Christ is our Savior. How can Jesus be less than God in such a description?

Titus 2:13,14 – Jesus is our great God and Savior Jesus Christ. He gave Himself to redeem us from sin so we might become His special people. (See notes on this passage under names of Deity.) (2 Peter 1:1,11; 2:20; 3:18)

Acts 4:12 – There is salvation in no one other than Jesus.

Mark. 2:1-12; Luke 7:48,49 – Jesus had power on earth to directly forgive sins. This is a work only God can do. So, for Jesus to claim this power would have been blasphemy if He were not God.

Ephesians 1:7 – We have redemption through Jesus' blood, even the forgiveness of sins. (Colossians 1:13,14)

Jesus is not classed with the creatures in need of redemption. He is the redeemer.

God is the Savior and besides Him there is no Savior, but Jesus is the Savior and salvation is found in no one else. God is the redeemer who offers forgiveness of sins, but Jesus is the redeemer who offers forgiveness of sins.

What man, angel, or other created being ever had power on earth to directly forgive sins? Who but God can forgive sins? If Jesus is not God, how could these expressions be anything but blasphemy? Jesus must possess Deity because Jesus can forgive sins as only God can do.

(Ephesians 5:23; Galatians 3:13; 1 Peter 1:18; Romans 3:24)

Judging Men's Lives

Judging man's eternal destiny is a unique work of God.

As the ruler of the universe, God has revealed His laws by which men ought to live. He will judge all men and reward them eternally for how they have or have not followed His rules.

Isaiah 33:22 – Jehovah is our lawgiver, king, and judge.

Psalm 50:6 – God Himself is judge. (94:1,2)

Psalm 96:10,13 – Jehovah reigns and will judge the people. He will judge the world with righteousness.

Only God, as the Supreme Ruler, has the right to so judge men and determine their eternal destinies.

(Romans 2:3,5,16)

Jesus is the judge who will do this work.

John 12 48 – All men will be judged according to Jesus' words.

Matthew 25:31-46 – All nations will be gathered before the Son of Man. He will separate them and send them into eternal punishment or eternal life.

2 Corinthians 5:10 – We must all be made manifest before the judgment seat of Christ to receive the things done in the body, good or bad.

John 5:22,23 – The Father does not judge anyone but has given all judgment to the Son. (Acts 17:31)

God of the Bible

Judging mankind for their lives and determining their eternal destiny are unique works of God. Yet Jesus is the one who will do that work. He is not classed with the created beings whose works will be judged by God. He is classed with God who will judge the works of the creatures.

Conclusion

All the works we have studied involve activity that only Deity can accomplish, yet Jesus does them all. So, Jesus possesses Deity.

Some people try to avoid the force of this evidence by claiming that Jesus does not do these works on His own authority but simply acts as an agent for God (the Father). He acts "in the name of" the Father or the Father does them "by" or "through" Jesus.

It is true that some passages say Jesus acted in the name of the Father or that the Father acted by Him, especially while Jesus was on earth as a man in the form of a servant (Philippians 2:6-8). However, it is also true that Jehovah God is said to act "by" Jehovah! See Hosea 1:6,7; Zechariah 10:12. Further, the Father is said to act "in the name of" Jesus – John 14:26. Does this prove that the Father is not God?!

In many of the above passages Jesus is said to do these unique works of God in His own name or using other expressions that imply He is the authority behind the work (see Acts 4:12; Colossians 1:16,17 – "through Him and *unto* Him"; Titus 2:13,14; Mark 2:1-12; John 4:42; Luke 7:48,49). What passage ever speaks of men, angels, or other creatures creating, sustaining, or ruling the universe? What passage speaks of them as the redeemer who has power to actually speak men's sins forgiven or to determine their eternal destinies? If men or angels spoke or acted as Jesus did in these examples, such would be blasphemy. God would not use a man for such things, because a man would not be adequate.

The fact is that Jesus is not classed, in these passages, with the created beings. He is classed with God doing the works of God. Jesus possesses Deity. And if He ever possessed it, He always possessed it, for God cannot cease to be God.

Jesus Deserves the Worship and Glory That Are Uniquely God's.

Just as only God deserves to wear certain unique names, to possess certain unique characteristics, and to do certain unique works, so there are certain unique forms of worship and honor that belong only to God. Because God created and rules the whole creation, it follows that all created things must honor and worship Him. No man or other created being may rightly receive such worship. To give such honor to men or created beings constitutes blasphemy or idolatry.

Worship

Only God deserves to receive spiritual worship from men.

The New Testament word for worship (προσκυνεω) means to do obeisance, reverence, or acts of homage (see Thayer, Vine, and Arndt & Gingrich). This word is often used to describe men worshiping God: John 4:20-24; Revelation 4:10; 7:11; 11:16; 14:7; 19:4; 15:4; 1 Corinthians 14:25.

Many verses forbid worshiping men, angels, or any created thing.

Acts 10:25,26 – Cornelius fell down to worship Peter. Peter forbade it saying that he himself was just a *man*. God deserves worship, but men do not. (Compare Acts 12:20-23; 14:8-18.)

Revelation 22:8,9; 19:10 – John sought to worship the angel, but the angel forbade it because he was a "fellow servant." "Worship God."

Romans 1:25 – People who worship and serve created things, rather than the Creator, have left the truth of God.

To worship any created thing – whether man, angel, heavenly body, or some other object in nature (mountain, ocean, etc.) – constitutes idolatry.

Only the true God deserves to be worshiped.

Matthew 4:9,10 – Worship the Lord your God and serve Him only.

Revelation 9:20 – Idolatry is forbidden because it constitutes worship of someone other than God (Exodus 20:3-6; Deuteronomy 6:13-15; Revelation 14:9-11). (See also Exodus 34:14.)

When used for *religious* honor, worship is forbidden toward any except God. In this sense, "worship" is like "lord," "father," "master," etc. The words may be acceptably used for earthly, physical relationships (Ephesians 6:1-9; Colossians 3:21,22), but we are forbidden to use such as religious honor to men or created things (Matthew 23:8-12). (On Revelation 3:9, compare to 1 Corinthians 14:25.)

The concept of Deity distinguishes the Creator from the creature. Things that are created do not have the unique characteristics of God, do not do the unique works of God, and therefore should not be addressed by the unique names of God nor should they be worshiped.

Note: worship (προσκυνεω) is forbidden when used for obeisance to men from a spiritual or religious motivation or purpose. The word is sometimes (but rarely) used in the New Testament non-religiously to refer to bowing in obeisance to a king, master, or other person in authority (see Matthew 18:26 – this usage is more common in the Old Testament).

God of the Bible

But Jesus received the unique worship God deserves.

He was often worshiped while He appeared on earth before His resurrection.

Matthew 8:2 – A leper came and worshiped Jesus. (9:18; 15:25; Mark 5:6)

Matthew 14:33 – After Jesus had calmed the storm, the disciples worshiped Him saying He was the Son of God.

John 9:38 – After Jesus had healed the blind man, He revealed Himself to be the Son of God (verse 35). The man said he believed, and he worshiped Jesus.

Note that such religious worship would have been blasphemy and should have been forbidden as it was in the case of Peter, the angel, etc., if Jesus had been just a man on earth.

Created beings also worship Him after His resurrection.

Matthew 28:9,17 – After His resurrection, His disciples worshiped Him. (Compare John 20:28,29.)

Luke 24:52 – Even after He had ascended back to heaven, they worshiped Him.

Hebrews 1:6 – Angels are instructed by God to worship Jesus.

Note that men were rebuked for worshiping men, angels, or created beings, but they were never rebuked for worshiping Jesus. Angels are even instructed by the Father to worship Jesus. The context of the above passages cannot fit the idea of obeisance to an earthly king or ruler. They refer to honoring Jesus as a religious authority – the very thing forbidden when offered to Peter, angels, etc.

So, Jesus accepted worship as an act of religious honor. The Scriptures, including Jesus' own teachings, would absolutely forbid this unless He possesses true Deity.

Glory and Honor

"Glory" (δοξα) means "...praise, honor ... magnificence, excellence, preeminence, dignity, grace ... majesty" – Grimm-Wilke-Thayer.

"Honor" (τιμη) means "...honor which belongs or is shown to one; the honor of one who outranks others, pre-eminence ... veneration ... deference, reverence..." – Grimm-Wilke-Thayer.

Like the words "power" and "wisdom," both these words can properly be used to refer to men in the physical realm (Matthew 6:29; 1 Peter 1:24). But they are also used to describe a special degree of glory which no one but God can possess.

God receives a special, unique glory and honor.

Psalm 24:7-10 – Jehovah is the "King of glory."

Psalm 29:3 – He is the "God of glory." (Acts 7:2; compare Isaiah 60:19; Galatians 1:5; etc.)

Revelation 4:9-11 – God deserves this glory because He created all things. Note again the distinction between the creature and the Creator. (Revelation 5:13; Romans 11:36)

Isaiah 42:8; 48:11 – This glory is unique to God in that He refuses to share it with anyone else. Idols and created things have no right to receive this glory.

It follows that it would be blasphemy for anyone but God to receive this unique kind of glory. If anyone does receive this glory with God's approval, then that one must possess Deity.

But Jesus receives the unique glory of God.

John 5:23 – All men should honor the Son "just as" they honor the Father. To fail to give this honor to the Son is to fail to properly honor the Father.

"Just as" (καθως) is translated "even as" in KJV, ASV, NASB, RSV (compare Thayer and Arndt & Gingrich). Other examples of its use in comparisons is found in Luke 6:31; 11:30; 17:26; John 3:14; 2 Corinthians 10:7; Colossians 3:13; etc.

The significance of the word, when used in comparisons, is that one item or action is just like the other regarding the aspect in which they are being compared. So, Jesus rightly receives honor just like the honor the Father receives. And if we refuse to give such honor to the Son, then we are refusing to honor the Father!

John 17:5 – Jesus prayed to the Father to "glorify Me together with Yourself, with the glory which I had with You before the world was" (NKJV, compare NASB, NEB; others are similar – ASV, KJV). Jesus asks to be glorified together with the Father with the glory He possessed "with" (παρα) the Father from eternity.

The clear implication is that Jesus and the Father both possessed the same glory before the world began. Jesus, in coming to earth as a servant, did not then appear to possess that glory but appeared as a man (this is part of what he gave up on coming to earth – Philippians 2:6-8). But having nearly completed His work on earth (John 17:4) and being ready to ascend to the Father, Jesus anticipated receiving this glory again (Philippians 2:9-11).

However, we have already learned that no one but God can receive the glory God has (Isaiah 42:8; 48:11). Jesus did receive that glory with the approval of the Father. Therefore, Jesus possesses Deity.

Revelation 5:12-14 – Both the Father and the Lamb (Jesus) were praised by the created things, who attributed to them "blessing and honor and glory and power." Note that the same glory and honor belongs to both Father and Son.

Hebrews 1:3 – Jesus is the brightness of the Father's glory (or the effulgence or radiance of His glory). That glory which shines from the Father also shines from Jesus because He is the creator (verse 2), upholds all things (verse 3), and is the express image of God (verse 3).

God of the Bible

1 Corinthians 2:8; James 2:1 – Jesus is called the "Lord of glory," just as God in the Old Testament is called the "King of glory" (Psalm 24:7-10).

Note that the glory Jesus possesses is not just the glory possessed by men or angels. His glory is above that of angels (Hebrews 1:6,13). He is above all principality, power, might, dominion, and every name that is named (Ephesians 1:21; Philippians 2:9-11). No created being possesses the glory and honor Jesus does.

We have seen, however, that Jesus deserves the glory, honor, and worship of Deity even as the Father does. God forbids this to be given to any but Deity, but Jesus does receive it. This would be blasphemy if Jesus were not God.

Conclusion

If Jesus is not Deity, then who is He? To understand God, we must realize that God is not part of the created things. God is the Creator, separate and far above the creatures. This distinction is made again and again in the passages we have studied. Jesus must be classed on one side or the other. Either he is a created being or else He is Deity. To say He is not Deity is to say He is a created being. To say He is not a created being is to say He is Deity. There are no other alternatives.

Men are creatures; angels are creatures that are above men. But Jesus is above the angels and is not classed with them (Hebrews chapter 1 – see especially verses 5,6,13). We have seen that He is not an angel nor an exalted man, but the Bible attributes to Him that which can only be said of God. We have learned that:

* Jesus is expressly stated to be God or to possess Deity.
* Jesus is called by names that may only be used for God.
* Jesus possesses characteristics that only God can possess.
* Jesus does work that only God can do.
* Jesus deserves worship and honor that only God deserves.

In all these areas Jesus is described as the Creator, not a created being. He is eternal, has the power, and did the work of creation. He deserves honor as the Creator. Clearly He is not to be classed with the created things but with Deity.

But we have also proved that there is only **one** true God who made the universe. If Jesus is "god," He is not an idol nor a false god. Since He possesses Deity and there is only one true God, then He must possess true Deity, not some lesser form of deity. He must be included in the one true God or Godhead along with the Father and the Holy Spirit.

Finally, if Jesus is God then He always has been God and always will be God, since God's unique nature cannot change (Hebrews 13:8). God cannot cease to be God nor can God lose the characteristics of God. He can take on non-Divine characteristics as Jesus added the characteristics of a man when He came to earth, and He can limit the use of His powers in order to accomplish His Divine purposes as Jesus did on earth. But He cannot cease to be God and He cannot lose the power and characteristics of God.

Jesus possesses Deity.

Notes

Two works that have been of special assistance in this study have been:

Jehovah's Witnesses by Maurice Barnett

Jehovah's Witnesses and Jesus Christ by Bruce M. Metzger

Many other works were consulted and have been credited where appropriate in these notes.

The Nature of the Holy Spirit

Introduction:

The purpose of this study is to consider the nature of the Holy Spirit

Specifically, we want to consider whether or not the Holy Spirit is a personal individual Being or just a force or power. Then we will consider whether or not the Spirit possesses Deity as part of the Godhead, like God the Father and God the Son.

Our understanding of the nature of the Holy Spirit is necessarily limited.

Many things about the infinite, spiritual God are beyond our ability to understand as finite, fallible humans. Can we answer every question about the nature of the Father? If not, why should we expect to answer every question about the nature of the Holy Spirit?

Many people are uncomfortable discussing the Holy Spirit, simply because we have neglected to study about Him. We talk about the Father so often that we get used to the fact that there is much about Him we do not know. But if we have neglected studying the Holy Spirit, it may bother us to discover how little we know about Him. But there are some things we'll never know this side of eternity (Job 26:14; 36:26; 37:5,23; 11:7-9; Isaiah 55:8,9; Deuteronomy 29:29).

On the other hand, there are many things we can know about Deity.

Even with our limited intelligence, we can know that the Father and the Son exist and that they are living individual Beings who possess Deity and possess the characteristics of Deity (eternal, all-knowing, all-powerful, etc.). Likewise, we can determine whether or not the Holy Spirit exists as a living, individual Being who possesses Deity and the characteristics of Deity. That is the purpose of this study.

The Names of the Holy Spirit

The Bible often uses interchangeable terms for things. For example:

* God is called Jehovah, Almighty, or the Most High.

* The church is called the kingdom, body, house, or bride.

* The gospel is called the New Testament, the truth, the Word of God, or the faith.

* Christians are called children of God, disciples, saints, or priests.

* Elders are called bishops, overseers, pastors, or presbyters.

In each case the different terms emphasize different aspects of the same thing, person, or concept. Likewise, we will see that the Scriptures use a number of names interchangeably to refer to the Holy Spirit.

The "Holy Spirit" (or "Holy Ghost")

Obviously this is a common expression. We will see it used repeatedly as the study proceeds.

(Psalm 51:11; Isaiah 63:10; Matthew 3:11; 12:32; 28:19; Mark 12:36; 13:11; John 14:26; Acts 1:5,8; 2:4; 5:3,32; 8:14-19; 1 Corinthians 6:19)

"The Spirit of Truth" and "the Comforter"

John 14:16,17,26; (15:26; 16:7,13) – Jesus promised to send to the apostles "the Comforter" even "the Spirit of Truth." But in 14:26 He calls the one He would send the "Holy Spirit."

So, "Spirit of Truth" and "Comforter" here are simply other names for the Holy Spirit. This demonstrates that different terms are used for the Holy Spirit.

"The Spirit"

Often the Holy Spirit is called simply "the Spirit."

Matthew 22:43 – David spoke Psalms 110:1 "in the Spirit." But the parallel passage in Mark 12:36 says He spoke it by the Holy Spirit.

Mark 1:10 and John 1:33 – At Jesus' baptism, "the Spirit" descended in a form like a dove. But Luke 3:22 says this was the Holy Spirit.

Luke 4:1 – Jesus was full of the Holy Spirit and led of "the Spirit."

Acts 2:4 – The apostles were filled with the Holy Spirit and spoke with other tongues as "the Spirit" gave them utterance.

1 Corinthians 2:10 – The apostles and prophets spoke the will of God by revelation from "the Spirit." But verse 13 (NKJV) and John 14:26; 16:7,13 show this was the Holy Spirit.

1 Corinthians 12:7-13 – Miraculous gifts were given to men by "the Spirit," but 12:3 shows that this was the Holy Spirit.

2 Corinthians 1:22; 5:5 – "The Spirit" is the earnest or pledge of our inheritance given us by God. But Ephesians 1:13,14; 4:30 say that this earnest or seal is the Holy Spirit.

In these passages "the Spirit" is simply another name used to refer to the Holy Spirit. But note that, in other contexts, "the spirit" may be identified as a spirit other than the Holy Spirit (see James 2:26; Matthew 26:41; Ephesians 4:23; etc.). The context must determine.

This should not surprise us, since we do similar things. People may say, "I'm going into the city today," but what city they refer to depends on the context. Likewise, in many contexts "the Spirit" refers to the Holy Spirit, but can refer to other spirits in other contexts.

"The Spirit of God"

The Holy Spirit is sometimes referred to as "the Spirit of God," or God may refer to the Holy Spirit as "my Spirit." Or in a context talking about God, other people may refer to the Holy Spirit as simply "His Spirit."

Matthew 3:16 says "the Spirit of God" descended on Jesus as a dove at His baptism, but remember Luke 3:22 says it was the Holy Spirit.

Acts 2:17,18 quotes Joel 2:28,29 where God said "I will pour out **My Spirit** upon all flesh." But this was fulfilled by the coming of the Holy Spirit (verses 4,33).

1 Corinthians 2:11,12 – "The Spirit of God" revealed God's will, but verse 13 (NKJV) and John 14:26 show that this refers to the Holy Spirit.

Ephesians 4:30 combines the terms as the "Holy Spirit of God."

1 Thessalonians 4:8; Psalm 51:11; and Isaiah 63:10 combine "Holy Spirit" with "My Spirit" or "His Spirit" speaking of God.

Acts 5:3,9 use Holy Spirit and "Spirit of the Lord" interchangeably.

So, "Spirit of God," "My Spirit" (God speaking), etc., are other names for the Holy Spirit. Question: Can you find any instance where you can **prove** these phrases refer to anyone other than the Holy Spirit?

(Matthew 12:18,28 with Isaiah 42:1; Matt, 12:32; Luke 4:1; Acts 10:38.)

A Living Spirit Being

Alternative Meanings of the Word "Spirit"

Like other Bible words, "spirit" can have different meanings depending on context. Let us consider some alternative ways "spirit" may be used in the Bible, then we will consider which of these meanings applies to the "Holy Spirit."

A living spirit being

When used in this sense, "spirit" refers to a living individual being who possesses the characteristics of a person – i.e., a living individual separate and distinct from other such beings. The Bible mentions several kinds of living beings or individuals who are spirit beings. In some cases, like man, a spirit may dwell in a physical body; but this is not true of all spirit beings.

* God the Father and Jesus the Son – John 4:23,24; Luke 23:46
* Angels – Hebrews 1:13,14
* Satan and demons – Matthew 8:16; 12:24,43-45; Mark 1:23-27
* Human beings – 1 Corinthians 15:35,44; 2:11; James 2:26; Luke 8:55; Acts 7:59; 17:16.

Note that the spirit of each such individual being is separate and distinct from the spirits of other living beings. For example, the Father is a Being whose spirit is separate and distinct from the spirits of angels and men, etc. The spirit of each angel is separate and distinct from the spirit of the Father and from other angels, etc.

The characteristics, qualities, or attitudes possessed or expressed by a person

When used in this sense, "spirit" refers to some particular aspect of a person's personality, disposition, nature, character, etc. Examples:

Luke 1:17 – John came in "the spirit and power of Elijah."

Romans 11:8 – A spirit of slumber ("stupor" – ASV)

1 Corinthians 4:21; Galatians 6:1 – A spirit of meekness.

2 Timothy 1:7 – A spirit of fear contrasted to a spirit of power, of love, and of a sound mind.

1 Peter 3:4 – A meek and quiet spirit.

Many other examples can be given. The spirit of man (in the personal sense of a living spirit being) is the inner man – the part that feels, wills, motivates, etc. So the real character of a man is determined by the nature or condition of his spirit. As a result, the word "spirit" came to refer to the various attitudes or qualities expressed by the personal spirit.

Note that each individual can have only one personal "spirit" – he is just one living individual being. Yet he may have many different

God of the Bible

"spirits" in the sense of different qualities or attitudes. And in fact, his spirit (in the latter sense) can even change as time passes.

(A third alternative meaning might be that the Holy Spirit is simply the spiritual aspect of God, if God consisted of two parts like man is body and spirit. This meaning cannot be correct, however, because God is entirely spirit – John 4:23,24. We will also show below that the Holy Spirit is a separate Being from the Father and the Son. When people deny the Spirit is a living being, they almost always argue that it is just a power or other characteristic of God.)

("Spirit" has other meanings in the Bible, such as the "spirit of a beast," physical wind, etc. We will not discuss these, since they cannot possibly apply to the Holy Spirit.)

The Holy Spirit as a Living Spirit Being.

Is the Holy Spirit a **living spirit being** in the personal sense, separate and distinct from other spirit beings like the Father and angels, etc.? Or is the Holy Spirit just a **characteristic or an attitude** possessed by God? Could the "Holy Spirit" be just a way of referring to the power, character, nature, attributes, or disposition of God?

The Holy Spirit possesses the characteristics and qualities of a living spirit Being.

Consider the following descriptions of the Holy Spirit. Is this the kind of language that would properly be used of a mere characteristic or attitude, or does this language demonstrate that the Holy Spirit is a personal being who possesses personal characteristics and qualities?

Personal Characteristics of the Holy Spirit

* He hears – John 16:13
* He can be lied to – Acts 5:3
* He makes decisions about right and wrong (like people do) – Acts 15:28
* He intercedes – Romans 8:26
* He has a mind – Romans 8:27
* He loves – Romans 15:30
* He searches – 1 Corinthians 2:10
* He knows (like the spirit of a living being knows) – 1 Corinthians 2:11
* He gives gifts – 1 Corinthians 12:8,11
* He wills – 1 Corinthians 12:11
* He grieves – Ephesians 4:30 (Isaiah 63:10)

The Holy Spirit is not just a characteristic or attitude. Rather, He is a living Being who possesses the characteristics of a person.

(See also Romans 8:26,27; 1 Corinthians 12:8,11; 6:11; Matthew 12:31; Hebrews 10:29; Acts 5:9; 7:51; 8:29; 16:6,7; 13:2,4; 1 Timothy 4:1; John 15:26; 16:13; 14:26; 16:7,8; Ephesians 3:5; Revelation 22:17; Nehemiah 9:20.)

He is referred to by masculine pronouns.

This evidence may not be conclusive by itself apart from the facts we just studied. But when considered with the preceding evidence, it confirms the personal nature of the Spirit.

John 16:13,14 – "***He***," the Spirit of Truth, will guide you into all truth, and "***He***" (the Spirit) will glorify Me (Jesus). ("Spirit" here is **neuter** in Greek, yet "He" in both cases is from a **masculine** demonstrative pronoun. Normally, a neuter pronoun would be used with a neuter antecedent. The use of a masculine pronoun with a neuter antecedent implies reference to a person.)

(Note that in other places in the context the translators refer to the Holy Spirit by personal pronouns "He" and "Who" – John 14:16,17,26; 15:26; 16:7-14. These cases are helpful, but they are not as conclusive as the point made on verses 13,14 above, because the pronoun refers back to "comforter/helper," which is masculine in Greek, so naturally a masculine pronoun is used. In contrast, in John 16:13,14 "the Spirit of Truth" is neuter, but "He" is masculine. Nevertheless, even this is not conclusive, since "spirit" is an appositive referring back to the demonstrative pronoun "He," which is the subject of the sentence. So even here "He" could refer back to "comforter," as throughout the context of verses 7-14.)

Ephesians 1:13,14 – The Holy Spirit "***who***" is the guarantee of our inheritance (NKJV). (Again, this is a masculine pronoun referring to the neuter "Spirit," which would imply that it refers to a person. But note that some manuscripts here have the neuter "which" – see ASV.)

The fact that the translators use "He" and "who" in these passages strongly indicates that they see the original language as referring to a living Being. This evidence is helpful, but not conclusive in the original language.

He is classed with the Father and the Son, who are surely living individuals.

Matthew 28:19 – Jesus commands people to be baptized in the name of the Father, Son, and Holy Spirit. Surely the Father and Son are living spirit Beings. How could the command make sense if the Holy Spirit is just a power or characteristic, rather than a living Being like the Father and Son?

2 Corinthians 13:14 – The grace of the Lord Jesus Christ, and the love of God, and the communion of the Holy Spirit be with you all. Since Christ and God are living Beings, how would this make sense if the Holy Spirit is just an attitude or characteristic?

1 Peter 1:2 – We are elect according to the foreknowledge of the Father, in sanctification of the Spirit, for obedience and sprinkling of Jesus' blood. The Father and Son are living spirit Beings, so the Spirit must also be. All three are listed here as being involved in our salvation.

Luke 3:21,22 – When Jesus was baptized, the Father spoke from heaven, and the Holy Spirit descended in a bodily form like a dove.

God of the Bible

This pictures the Holy Spirit as having life of Himself, like the Father and Son, and He took a separate bodily form.

These verses show that the Holy Spirit acts jointly with other persons. Since He acts like a person along with other persons, this implies that He is a person like the other persons.

When all this evidence is considered as a whole, it proves that the Holy Spirit is a living person or individual being, not just a characteristic, attitude, power, or influence. (This does not deny that He **possesses** characteristics and attitudes. But He is **more** than just a characteristic or a power.) (See Romans 15:13,19.)

So the Holy Spirit is a living being, who possesses the characteristics of a person. He is referred to by terms that imply He is a personal Being. He acts and does work like a living Being. And He is described and classified along with other personal beings. We conclude that the Holy Spirit is a living Spirit Being, not just a characteristic or a part of another Being.

(Some passages "sound like" the Holy Spirit is inanimate, but note that Jesus is also called "the Word" in John 1. This may "sound like" something inanimate, but it really just describes the **work** He did in revealing God – verse 18. Other passages show He is a living Spirit Being. Likewise, other passages show the Holy Spirit is a living Being, and the passages that sound otherwise are simply describing some **work** He has done.)

(When folks claim the Holy Spirit is just power from God, consider also the following verses where the Holy Spirit is listed separately from His power: Acts 10:38; Luke 1:35; 1 Thessalonians 1:5.)

(See also John 14:26; 14:16,17; 15:26; 20:21,22; Acts 1:4,5; 2:32,33; 10:38; Luke 1:35; John 3:34; 1 Corinthians 12:4-6; 2 Corinthians 1:21,22; Ephesians 2:18; 4:4-6.)

Distinction from Other Spirit Beings

Since the Holy Spirit is a living spirit Being, we must consider next whether He is a separate and distinct individual from other spirit beings. Or could "Holy Spirit" just be another name for the Father or the Son or some other spirit being?

Distinct from Demons, Humans, and Angels

The Holy Spirit is distinct from Satan and demons.

Obviously He is distinct from Satan and demons, since by nature He is the **Holy** Spirit, whereas Satan and demons are not holy. Surely the Holy Spirit is not Satan or a demon.

This point should also distinguish the Holy Spirit from humans, since all humans at times are not holy. But notice further:

The Holy Spirit is distinct from humans and from angels.

1 Peter 1:10-12 – Angels and Old Testament prophets alike desired to look into the things that had been prophesied in the Old Testament and then were revealed in the New Testament. But the Holy Spirit sent from heaven revealed these things. So, the Holy Spirit is here distinguished both from angels and from humans.

1 Corinthians 2:10-13 – Men cannot know the things of God until they are revealed to us, but the Holy Spirit knows and reveals the things of God. This distinguishes the Holy Spirit from people. But the previous passage showed that the angels also did not know the things of God till the Holy Spirit revealed them. So, the Holy Spirit is neither an angel nor a human.

It also follows from these facts that, not only is the Holy Spirit not an angel (or a human), but in fact He is **above** the angels, even as He is above men.

(Acts 5:3,4; Mark 13:11; 2 Peter 1:21; Ephesians 3:3-5)

Distinct from God the Father and Jesus.

If the Holy Spirit is not a human or an angel, could it be that "Holy Spirit" is just another name for, or perhaps part of, the Father or Son? Or is the Holy Spirit a distinct individual from the Father and Son?

The Holy Spirit conceived Jesus in the womb of Mary – Matthew 1:18,20.

Did Jesus conceive Himself in Mary's womb? Surely not, so the Holy Spirit must be a separate and distinct person from Jesus. (Luke 1:35)

All three were present at Jesus' baptism – Luke 3:21,22.

Jesus was on earth being baptized. The Father spoke from heaven and acknowledged Jesus as His Son. And the Holy Spirit appeared in a bodily form like a dove. All three were present and distinguished one from the other. So just as the Son is here distinguished as a separate individual from the Father, so the Holy Spirit is distinguished from both the Father and the Son.

Blasphemy against Jesus is not blasphemy against the Spirit – Matthew 12:31,32

Blasphemy against the Son would be forgiven but not so blasphemy against the Holy Spirit. But if the Holy Spirit is just another name for Jesus or just part of Jesus, then blaspheming the Holy Spirit would be blaspheming Jesus.

We are baptized in the name of the Father, Son, and Holy Spirit – Matthew 28:19.

The Father and the Son are separate and distinct persons. The Son is not just another name for the Father, nor just part of the Father. So likewise, the Holy Spirit is not just another name for the Father or the

God of the Bible

Son, nor is He just part of the Father or the Son. The verse lists three distinct living spirit Beings.

The Father and the Son sent the Holy Spirit

John 15:26; 16:7 – Jesus was about to die and return to the Father in heaven (14:12,28; 16:7,10). He promised that He would then send the Holy Spirit to guide the apostles. Here you have one living individual Being sending another individual to do a work.

John 14:16,26; 15:26 – The Father also sent the Spirit. So, both the Father and the Son joined in sending the Holy Spirit. But if the fact that the Son sent the Holy Spirit proves that the Son is a different Being from the Spirit, then the fact that the Father sent the Spirit must likewise prove that the Father is a separate Being from the Holy Spirit.

The Spirit is another comforter besides Jesus – John 14:16.

In sending the Holy Spirit, Jesus sent "another" Helper. ("Another" is from a Greek word meaning "another one of the same sort.")

But if the Holy Spirit is just another name for Jesus or for part of Jesus, then the Holy Spirit would not be "another" comforter at all.

Ephesians 4:4-6 also lists the Spirit separately from the Father and from Jesus.

This passage mentions seven things of which there is only one each in God's true plan for man's unity (verse 3). But each item listed is separate and distinct from all other items listed: The body is not the hope, the baptism is not the Lord, the faith is not the God, etc. Likewise, the one Spirit (remember, this is a name for the Holy Spirit) is distinct from the one Lord (Jesus) and from the one God and Father.

So the Holy Spirit is a living spirit Being, just as surely as are the Father and Son. But He is not the Father nor the Son, nor is He just a part of the Father and Son. Rather, He is a distinct individual. If we can understand how the Father and the Son can exist as separate individuals, then we can understand how the Holy Spirit can exist as a separate individual.

(2 Corinthians 13:14; 1 Peter 1:2; Acts 10:38)

Deity of the Holy Spirit

If the Holy Spirit is a living Spirit Being, but He is not the Father or the Son, then what position does He hold? What level of authority does He possess and how should we view Him?

He Is Above the Demons, the Humans, and the Angels.

The Holy Spirit is a living Spirit Being, but we have proved He is not a demon, a human, or an angel. The only position left is that of Deity.

The Bible describes no other kinds of spirit beings other than those we have considered. Since the Holy Spirit is not any of the other kinds of beings, He must be Deity.

Further, we have learned that He is above all the other levels of beings, so this confirms that His position must be Deity. In order to believe otherwise, we would have to prove that some other level of authority exists.

He Is Referred to by Terms of Deity.

Acts 5:1-11

Ananias lied to the Holy Spirit – verse 3.

In so doing, he lied, not to men, but to God – verse 4.

In lying to the Holy Spirit, Ananias did not lie just to men; it follows that the Holy Spirit is more than just a man. And if the lie was told to God, then the Holy Spirit must partake of the character and nature of God. He possesses Deity.

(In this they tested the Spirit of the Lord – verse 9. It is wrong to test God – Matthew 4:7. But we are commanded to test other spirits – 1 John 4:1.)

He is the "Spirit of God."

In studying the names of the Spirit, we examined passages where the Holy Spirit is called "the Spirit of God." (See Matthew 3:16, compare Luke 3:22; 1 Corinthians 2:11,12, compare John 14:26; Ephesians 4:30). But how can He be "the Spirit of God" unless He possesses and partakes of the character and nature of God?

The spirit of a **man** possesses and partakes of the character and nature of man – humanity. The spirit of a **demon** possesses and partakes of the character and nature of demons – demonic. The spirit of an **angel** possesses and partakes of the character and nature of angels – angelic. It follows that the Holy Spirit could be the "Spirit of God" only if he possesses and partakes of the nature of **God** – Deity.

But we have already proved that the Holy Spirit is a living Spirit Being, and He is a distinct individual from the Father and the Son. So, the Holy Spirit is a living Spirit Being who possesses the character and nature of Deity. He must be a third Being in the Godhead, along with the Father and the Son.

(Compare Acts 2:17,18,4,33; 1 Thessalonians 4:8; Psalm 51:11; and Isaiah 63:10; Consider also "Spirit of Truth" in John 14:16,17; 15:26; .16:7-14; "Spirit of glory" in 1 Peter 4:14; "Spirit of life" in Rom, 8:2.)

(Compare also the expression "Son of God." Jesus is the "Son of God" in the sense that He partakes of the character and nature of God, yet He is a separate individual from the Father. Likewise, the "wife of Dave Pratte" is a separate individual from me, yet our relationship is so close that we are said to possess one another. So, the Holy Spirit is a separate spirit Being from the Father and Son, yet partakes of His nature and is so close that the Father and Son are said to possess Him.)

He Possesses the Character and Does the Works of Deity.

Creation, sustaining creation, and eternal existence

Genesis 1:2 – The Spirit of God (the Holy Spirit) was present at creation and was involved in it, even as were the Father and the Son.

Psalms 104:30 – The context describes God's provision for animals and the creation. He sends forth His Spirit and they are created and renewed.

Job 26:13 – By His Spirit He adorned the heavens.

So, the Holy Spirit was involved in doing the work of creating and sustaining the universe. This is the work of Deity.

(Job 33:4; 34:14,15)

Everywhere present

Psalms 139:7-12 – In describing God as all-knowing (verses 1-6) and present everywhere, David asked, "Where can I go from your Spirit?" He then describes how the Spirit would see him everywhere.

So, the Holy Spirit is omnipresent, which is a characteristic of Deity.

All-knowing source of Divine revelation

Mark 13:11 – When inspired men spoke for God, it was not they who spoke but the Holy Spirit.

John 16:13 – He guided inspired men into **all** truth. He is the source of all knowledge. This is surely the work of Deity. What other being would be so described if it did not possess Deity? (14:16,17,26; 15:26; 16:7-14) (The fact He does not speak on His own does not prove that He does not know all things. It means that He spoke in agreement with the Father and Son. – John 16:13)

1 Corinthians 2:10-14 – The Holy Spirit (verse 13) knows the mind of God (like a man's spirit knows his mind) and reveals it to men. How could this possibly be said of anyone who is not Deity? How could any lower being be said to know the mind of God?

Ephesians 3:3-5 – The Spirit made known the mystery of Christ, which had not been made known to men in earlier ages.

2 Peter 1:21 – Prophecy never came by man's will, but holy men spoke as they were moved by the Holy Spirit.

The message of the Scriptures is the message of God (2 Timothy 3:16). But the Holy Spirit is the Source Who had the power to reveal it.

Men acted as spokesmen or messengers, but they made clear it was not their message. They were not the source of origin of it, nor was it based on their authority. The same is true of angels. But the work of the Holy Spirit is contrasted to the work of the human teachers, in that the Spirit (along with the Father and the Son) is viewed as the source of the message and the authority behind it. This classes the Holy Spirit with Deity, not with lower beings. It attributes to the Holy Spirit the work and power of Deity.

(Acts 1:16; Mark 12:36; Acts 28:25; Hebrews 3:7; Isaiah 40:13)

Unlimited authority and power

Miracles

Throughout the Bible, the Holy Spirit is spoken of as the source of miracles. But miracles, by their very nature, are works that only God can do.

Matthew 1:18-20 – In the Virgin Birth, Mary conceived by the power of the Holy Spirit.

Acts 1:8; 2:4,33 – The Holy Spirit gave the apostles power to speak in tongues. (10:44-46; 19:6)

Hebrews 2:3,4 – God bore witness to the message of inspired men by signs, wonders, miracles, and gifts of the Holy Spirit.

1 Corinthians 12:4-11 – All miraculous powers are from the Spirit (the Holy Spirit – verse 3). He distributed these to men **according to His own will**.

Who besides Deity is spoken of as being the source of miracles? What man or angel could be described as distributing miraculous powers according to his will?

Miracles were often done through inspired men or angels, but they repeatedly denied that they were the **source** of the power (compare Acts 3:12; 4:10). The very nature and purpose of miracles demands that their source must be God – Deity. Yet the Holy Spirit is repeatedly spoken of as the source of the power. The only possible explanation for this is that the Holy Spirit possesses Deity.

Baptism

Matthew 28:19 – People of all nations are commanded to be baptized in the name of the Father, Son, and Holy Spirit. This passage places the Holy Spirit on equal authority with the Father and Son. Baptism is in the name of all three. The name or authority of the Holy Spirit is the basis of baptism right along with the Father and Son.

To see the significance of this, would God ever issue a command in the name of the Father, the Son, and a human being or even an angel? If a thing must be done in the name of Deity, what significance is there in adding the name of a man or an angel? Such would be foolish to the point of blasphemy.

Compare 1 Corinthians 1:10-13 – The Corinthians were divided over preachers. Paul teaches them in chapter 1-4 to emphasize Deity, not men, since men are just messengers for God (3:3-11; 4:1,2). We should glory in the Lord (Deity), not in men (1:29,31; 2:5; 3:21).

God of the Bible

To illustrate, Paul asks if he was **crucified** for us (verse 13). No, so Deity is important, not man. It would be blasphemy to exalt a man or angel as if he had died for us.

Then he asks if we are **baptized** in the **name** of Paul (verse 13). No. So, again, we should glory in Deity, because **we are baptized in the name of Deity**.

Note carefully: It would be blasphemy to be baptized in the name of any being that is not Deity. But we are baptized in the name of the Holy Spirit right along with the Father and Son. Therefore, the Holy Spirit possesses Deity as surely as do the Father and the Son.

The Holy Spirit does work and possesses a name/authority that only God can possess. Therefore, the Holy Spirit possesses Deity. (Matthew 12:28; Romans 15:19; 2 Corinthians 13:14)

Forgiveness, redemption, and sanctification

Matthew 28:19 – We are baptized in the name of the Father, Son, and Holy Spirit. But what is the purpose of baptism? To forgive sins! See Mark 16:15,16; Acts 2:38; 22:16; Romans 6:3,4; Galatians 3:27; 1 Peter 3:21. So sins are forgiven by the power and name of the Holy Spirit, right along with the Father and the Son.

But only God can forgive sins – Mark 2:5-7. Since sins are forgiven in baptism, then to be baptized in the name of anyone other than Deity would be blasphemy! But we are baptized in the name of the Holy Spirit, as well as the Father and the Son; so, the Holy Spirit possesses the power of Deity to forgive sins. (Compare 1 Corinthians 12:13.)

1 Corinthians 6:11 – Sinners are **justified** in the name of the Lord Jesus and by the Spirit of our God (the Holy Spirit). So the Holy Spirit justifies from sin. But only God can justify from sin, so the Holy Spirit is God.

1 Peter 1:2; Romans 15:16 – We are elect according to the foreknowledge of the Father, in **sanctification** of the Spirit, for obedience and sprinkling of the blood of Jesus. Again, all three Beings are involved in our salvation. Sanctification is essential to our salvation as surely as election and the blood of Jesus. Only Deity can sanctify men. The passage involves the Spirit in our salvation as fully as the other Beings of Deity.

The Holy Spirit has characteristics that only Deity possesses and does works that only Deity can do. Therefore, the Holy Spirit possesses Deity as surely as the Father and the Son do. (2 Thessalonians 2:13; Galatians 6:8; Ephesians 2:18)

Conclusion

The purpose of this study has been to increase our understanding of the Holy Spirit. But that understanding should lead us to a greater appreciation of Who the Holy Spirit is.

Our study has shown that the Holy Spirit is not just a force or a characteristic but is a living spirit Being who possesses the personal characteristics and does works that can only be true of Deity. We understand that the Father and the Son are separate and distinct living Spirit Beings, yet each possesses Deity. In the same way we should understand that the Holy Spirit is a third distinct individual who also possesses Deity. So, the God we worship consists of three separate and distinct Beings, yet together they make up the one true and living God.

If this is true, then we should realize that we can have a personal relationship with the Holy Spirit just as surely as we do with the Father and the Son. This is called "fellowship" with the Spirit – 2 Corinthians 13:14. We need to love, honor, and respect the Holy Spirit even as we do the Father and the Son, even as He loves us – Romans 15:30.

The Nature of Spiritual Gifts

Introduction:

Much confusion exists about the work of the Holy Spirit. As already learned in previous studies, the Holy Spirit is a living spirit Being in the Godhead, like the Father and Jesus Christ the Son. The purpose of this study is to learn what the Bible says about the work of the Spirit in miracles and spiritual gifts, especially in the New Testament age.

The Spirit has used miraculous gifts to **reveal** the will of God and to **confirm** that the message revealed really came from God (1 Corinthians 12:1-11). In this section, we wish to study the **nature** of those gifts. What were they like and what did they empower men to do?

The Holy Spirit has done various different works in history.

This study concerns mainly His work in New Testament times. Prior to the birth of Jesus, He did the following things:

* Active in creation and in sustaining the universe – Genesis 1:2; Job 33:4; 26:13; Psalm 104:30

* Guided Old Testament prophets – 2 Peter 1:21; Mark 12:36; 2 Samuel 23:2; Acts 1:16; 28:25; Hebrews 3:7; 10:15

* Conceived Jesus in Mary's womb – Matthew 1:18,20; Luke 1:35

Many miracles, which God or the Spirit did in the past, have ceased and will not be repeated.

* Creation – Genesis 1,2 (compare 2:1,2)

* The Flood of Noah's day – Gen 6-9 (note 9:8-17)

* The virgin birth – Matthew 1:18,20; Luke 1:35

* Jesus' resurrection

* The work of apostles living on earth (Acts 1:21,22).

Sometimes folks claim that the Spirit/God did miracles in the past, so He must do so today. They claim God is the same yesterday, today, and forever. If we teach that there are no miracles today, such folks claim we are saying God does not have the power He used to have or does not love us like He used to, etc.

To admit there are any miracles He has done but is not doing today is to admit all such arguments are not valid. But we just listed a number of miracles He has done, which we must agree He is not doing today. The question then becomes whether He is doing any miracles at all today.

Note that Satan has always produced lying counterfeits in imitation of what God does.

In particular, the Bible warns about:

* False prophets – Matthew 7:15; 2 Corinthians 11:13-15; 1 John 4:1; 2 Peter 2:1; Matthew 15:14; Acts 13:6-12; Revelation 2:2.

* False miracles (amazing works claimed to be from God) – Acts 8:9-13; 2 Thessalonians 2:9-12; Matthew 7:21-23; Exodus 7:8-12,20-22; 8:6,7,17-19; Matthew 24:24

Our study of the characteristics of **true** spiritual gifts will help us distinguish them from Satan's counterfeits. We will see that the nature of true spiritual gifts was such that Satan's false workers cannot duplicate them. So, we can distinguish the true from the fake by their characteristics.

Gifts of Direct Revelation

Until the Bible had been completed, God gradually revealed new revelation to people by direct guidance of the Spirit. But Satan has sent false prophets to mislead people. Many people claim to be "led" by the Spirit in addition to Bible teachings.

1 John 4:1 – Test the prophets to see if they are from God. This is a Divine command.

Matthew 7:15-21 – You can know false prophets by their fruits. The major fruit of a prophet is his teaching. One major way of testing prophets is by comparing the nature of their alleged revelations to true Bible revelations.

What were true revelations like? Do people today have direct guidance like the Bible describes? Let us consider the nature of direct revelations from God and then test other prophets by comparing their revelations to true revelations.

Consider some definitions:

Prophecy

Compare Exodus 4:10-16 to 7:1,2 as an example. Moses' was God's mouth because God told him what to say. So Aaron was Moses' mouth or spokesman, because Moses' told him what to say. But Exodus 7:1,2 calls this the work of a "prophet."

God ➔ Moses ➔ Aaron ➔ People

So, a prophet was a mouthpiece or a spokesman. Prophecy was the ability to speak the will of God by the direct guidance and inspiration of the Holy Spirit.

(Vine on "prophecy": "...prophecy is not necessarily, nor even primarily, foretelling. It is the declaration of that which cannot be known by natural means...it is the forth-telling of the will of God, whether with reference to the past, the present, or the future ...")

(Thayer on "prophet": "...one who, moved by the Spirit of God and hence his organ or spokesman, solemnly declares to men what he has received by inspiration...")

Other gifts

* Wisdom – the supernatural ability to make practical application of truth. (1 Corinthians 12:8; Luke 21:14,15; 1 Corinthians 2:6,7,10-13; 2 Peter 3:15)

* Knowledge – the supernatural ability to learn facts, information, or truths from God. (1 Corinthians 12:8; 2:12; Ephesians 3:3-5)

* Discerning of spirits – the supernatural ability to distinguish true prophets or teachings from false (1 Corinthians 12:10; compare 1 John 4:1).

Consider now the characteristics of true direct revelation.

The Revelation Always Gave God's Exact Will in Words God Selected.

The message was **divine** in origin, not in any sense **human**.

Direct revelation in the Bible

General passages

Matthew 10:19,20 – Men did not need to study what to say, because God would speak through them. It was not the men who would speak. God would give them **what** and **how** to speak.

1 Corinthians 14:37 – What was taught was the commands of the **Lord**.

Deuteronomy 18:18,19 – God put his words in the prophet's mouth. Then the prophet spoke to the people.

2 Peter 1:21 – Prophecy did not come by will of men, but men spoke as moved by the Holy Spirit.

2 Samuel 23:1,2 – God's word was on the prophet's tongue. The Spirit spoke by him.

(Exodus 4:10-16; 7:1,2; 1 Corinthians 2:10-13; 2:3-5; John 16:13; 14:26; Galatians 1:8-12; 1 Thessalonians 2:13; 2 Timothy 3:16,17; Luke 10:16; Ephesians 3:3-5; Exodus 24:3,4; Deuteronomy 30:9,10; Matthew 15:1-9; Isaiah 51:16; 59:21; Jeremiah 1:4-9; 30:1-4; 36:1-4; Ezekiel 3:4; Zechariah 7:12)

Some methods used

* Audible voice – 1 Samuel 3:1-18
* Vision – Acts 10:9-16
* Angel – Acts 10:3-8; Matthew 1:18-25;
* Dream – Genesis 37; Daniel 2; etc.
* Appearance of Jesus – Acts 9:3-6

Note that every direct revelation was capable of being described in **words:** God gave the words that could be repeated to others. This could be done even if the one who received the revelation did not fully understand the lesson taught by those words.

(Often the prophet who received the revelation, though he knew what had been done and said, still had to study and meditate on the revelation in order to understand it, just as we have to study the Scriptures to understand them or as people who heard the prophet speak would have to study what he had said to understand it – Acts 10:17; 11:1-18; 16:10; Daniel 12:8; 1 Peter 1:10-12; Revelation 17:6.)

Modern "revelations"

In contrast to Bible examples of direct revelation, consider the claims of people today who say they are led of the Spirit.

Vague "leadings"

Often people today have an emotional experience, a vague feeling or impression, or some overwhelming sense of assurance. As a result, they are convinced that they have been saved or that some church or doctrine is true or that they should follow a certain course of action. Then they say the Spirit has "revealed" this to them, or they were "led" by the Spirit, and they claim it is God's will.

When questioned about the nature of the revelation, they often cannot clearly describe what happened or how the revelation came – they cannot put this into words. They usually acknowledge, "It is not as though I heard a voice or saw an angel." They say it is "better felt than told."

An excellent example of this is Mormon "testimony" by which they claim to know Mormonism is true. When asked to describe it, the best they can say is "burning in the bosom" and an overwhelming sense of assurance that Mormonism is true. This is nothing but an emotional experience, but they are convinced it is a revelation from the Holy Spirit.

Such "revelations" are Satan's counterfeits for true revelations. When people receive true revelations from God they are always able to describe exactly in what *form* the revelation came, and they can put into **words** the **content** of the message.

God of the Bible

"Understanding" of Scripture

Other people claim that the Holy Spirit directly reveals to them an understanding of the Bible, when they study it. But this is not prophecy nor is any such spiritual gift described in Scripture. Prophecy and direct revelation did not involve study and understanding Scripture; they involved *infallible revelation that was not learned by study*.

(The Bible does teach us to pray for wisdom and understanding – James 1:5; Colossians 1:9; etc. But this comes through natural means as one studies the Scripture and applies it in life. Nothing about this involves direct revelation or supernatural spiritual gifts.)

The Revelation Was Always True, Inerrant, and Infallible.

Bible examples

John 17:17 – God's word is *truth.* (Psalm 119:160,142)

Deuteronomy 18:20-22 – A prediction may claim to be from God, but if it does not come true, then it is not from God. (Jeremiah 28:9

Psalm 33:4; 119:128; 19:8 – God's word is *right*.

Revelation 21:5 – These words are true and faithful. (19:9)

Matthew 22:32 – Even the tense of verbs must be accurate. (Galatians 3:16?)

So true Divine revelations could not be false in any sense, including in their predictions of the future. Everything they say is accurate and true, and everything they predict must come true. If their predictions do not come true, they are not true revelations from God.

(Titus 1:2; Hebrews 6:18; 1 Corinthians 14:33; Psalm 147:4,5; Job 37:16; Numbers 23:19)

Modern examples

Modern "prophets" often make predictions that do not come true.

Note that the Scriptures expressly state that we ought to test whether or not revelations are from God by seeing whether or not their predictions of the future come true. So let us do this with predictions some have claimed to be from God.

* Many groups have mistakenly predicted the time of Jesus' coming, etc. (Jehovah's Witnesses, Adventists, and others).

* Jean Dixon became famous by predicting the death of President Kennedy. But one rarely hears about her predictions that failed. These include:

World War III would begin in 1958. (Did it?)

Russia would put the first man on the moon. (A good guess since they led the space race at the time. But America was first; Russia still has not done it.)

Lyndon Johnson would be the democratic candidate for president in 1968. (Since he was already president, he would have been the logical choice. But he refused to run.)

President Ford would resign and Rockefeller would replace him. (Ford never resigned; Rockefeller was never president.)

Reagan would be the Republican candidate for president in 1976. (Ford won the nomination instead).

(Others: Red China would enter the UN in 1958 – it didn't happen till much later. Vietnam war would end within 90 days of May 7, 1966 – it did not happen till much later. See Halbrook, 1974 Florida College lectures; O'Neal, *Searching the Scriptures*, 6/78)

* Joseph Smith, Jr.

Jesus would come within 56 years of 1835

The temple would be rebuilt within a generation of 1832

Several Mormon apostles (alive in his day) would live to see Jesus return

The Civil War would be a "full end of all nations"

He "translated" the *Book of Abraham* as part of Mormon Scripture. Eventually it was translated by language experts and turned out to be a book of heathen Egyptian burial rites, totally different in meaning from what Smith "translated."

* Faith healer Robert Tilton – Beverly Crowley sued Tilton because he kept sending requests for donations to Mrs. Crowley's husband and promising to heal him. One such letter said, "God spoke to me this morning specifically about you, Tom, and He's going to heal you." When the letter was written, Mrs. Crowley's husband had been dead for five months! – via Greg Gwin, West Knoxville bulletin.

* National Enquirer psychics

22 false predictions in 1975 (R. Harris, *Contender*, 1/76)

14 misses in second half of 1977 (O'Neal, *Searching the Scriptures* 6/78)

Of 58 predictions, only two were right, and these were easy guesses (Bob Craig, *Gospel Anchor*, 5/79)

* Mohammed – He once predicted there would be 73 sects of Islam, of which only one would survive. But Muslims admit there have been far more than 73. And today many sects, not just one, still survive. (*Encyclopedia Britannica*, XII-711)

Often people follow some "leading" that proves to be untrue.

They have some urge that is just like other urges that they attribute to the Holy Spirit. But when they follow the "leading," they get into trouble or it does not work out like they supposed it would.

Specifically, I have had such people tell me how the Holy Spirit would lead them to talk to someone about the gospel. Some have said the Holy Spirit "led" them to study the Bible with me. However, after studying together they soon learned that I was presenting Bible evidence that contradicted their beliefs and they could not answer with Scripture. So they refused to continue studying with me!

Usually, such people just forget about these "leadings" that don't work out and continue to emphasize the ones that they think had a favorable outcome. Some even admit that the "leading" wasn't from God. But then how can they trust other "leadings"? The truth is that none of them are from God, because they don't have the characteristics of true revelation.

People who claim to be led of the Spirit often contradict one another.

Mormons, Pentecostals, Catholics, etc., all claim that their leaders are led by the Spirit, but their teachings are completely contradictory, and often they teach that the other groups are in error.

Remember that real Divine revelation is true and faithful with no errors. How can the "revelations" of these groups all be "true" when they disagree with one another (1 Corinthians 1:13; 14:33)?

These examples illustrate how prophets (since the completion of Scripture) fail when they attempt to predict the future. When we compare them to Bible prophets, exactly as the Scripture tells us to do, we find they are not true or infallible.

The Revelation Always Harmonized with Other Divine Revelation.

Divine revelation is always harmonious. It never contradicts other Divine revelation. So, one way to check messages that claim to be revealed from God is to compare them to other revelation that we already have. If they contradict, then they cannot be from God.

Bible examples

Acts 17:11,12 – The Bereans checked the new revelations by comparing them to old ones.

Galatians 1:6-9 – Any new revelation, which differs from previous ones, is false.

2 John 9-11 – How do we know which teachers to accept? By comparing what they teach to the doctrine of Christ (which is found in the Bible).

In this way, New Testament prophets often used the Old Testament to prove they were of God – Luke 24:25-27,44-46; Acts 2:14-36; John 5:39,46; etc.

Teaching must be false if it contradicts other Divine teaching. We know the Bible is from God, so we can determine whether or not other teaching is true by comparing it to the Bible.

(Matthew 7:15-27; 1 Corinthians 14:33; John 16:13; 1 John 2:3-6; 4:1,6)

Modern examples

Many people today may claim direct revelation, yet they teach things that directly contradict the Bible. Some examples:

(1) Some teach we are saved before or without immersion in water (Compare Mark 16:15,16; Acts 2:38; 22:16; Romans 6:3,4; Galatians 3:27; I Peter 3:21)

(2) Others teach that the Old Testament law is still binding (Compare Hebrews 10:1-10; 7:11-14; 8:6-13; 9:1-4; 2 Corinthians 3:6-11; Galatians 3:24,25; 5:1-6; Romans 7:1-7; Ephesians 2:11-16; Colossians 2:13-17)

(3) Some have women preachers (Compare 1 Corinthians 14:34,35; 1 Timothy 2:11,12)

These doctrines directly contradict the Scriptures that we know are from God. It follows that the groups that teach them are in error. When such groups claim to be following direct revelations from God, we can know those revelations are false and the men who teach them are false teachers.

A fourth characteristic of direct revelation is that it was confirmed by miraculous signs. This will be discussed under a later point.

God has warned us to test those who claim to have the gift of direct revelation to see whether or not they are from God. We should not just accept that they are teaching the truth. Three ways the Scriptures give us to test such teachers is by examining how the person claims to have received the revelation, by seeing whether or not their predictions of the future come true, and especially by comparing their teaching to the Scriptures we already have from God.

Today, the result of such examinations will always be that modern revelations do not measure up to the characteristics of Divine revelation. That is because the Bible as we have it is complete, and spiritual gifts ceased when it was completed (1 Corinthians. 13:8-11). What is the basis of your faith? Do you follow the true word of God found in the Scriptures?

Gifts of Miraculous Confirmation

In order to prove that certain people had a message from God, the Spirit accompanied their preaching by miraculous powers. People today often claim to have these powers like Jesus and His apostles did. Remember that Satan sends counterfeit miracles to confuse people. One way to recognize counterfeit miracles is to compare them to true New Testament miracles.

God of the Bible

There are three terms used in the New Testament to refer to miracles (see Acts 2:22; 2 Corinthians 12:12; Hebrews 2:3,4). Consider some definitions of them.

"Miracle"

Translated "mighty work" or "power" in ASV.

Defined "power, inherent ability ... works of supernatural origin and character, such as could not be produced by natural agents and means..." – Vine.

This term emphasizes the **power** possessed by the One (God) who is the source of the event.

"Sign"

Defined "a sign consisting of a wonder or miracle, an event that is contrary to the usual course of nature..." – Arndt and Gingrich.

This term emphasizes the **unique nature** of the event. It is impossible by the normal laws of nature or human ability, so that its very occurrence proves it happened by the power of God.

"Wonder"

Defined "something strange, causing the beholder to marvel" – Vine. This word is always used in connection with "sign," so it too refers to that which is impossible by natural law. It emphasizes the **amazing** or surprising character of the event.

To help us understand the nature of true Biblical miracles, consider the following characteristics of true miracles.

Note that every New Testament miracle possessed all four of these characteristics. In some cases, as with all eyewitness testimony, certain details are not mentioned; but when the details are mentioned, they always harmonize with these characteristics. As we proceed, we will note the differences between these true Bible miracles and those events which people today claim are miracles like those in the Bible.

There Was Conclusive Evidence that the Event Really Occurred.

The occurrence of the event was unmistakably evident to observers.

Bible miracles

There was no sleight of hand or trickery. In regard to healings, there was clear evidence that the people had organic disorders, and there was conclusive proof that the problem was removed. There were no invisible or undetectable diseases, no psychosomatic problems (caused by the person's mental or emotional state, such that an improvement in their mental or emotional state would cause the removal of the problem).

Consider some examples:

* Lazarus – John 11:17,38,39,43-45. All the witnesses could see for themselves that he had been dead but came alive again.

* Blind man – John 9:1,7,18-20,21,25 – Unquestionably the man was blind from birth, but then he was so healed he could see.

* Woman bowed together – Luke 13:11,13,16 – All could see she was hunchbacked, but then she was straightened.

* Lame man – Acts 3:2,7,8,10; 4:22 – Many people knew he could not walk, but it was obvious that he was enabled to do so. (Compare 14:8-11.)

(Compare Luke 7:11-17; Acts 13:6-12; Mark 1:44; 2:1-4, 10-12; 4:35-41; 7:32-37; Matthew 12:9,14; 14:22-33; John 6:5-14; 2:1-11.)

Modern so-called miracles

Often today there is no evidence the person really had a physical disease, or there may be no proof the disease was removed. Or the problem may have been the result of a person's state of mind and was relieved because of his trust in the healer, combined with the emotions of the moment, the desire to be healed, the power of suggestion, and the hypnotic powers of the healer.

Some examples:

> ...a very pretty young girl limped up to the stage. She waved her leg brace in the air and stood, with her pelvis tilted badly, on one good leg and one short, withered leg ... Everyone applauded. The girl cried.

> This scene was, to my mind, utterly revolting. This young girl had a withered leg, the result of polio. It was just as withered now as it had been ten minutes earlier, before Kathryn Kuhlman called for someone to remove her brace. Now she stood in front of ten thousand people giving praise to the Lord – and indirectly to Kathryn Kuhlman – for a cure that hadn't occurred and wasn't going to occur – Nolen, *Healing: A Doctor in Search of a Miracle,* page 65.

> Not once, in the hour and a half that Kathryn Kuhlman spent healing, did I see a patient with an obvious organic disease healed (i.e., a disease in which there is a structural alteration) – Nolen, page 66.

Local people were personally involved in the miracles.

Bible examples

When inspired men sought to convince people that they had power to do miracles, they did not tell testimonies of miracles they had done elsewhere. They simply did miracles on people in the local area. Local people received the effects of the miracles, and local people could observe the evidence for themselves.

People could then check the matter out. They could question the people involved, check out whether they had really been ill, observe if there was a complete healing or whether there were relapses, etc. So, they could determine for themselves whether there had been a real miracle.

* Lazarus – John 11:1,17-19,31,45 – Lazarus was healed in his own hometown, where he was known to be dead and could then be observed alive. People could question those who knew him.

* Blind man – John 9:1,7-9,18-20 – To determine the validity of the event, people could contact witnesses. Jesus was not afraid to have people check out the validity of His miracles. He did not accuse them of evil simply because they checked (though He did rebuke those who, having checked out the evidence, still did not believe).

* Son of the widow of Nain – Luke 7:11-17. This young man was raised from the dead in the presence of his own funeral party – the very people who knew him best, knew of his death, and could see for themselves that he had come back to life.

* Lame man – Acts 3:2,9,10; 4:22,16. This man was known by the people of the city to be lame. Multitudes of these people saw him after he was healed.

(See also Acts 13:6-12; Mark 2:1-4,10-12.)

Modern so-called miracles

When questioned about the validity of the miracles they claim happened, people today want to argue and debate about it. They give testimonials of miracles they have done or seen. Usually the most impressive accounts involve people far away and/or long ago, whom no one locally can know or question or check out.

Or they will argue at length about Bible passages, which they affirm prove miracles are for today. Why not dispense with all the testimony and argumentation? If people have power like Jesus and His apostles did, let them do like Jesus and His apostles did. Just do miracles that we can observe and check out for ourselves!

Miracles were often done in the presence of unbelievers, false teachers, and even false miracle-workers.

Even opponents of the truth could not deny the occurrence of the miracles.

Bible miracles

When men had true power to do miracles, they were not afraid to do them in the presence of people who had questions or doubts or even openly opposed their teaching. Often they deliberately did miracles in the presence of those who did false miracles, so that people could see the difference. Opponents could not deny that God's prophets could do miracles; often they even admitted the power.

* Ten plagues – Exodus 8:17-19. Pharaoh's magicians tried to duplicate Moses' miracles, but eventually they admitted Moses did miracles by the power of God.

* Crossing the Red Sea – Exodus 14:21-31. The sea parted so Israel could cross on dry ground. When Pharaoh's army tried to cross, the sea collapsed and they drowned.

* Elijah on Mt. Carmel – 1 Kings 18:20-40 – Elijah challenged the prophets of Baal to a showdown to see who had real power of miracles.

* High priest's servant – Luke 22:50,51. In the presence of the men who came to arrest Him, Jesus restored the ear that had been cut off one of those who arrested Him!

* Lazarus – John 11:47,48. After Jesus raised Lazarus, His enemies admitted His miracles.

* Jesus' miracles – Acts 2:22. Peter said the people who killed Jesus knew of His miracles.

* Lame man – Acts 4:10,14-16. After Peter and John healed the lame man (3:1-10), the Jewish opponents admitted it was a great miracle known to all the people.

* Philip and Simon – Acts 8:5-13. Simon did works claimed to be from God. But when Philip did true miracles in his presences, Simon was so amazed he was converted.

* Saul of Tarsus – Acts 9:1-9 – After His resurrection, Jesus appeared to the persecutor Saul to convince Him of the resurrection.

* Paul and Elymas – Acts 13:6-12. When Elymas opposed the truth, Paul struck him blind. Elymas could neither prevent nor overcome it. He admitted the miracle by seeking a guide.

These examples show that one way to recognize counterfeit "miracles" is to compare them to the characteristics of true miracles in the Bible. When people claim to do miracles but those "miracles" do not measure up to the character of Bible miracles, then those teachers are false teachers, just like people in the Bible who claimed to do miracles but could not do as true miracle-workers did.

(Numbers 16:28-35 & chapter 17; Matthew 12:22-24; Luke 5:17-26; 6:6-11; 13:10-17; 1 Kings 13:1-6; chapter 22; 2 Kings 1 & 6; Daniel 2,3,&5; Jeremiah 28; Acts 19:11-17)

(Note: In the above cases, miracles were done to convince either the false teachers or else the audience to believe. When no such outcome was possible, miracles were not done. At Nazareth Jesus refused to do many miracles because of the unbelief of the people – Matthew 13:54-58; Mark 6:1-6. In light of the above evidence, this does not mean He was afraid or unable to do them, but simply He saw no purpose to it. He knew people would not believe anyway, because they had seen His miracles and still disbelieved. Even so He did do a few miracles there, and He gave the greater sign of His resurrection. Jesus refused to cast pearls before swine – Matthew 7:6.)

God of the Bible

Modern so-called miracles

Today, those who claim miracle power often refuse to even attempt them if opponents are present. They may say they cannot do them because of the unbelief in the audience.

Whereas even the opponents of God's teachers often admitted that Bible miracles occurred, today many of us deny they are occurring (see again Nolen, page 66 above and page 90 below). And when we do, none of us suffer consequences such as happened to Elymas, Pharaoh, etc. Who today will do to false teachers what Paul did to Elymas?

Their false claims regarding miracles demonstrate them to be false teachers.

True Miracles Were Sudden.

True miracles

The miraculous event took place quickly at precisely the time the inspired man attempted to do it or said it would occur. It did not take days, weeks, or months to gradually develop.

* Acts 3:7 – The lame man immediately leaped and walked.
* Luke 13:11-13 – The hunchbacked woman was immediately made straight.
* Mark 2:10-12 – The paralyzed man got up immediately.
* Mark 5:25-29 – The woman who had bled for 12 years was healed immediately.
* Mark 5:35-42 – Jairus' dead daughter arose immediately when Jesus raised her.
(Acts 13:11; 14:8-11; John 9:1,6,7; Mark 1:42; Luke 7:14,15; 1 Kings 18:25-30,35-39; etc.)

Modern "miracles"

In most modern cases, if healing occurs at all, it takes days, weeks, or months. Such gradual healings could be explained as simply natural processes, yet they are claimed as miracles.

Examples from Oral Roberts' *Abundant Life* magazine, Sept., 1974:

> She phoned the Prayer Tower and requested prayer for me ... 3 days went by, and to everyone's amazement I was not only still alive, but improving. And as the days passed I kept improving. Although my healing was slow, I now realize God might have planned it that way... – *Abundant Life*, page 17

> I can't say the miracle I needed came right away, or even that the year of 1973 wasn't a nightmare at times. Immediately following surgery, Joe went through 6 months of extensive chemotherapy. Then came the radiation treatments ... By the end of the year, I believe the doctors can pronounce him cured – *Abundant Life*, page 20.

Another Christian and I visited the "Hallelujah House" in Ft. Wayne, Indiana, where a leader testified of his "miracle." He broke his back but decided the Lord would heal him, so he left the hospital despite the doctors' warnings. I asked if he jumped out of bed and ran home. He said he couldn't with a broken back! They wheeled him out, he went home and fifteen weeks later he was well. He offered to have us feel on his back the place where it had been broken but healed. I said it was not a miracle because it was not immediate, and a miracle would leave no sign the problem ever existed.

On a radio program in Louisville, KY, Ken Green challenged a healer to come on his program and do a miracle. A preacher accepted the challenge, so Ken had a blind man come to be healed. The preacher tried to heal him, but the man still could not see. The preacher said, "It may happen tomorrow, next week, or next month. If it ever happens, it's a miracle." (Can you imagine Jesus ever saying this?)

Remember, when modern "miracles" lack the characteristics of Bible miracles, we can know they are frauds, and those who perpetrate them are false teachers.

True Miracles Were Always Successful.

True miracles

Neither Jesus nor His apostles (after they received Holy Spirit baptism) ever attempted a miracle and failed. There was no kind of disease they were unable to heal.

Matthew 4:23,24 – Jesus healed **all manner** of diseases.
Matthew 14:34-36 – **All** were healed.
Acts 5:12,15,16 – They were healed **every one**.
Jesus and His apostles did all the following:
* Healed one born blind (John 9:1)
* Healed one born lame (Acts 3:2; 4:22)
* Healed lepers (Mark 1:40-45)
* Raised the dead (John 11; Luke 7:11-17; Acts 9:36-42)
* Healed missing or withered body parts (Luke 22:49-51; Mark 3:1-5)
* Turned water to wine (John 2:1ff)
* Walked on water (Matthew 14:25-33)
* Calmed storms (Mark 4:25-41)
* Fed thousands with a few loaves and fishes and had more left over than they started with (Matthew 8:16,17; 10:1; 9:35; 12:15; Mark 7:32-37; 16:17,18).

God of the Bible

They did not fail even when unbelievers were present (see previous notes), or when the person who received the effect of the miracles had no faith.

* Pharaoh, his magicians, and the Egyptians suffered the plagues exactly because of their lack of faith – Exodus 8:17-19; 14:21-31.

* Elijah called fire from heaven when the people lacked faith – 1 Kings 18:20-40.

* Peter was rescued though he lacked faith – Matthew 14:25-33.

* Jesus calmed a storm though the disciples lacked faith – Mark 4:35-41.

* Dead people have no faith – Luke 7:11-17; John 11:38-44.

* Surely the high priest's servant who came to arrest Jesus lacked faith- Luke 22:50,51.

* Elymas received a miracle because he lacked faith – Acts 13:6-12.

People did not need faith to receive a miracle, but sometimes miracles were done as a reward for faith. In these cases, the man of God knew miraculously that the faith existed (Acts 14:8-10; Mark 6:1-6). In any case, they never attempted a miracle, failed, and blamed it on the people's lack of faith.

(Compare John 9:1,6-8,35-38; Acts 3:1-12; 8:5-13.)

(In two cases, the apostles failed – Matthew 17:14-20; 14:25-33. But this was before they received Holy Spirit baptism, and in both cases it is stated that they failed because **they** – the ones attempting to do the miracle – lacked faith, not because the people wanting to receive the miracle lacked faith.)

Modern "miracles"

Modern "miracle-workers" never cure all the people who come, they often attempt and fail, and often there are certain kinds of cases they will not even attempt to heal. Sometimes when they fail, they blame the failure on a lack of faith of those who want the miracle.

Examples:

...I can detect the presence of the evil spirit, to know what his name is, or the number of them. Now sometimes it doesn't work that clearly, but when it does work that clearly I know their number and their name, and usually have the power to cast them out. I don't always. – Oral Roberts, *Twelve Greatest Miracles of My Ministry*, page 116.

Our daughter Sharon knew a Christian who had lost an eye and wore a patch over the empty socket. He attended a service of a woman healer. As the service progressed, she called on him to stand up. No doubt thinking he just had a diseased eye, she said the Lord had healed him so he should take off that eye patch! He turned to the audience displaying his empty socket, saying, "What has she done to my eye? Make her give me back my eye!" The meeting broke up and the woman had to leave town!

At one point the young man with liver cancer staggered down the aisle in a vain attempt to claim a 'cure.' He was turned away, gently, by Maggie. When he collapsed into a chair I could see his bulging abdomen – as tumor-laden as it had been earlier – Nolen, page 66.

Finally it was over ... I spent a few minutes watching the wheelchair patients leave. All the desperately ill patients who had been in wheelchairs were still in wheelchairs ... I stood in the corridor watching the hopeless cases leave, seeing the tears of the parents as they pushed their crippled children to the elevators – Nolen, page 67.

Remember, when people claim to do miracles but do not measure up to the characteristics of Bible miracles, they are frauds like the false miracle workers in the Bible.

True Miracles Were Complete and Perfect

True Miracles

True miracles always completely accomplished what the inspired man said they would and always completely satisfied the need. In healings, people returned immediately to complete and normal health. Every symptom of the disease was removed. There were no partial improvements, no relapses, and no need for further medical care and treatment.

* Matthew 12:10,13 – A man's withered hand was restored whole as the other hand.

* Mark 1:40-45 – A leper showed himself to the priest as testimony of a complete healing.

* Mark 2:10-12 – The paralyzed man could walk and carry his bed.

* Acts 3:8 – The lame man leaped and walked.

(Compare Matthew 14:36; 1 Kings 18; John 9:7,11; Acts 13:11; Luke 13:11-13; 7:14,15; Mark 7:32-37.)

Modern "miracles"

Modern healers claim miracles in cases where there is only slight apparent improvement or temporary gain, even if recovery is not complete, even if further medical treatment is required, or even if people soon have a relapse.

Examples:

...the man with kidney cancer in his spine and hip ... and who had his borrowed wheelchair brought to the stage and shown to the audience when he had claimed a cure, was now back in his wheelchair. His 'cure,' even if only a hysterical one, had been extremely short-lived – Nolen, page 67.

[Mrs. Sullivan had claimed a cure of back cancer.] 'At four o'clock the next morning, I woke up with a horrible pain in my back. It was so bad that I ... didn't dare move ... In the morning we called the doctor. He took me to the hospital and got some X-rays that showed one of my vertebrae had partially collapsed. He said it was probably from the bending and running I had done [at the healing service]. I stayed in the hospital, in traction, for a week. When I went home I was back in my brace'... Mrs. Sullivan died of cancer four months after she had been 'cured' at Kathryn Kuhlman's miracle service – Nolen, page 99.

Again, when people claim to do miracles but cannot duplicate the characteristics of true Bible miracles, then they are frauds like those in the Bible who falsely claimed to do miracles.

Summary: True Miracles Are Impossible by Natural Law

Every true miracle possessed all four of the above characteristics.

This demonstrated that the event was impossible by natural law, but had to be God's intervention. We will see that this was necessary in order for miracles to accomplish their purpose of confirming the word. When people today claim as miracles events that do not possess all these characteristics, they demonstrate: (1) either they misunderstand Bible miracles, or (2) they are false miracle workers, like those in the Bible whose works could not measure up to true miracles.

We have already given many examples in which modern preachers claim to do miracles yet their works lack the needed characteristics. Many other examples can be given of events clearly not impossible by natural law, yet which are claimed as miracles.

With my next letter to Brother Roberts I included an increased Seed-Faith amount ... First, my husband got a raise in salary. Then the Lord threw the miracle-doors wide open. We were able to build a new home! – *Abundant Life*, page 17.

This University is one of the few colleges ever to have achieved full accreditation in [six years] – and ... granted the full ten-year term when first accredited ... Another miracle! – Roberts, *Twelve Greatest Miracles* ..., page 131

"The Miracle of Our Athletic Programs" – In 6 years ORU's basketball team set an NCAA scoring record, led the nation in rebounding, went to the NIT and won a game! It "was unbelievable unless you believe in miracles." – Roberts, *Twelve Greatest Miracles* ..., page 133.

The Bible distinguishes miracles from events that happen in answer to prayer according to natural law.

We have already described the distinction between true miracles and false miracles. But there is a third category of events in which God answers prayer, but does so by working through natural law. These events are blessings from God for which He should be thanked, but they are not properly classed as miracles because they are capable of occurring according to natural law. They do not have the characteristics nor accomplish the purposes of miracles.

Consider some examples that show the difference between miracles and answers to prayer through natural law:

Obtaining food

If we pray for daily bread (Matthew 6:11), then get a job and work for it (Ephesians 4:28) or grow it from the ground, that is a blessing from God in answer to prayer through natural law. But is not a miracle in the Bible sense of the term.

But a miracle would be: (1) using a boy's lunch to feed thousands of people and having more food left over than you started with (Matthew 14:13-21), or (2) manna coming directly from heaven and lying on the ground to be picked up (Exodus 16:14-16), or (3) turning water to wine (John 2:1ff).

Conception of a child

If a man and his wife conceive a child by natural procreation (Genesis 4:1,2), that is a blessing from God (Psalm 127 & 128). If they prayed for a child, it would be an answer to prayer. But it is not a miracle, since it happened according to natural law.

But miracles would be as when God created woman from the man's rib (Genesis 2:21,22) or caused Jesus to be conceived in the womb of a virgin (Matthew 1:18-25).

Healing from disease

If we pray for good health (3 John 2), God may bless us by healing in accordance with the gradual natural body process of healing, perhaps aided by medical or surgical treatment, diet, exercise, etc. This would be a blessing from God in answer to prayer, but it is not a miracle since it is in accord with natural law.

Miraculous healings, however, had the characteristics we have described and therefore did not occur according to natural law.

We should believe that God does answer prayer and meet our needs today through natural law. This does not mean, however, that these events are miracles. They do not fit the characteristics of miracles, nor do they accomplish the purpose of miracles. The Bible never calls such things as these miracles.

Conclusion

At the end of his investigations of Kuhlman's miracles, Dr. Nolen concluded:

> In talking to these patients I tried to be as honest, understanding and objective as possible. The only things I refused to dispense with – couldn't have dispensed with even if I

God of the Bible

had tried – were my medical knowledge and my common sense. I listened carefully to everything they told me and followed up every lead which might, even remotely, have led to a confirmation of a miracle. When I had done all this I was led to an inescapable conclusion: none of the patients who had returned ... to reaffirm the cures they had claimed at the miracle service had, in fact, been miraculously cured of anything, by either Kathryn Kuhlman or the Holy Spirit.

We believe God can and does heal people today in answer to prayer through natural law. But we thoroughly deny that modern miracle-workers are doing the kind of true miracles done by Jesus and His apostles. They deceive the people and are really doing counterfeits.

Speaking in Tongues

The Bible contains several examples of the gift of speaking in tongues – Acts 2:1-13; 10:44-46; 19:1-7; 1 Corinthians 12-14; Mark 16:17-20. This gift served both the purpose of revelation and the purpose of confirmation.

People often claim this gift today saying they want to receive the "Pentecost experience." Do these people possess the same gift as recorded in the Bible, or do they have a counterfeit? Remember that Satan often sends false miracles to try to mislead people.

One way to determine whether or not modern "tongues" are genuine is to compare them to Bible examples of tongue speaking. Are they the same or different?

Notice carefully the characteristics of tongue speaking.

Tongues Were Existing Native Languages.

One definition of the English word "tongue" is: "the language or dialect of a particular people" (*Random House College Dictionary*). We often say people speak "their native tongue."

(Vine defines the Greek word (γλωσσα) "...(3) (a) a language ... (b) the supernatural gift of speaking in another language without it having been learnt.")

Natural "tongues" refer to existing native languages

New Testament

Revelation 5:9 – Jesus redeemed people of every tribe and **tongue** (γλωσσα) and nation.

Revelation 14:6 – An angel preached to every nation, tribe, **tongue** (γλωσσα) and people.

(See also Revelation 7:9; 10:11; 11:9; 13:7; 17:15; etc.)

Old Testament

1 Corinthians 14:21, discussing the gift of tongues, quotes Isaiah 28:11 about people speaking other "tongues." The Hebrew word for "tongue" in Isaiah 28:11 is LASHON, which is used for native, natural, human languages in several passages.

Deuteronomy 28:49 – The Lord will bring a nation against you from afar, ... a nation whose **language** (tongue) you will not understand.

Daniel 1:4 – Daniel and his friends were taught the **language** (tongue) of the Chaldeans. Note that tongues were languages that could be learned by natural means.

So, tongues were languages, such as English, French, Spanish, German, Russian, etc.

Supernatural tongues also refer to existing native languages – Acts 2

This is the first and the clearest Bible example of tongues.

Verse 4 – The Holy Spirit empowered the apostles to speak in other "tongues" (γλωσσα). (*The NKJV Greek-English Interlinear New Testament* gives an alternative translation: "different languages.")

Verses 5,9-11 – Men from different nations were gathered in Jerusalem. These men would speak different natural, native languages.

Verses 6,8,11 – These people heard the apostles speak in the **languages or tongues** in which they were born. (Verses 6,8 use the word διαλεκτος, but verse 11 uses γλωσσα.)

The passage defines "tongues" for us. They were the native "languages" of the hearers. The true "Pentecost experience" involved speaking existing native languages.

(Note: The gift that came on Cornelius' household in Acts 10 was a 'like gift' – see 11:15-17.)

Do modern "tongues" refer to existing native languages?

1 John 4:1 – Many false prophets exist, so we should try the prophets. It is right for us to put to the test those who claim to have the Bible gift of tongues today.

John 8:17 – Jesus said facts regarding historical events (such as what people have or have not done) can be determined on the basis of the testimony of witnesses. (Matthew 18:16; 2 Corinthians 13:1; 1 Timothy 5:19; Hebrews 10:28; Deuteronomy 17:6; 19:15)

We determine what is pleasing or displeasing to God, not on the basis of the testimony of witnesses, but on the basis of God's word. But witnesses can testify regarding what people have done. We quote witnesses here to show what modern so-called tongue-speakers practice; then we compare that to the Bible, to determine whether their practice is right and wrong.

(Note: Many quotations below are from *Handbook of Religious Quotations* by Dawson and MacArthur, abbreviated HRQ.)

God of the Bible

Most modern "tongue-speakers" do not claim to speak human languages.

Since Bible tongues were languages and people today claim to have the same gift, it is reasonable to ask them: "What language do you speak?" Most make no claim to speak a language, until they are shown the above evidence (and many will not claim it even then).

One "tongue-speaker," when shown the above evidence, said he thought he was speaking Korean. I offered to find some Koreans to listen to his speech and tell us what he was saying. He refused!

The apostles deliberately used their tongues to communicate to people who knew the languages. If modern tongue-speakers have the real "Pentecost experience," they too should speak known, existing, native languages and should be glad to use them to communicate to people who know the languages. Why would they refuse?

Evidence shows that modern tongues are *not languages*.

Language experts were given recordings of modern tongue-speakers. Consider the results:

"The types of inventory and distribution would indicate clearly that this recording bears no resemblance to any actual language which has ever been treated by linguists" – Eugene Nida as cited by V. Raymond Edman, "Divine or Devilish?" *Christian Herald*, May 1964, page 16 (via HRQ, page 169).

"And I must report without reservation that my sample does not sound like a language structurally" – Wm. Welmes, Professor of African Languages at UCLA, Letter to the Editor, *Christianity Today*, Nov. 8, 1963, pages 19-20 (via HRQ, pages 168,169).

Language experts recognize the sound patterns of languages. They conclude that **modern "tongues" are not languages**. Regardless of the sincerity of those who seek to practice them, they do not constitute the "Pentecost experience" at all!

Tongues Conveyed a Message with an Understandable Meaning

Natural languages exist to convey a message: a meaning capable of being understood by those who know the language. The same is true of supernatural tongues.

Bible tongue speaking conveyed a message capable of being understood.

Those who knew the language could understand the meaning of what was said in such a way that they could be instructed or informed by it.

Acts 2:11 – Those who heard the tongues, not only recognized the language, but understood the message as expressions of praise to God. As with other Divine revelation, tongues conveyed a true message or meaning that gave instruction or information to those who knew the language.

1 Corinthians 14:5-12,19,26 – In church meetings speakers should convey messages that all could understand and be edified. So tongues could only be used in church meetings only if they spoke a message people could understand. Note verse 9 – Those who spoke in tongues were required to give a message easy to understand.

1 Corinthians 14:28 – But if no one understood the message so as to interpret it to others, the tongue speaker should keep silent in church.

So, the true "Pentecost experience" involved speaking a message capable of being understood, so as to edify.

Do modern tongue-speakers convey a message capable of being understood?

The language experts cited earlier said that modern "tongues" are not languages. It follows that they are not likely to convey an understandable message. Then what are they?

> The consonants and vowels do not all sound like English (the speaker's native language), but the intonation patterns are so completely American English that the total effect is a bit ludicrous – Wm. Welmes, Professor of African Languages at UCLA, Letter to the Editor, *Christianity Today*, Nov. 8, 1963, pages 19-20 (via HRQ, pages 168,169).

> On the basis of what I have learned about this type of phenomena of 'tongues' in other parts of the world, apparently there is the same tendency to employ one's own inventory of sounds, in nonsense combinations, but with simulated 'foreign' features – Eugene Nida as cited by V. Raymond Edman, "Divine or Devilish?" *Christian Herald*, May 1964, page 16 (via HRQ, page 169).

So, language experts recognize the sound patterns of languages. They not only concluded that modern "tongues" are not languages, but they know what they **are.** "Tongues" are the speakers' "own inventory of sounds, in **nonsense** combinations, but with **simulated** 'foreign' features." The speaker does not make the **sound patterns** of foreign languages; instead, subconsciously he takes the speech patterns that he already knows and combines them to imitate what he thinks sounds like a foreign language.

In short, subconsciously or unknowingly, modern tongue-speakers speak nonsense gibberish. They are like little kids making meaningless sounds to imitate a "foreign language." So not only do tongue-speakers not know what language they are speaking, but the fact is that we can know what they are speaking. It is nonsense gibberish and not a language at all!

On Pentecost the apostles spoke existing languages with a message capable of being understood by those who knew the language. No matter how sincere they may be, people who claim to speak in tongues today do not do what the apostles did.

Tongues Revealed a Message Capable of Interpretation.

Natural tongues convey a message that can be interpreted into other languages.

Acts 9:36 – A certain disciple was named Tabitha, which is translated Dorcas.

John 1:38 – They called Jesus "Rabbi" (which is translated, Teacher)

John 1:42 – Jesus called Peter "Cephas" (which is translated, A Stone).

John 9:7 – The pool of Siloam (which is translated, Sent).

Hebrews 7:2 – Melchizedek is translated "king of righteousness," and also king of Salem, meaning "king of peace."

So, the message spoken in the tongue could be translated to other languages.

Supernatural tongues conveyed a message or meaning that was capable of interpretation or translation to another language.

1 Corinthians 14:5 – He who prophesies is greater than he who speaks with tongues, unless he interprets (διερμηνευω) so the church may receive edification.

1 Corinthians 14:27 – If anyone speaks in a tongue, let there be two or at the most three, each in turn, and let one interpret. (διερμηνευω)

(1 Corinthians 12:10; 14:13,26)

(The word for "interpretation" in these passages is the same or closely related word to the words used in the Bible for translating one language into another by natural means: Greek: `ερμηνια and related verbs `ερμηνευω and διερμηνευω.)

Some claim "tongues" in 1 Corinthians 12-14 are different from Acts 2.

They say these "tongues" are not human languages but an emotional prayer language or "the tongues of angels" (1 Corinthians 13:1), which no one understands (14:2,14,19).

* If people do not speak languages capable of being understood, then they **do not have the "Pentecost experience"!** The apostles on Pentecost spoke understandable languages. Why do people claim to have the "*Pentecost* experience," but when examined they claim that what they have is *different* from Pentecost?

* "Tongues" in 1 Corinthians 14 refers to a miraculous spiritual gift, just as in Acts 2. Why assume it is a different gift unless we have some compelling reason?

* As in Acts 2, tongues in 1 Corinthians contained an understandable message which could be interpreted, provided someone knew the language (1 Corinthians 12:10; 14:5,13,27,28). **The reason they could not be understood, the way Corinth was using them, was that no one present knew the language (14:2).** And Paul said, in that case, to quit using them!

* When Paul mentioned "tongues of men and of angels," the word "tongues" must mean the same for "angels" as it does for "men": languages capable of translation. Whether used by men or by angels, tongues were existing languages used to convey a message with meaning. They were never a special prayer language that no one can understand.

* Paul's expression implies that speaking the tongues of angels would be rare. "Though I speak" implies an extreme case, which probably even he had not done. Had he given all his goods to feed the poor and his body to be burned (verse 3)? He means that, even if one were to go to the unusual extremes he described, it would do no good if not motivated by love. So speaking the tongues of angels would be a rare extreme.

So why do people today almost **never** speak the "tongues of men" (the usual gift), but claim to speak the tongues of angels (the rare gift)? The example of Acts 2 shows God's intended purpose for tongues: speaking languages so men could understand and be instructed. Even the tongues of 1 Corinthians 14 could be interpreted. Why do people today almost always speak that which no one can understand?

* We have already shown that modern tongue speakers do not speak any language at all, human or angelic. Language students recognize what it is: sounds the speaker already knows, but combined in nonsense ways. It is recognizable as gibberish!

* We will further see that modern tongues do not fit 1 Corinthians 14 because they have no consistent interpretation.

So, the tongues in 1 Corinthians 14 were not different in nature from those in Acts 2, they were just being used differently. And Paul, by inspiration, said to stop it in church meetings!

Do modern "tongues" convey a message that can be interpreted accurately?

Modern "tongues" are often used in assemblies without interpretation, so there is no understandable message and no one is edified. This clearly violates 1 Corinthians 14.

Again, "tongues" have been studied and proved to be incapable of interpretation, because they are not languages. They are gibberish with no real meaning.

We attended many meetings where glossolalia both occurred and was interpreted, and noted that the interpretations were usually of a very general nature. After a segment of tongue-

God of the Bible

speech, an interpreter commonly offered the explanation that the speaker had been thanking and praising God for many blessings. Another frequent theme was that the speaker was asking for strength and guidance for himself and for others.

However, perhaps a third of the time, the interpreter offered specific interpretation of what glossolalists said. More rarely, an interpreter 'translated' phrase by phrase and sentence by sentence. In order in investigate the accuracy of these interpretations, we undertook to play a taped example of tongue speech privately for several different interpreters of tongues. In no instance was there any similarity in the several interpretations. The following typified our results: one interpreter said the tongue-speaker was praying for the health of his children; another that the same tongue-speech was an expression of gratitude for a recently successful church fund-raising effort.

We know of a man who was raised in Africa, the son of missionary parents, who decided to test the interpretation of tongues. He attended a tongue-speaking meeting where he was a complete stranger. At the appropriate moment, he arose and spoke the Lord's Prayer in the African dialect he had learned in his youth. When he sat down, an interpreter of tongues at once offered the meaning of what he had said. He interpreted it as a message about the imminent second coming of Christ. – Dr. John Kildahl, *The Psychology of Speaking in Tongues*, Harper and Row, 1972, pages 62,63 (via Handbook of Religious Quotations, pages 169,170).

So, modern "tongues" are not languages of any kind (men or angels), they do not contain a consistent message, and they are not capable of interpretation. Therefore, they are not the true gift of tongues as in the Bible. They are a counterfeit.

Tongues Were Not Learned by Those Who Spoke Them.

Supernatural tongues came suddenly without training.

People were **never taught** how to speak in "tongues." The power came upon them suddenly and instantaneously.

Acts 2 – The apostles were "suddenly" empowered by the Spirit to speak in tongues (verses 2-4). The men who spoke were all of one place (Galilee – verse 7), but they spoke in the languages of men from all over the world (verses 5,8-12). The hearers were amazed, because they knew these men were speaking languages they could not have learned. (Acts 4:13 – These men were "ignorant and unlearned." This confirms that they had not learned these languages by natural means.)

Acts 10:44-46; 19:6 – People began speaking in tongues suddenly with no preparation.

The true gift of tongue speaking was not learned or taught by any form of training. Like miraculous healings, it came suddenly. Generally, people had no idea it was coming, were not expecting it, and had no control over when it came.

The miracle of tongues was that people could speak existing languages, which they had never studied. And they could speak them so well that people who knew the language, as their own native tongue, could recognize the language and understand the message!

Do modern tongues come suddenly with no training?

Modern so-called tongue speakers often "learn" to speak in tongues by listening to others, trying to do it, and even being trained. Whether consciously or subconsciously, they are taught.

Harold Bredesen instructs tongue-seekers:

> (1) To think visually and concretely, rather than abstractedly; for example, to try to visualize Jesus as a person; (2) consciously to yeild [sic] their voices and organs of speeck [sic] to the Holy Spirit; (3) to repeat certain elementary sounds which he told them, such as "bah-bah-bah," or something similar. He then laid his hands on the head of each seeker, prayed for him, and the seeker did actually speak in tongues – Cited by Stanley D. Walters, *Youth in Action*, May, 1964, page 11 (via HRQ, page 167).

> I have observed the same routine everywhere I have been: (1) a meeting devoted to intense concentration on tongue-speaking, followed by (2) an atmosphere of heightened suggestibility to the word of the tongue-speaking leader, after which (3) the initiate is able to make the sounds he is instructed to make. – Kildahl, *op cit*, page 74 (via HRQ, page 171).

If people today were really speaking in tongues, they would suddenly be able to speak French, Spanish, Russian, etc., without ever having studied the languages or practiced them. That is not what happens in modern tongues. They do not speak real languages, and what they do speak is learned by observing others and even by being instructed how to do it.

Tongues Were Impossible by Natural Law

Supernatural tongues occur in a way impossible by natural law.

Many Bible miracles consisted of acts that might occur naturally, if done in a different way. What made them supernatural or miraculous was the way they occurred.

Examples:

* People can be healed of many diseases naturally (by medicines, exercise, etc.), but Jesus and the apostles healed instantaneously just by speaking, etc.

* Storms can calm naturally (by change of weather), but Jesus calmed a storm immediately by speaking to it.

* Food can grow over a period of months from seeds planted in the earth, but God provided manna from heaven that lay on the ground, and Jesus fed thousands from a boys' lunch.

* People can learn God's word when taught it, but supernatural gifts of revelation involved direct knowledge of things one had not studied.

* God today can work by providence through natural processes to bless people, answer prayer, etc. It is God's power, but involves no miracles. Miracles were acts impossible by natural law.

In the same way, the word "tongue" refers to native languages that can be learned naturally. But what made them miraculous was the fact the Spirit empowered people to speak them suddenly without ever studying or learning the language.

Modern tongues can be explained by natural processes.

One does not have to be a glossolalist to produce glossolalic speech. Al Carlson at the University of California recorded the speech of glossolalists during their spiritual exercise; Later he recorded the speech of non-glossolalist volunteers whom he asked to speak spontaneously in an unknown language. Glossolalists were asked to rate the different recordings. They were unable to distinguish them. A similar test was made by Werner Cohn of the University of British Columbia with identical results – *Glossolalia*, Jividen, page 163

Incidents of glossolalia can be multiplied from religions ancient and modern; eastern and western; established and heretical. The glossolalia experience is to be found in all different cultural strata from non-Christian priests to medicine men. The experience is to be found among the Hudson Bay Eskimos, North Boreno pagans, 'demoniacs' in China and east Africa as well as Christianity. Burdick concludes:

"This survey has shown that speaking-in-tongues is widespread and very ancient. Indeed, it is probable that as long as man has had divination, curing, sorcery, and propitiation of spirits, he has had glossolalia ... Whatever the explanation, it is clear that pagans as well as Christians have their glossolalia experiences." – Jividen, pages 74,75

I have observed the same routine everywhere I have been: (1) a meeting devoted to intense concentration on tongue-speaking, followed by (2) an atmosphere of heightened suggestibility to the word of the tongue-speaking leader, after which (3) the initiate is able to make the sounds he is instructed to make. It is the same procedure that a competent hypnotist employs. Like the hypnotist, the tongue speaking leader succeeds with some subjects and with others does not – Kildahl, *op cit*, page 74 (via HRQ, page 171).

The Moslem claims miracles. He believes that these miracles show God's favor and confirms the correctness of his faith. Tongue speaking is one of the miracles which is claimed. Hudjwiri describes the miraculous powers of an Islamic saint. He says that "he can transform himself, transport himself to a distance, speak diverse tongues, revive the dead..." Other examples are cited in Kenneth Morgan's book entitled, *Islam the Straight Path*. – Jividen, page 75

All these experiences have left me with the conviction that glossolalia especially can be psychologically explained, and is not, in general, a "spiritual" phenomenon – Stuart Bergsma, "Speaking with Tongues, Part II," *Torch and Trumpet*, XIV, No. 10, page 10 (via HRQ, page 170).

As far as I know, there is no case of speaking in strange tongues which has been strictly and scientifically investigated that cannot be explained by recognized psychological laws – George B. Cutten, *Speaking with Tongues: Historically and Psychologically Considered*, New Haven, Yale University Press, 1927, page 181 (via HRQ, page 170).

So modern tongue speaking is not a supernatural phenomenon incapable of natural explanation. Speakers do not speak an existing language. What they do speak is based on what they have learned, and the means used to teach it are known. The methods are similar to **hypnotism**.

The same conduct has been duplicated around the world by people who are clearly in error, including pagans and people who are deliberately "faking it." If what tongue speakers do can be duplicated by people in error, then how can the tongue speakers know they have a genuine gift? How can they use their gift (as they often do) to prove they are pleasing to God?

Clearly modern "tongues" are not supernatural or miraculous.

Conclusion

A topic for future study would be the purpose of miracles. We will see that modern tongues also fail to accomplish the Biblical purpose of true tongue speaking.

When compared to true Bible tongues, modern "tongue speaking" fails on every count. It is a counterfeit, a fake, sent by Satan to fool people into accepting false doctrines. So why study it?

God of the Bible

First, so we are not misled to accept false practices or false doctrines (1 John 4:1).

Second, so we can help other people avoid false practices and false doctrines.

Third, by understanding what the Bible says, we can appreciate the nature and purpose of true spiritual gifts. These gifts existed to reveal God's will and give proof the message was from God. That message is now recorded in the Bible, so we today can learn the truth by studying it. And we can know that it is the truth from the eyewitness testimony of the miracles recorded in the Bible to confirm that it truly is from God. Fake "miracles" undermine the power of true miracles.

Studies like this should help us avoid error and at the same time appreciate truth.

The Purpose of Spiritual Gifts

Earlier we observed the undeniable fact that many of God's miraculous works have ceased and will not be repeated (creation, the flood, etc.). A major question we must consider is whether or not all of His miraculous works have ceased so that He is not doing any miracles today at all.

We then studied the characteristics of gifts of direct revelation, miraculous signs, and tongues. We pointed out that one way to know whether or not events today are true miracles is by comparing them to the characteristics of Bible miracles. Observing modern so-called gifts of the Spirit shows that they do not possess the characteristics of true miracles and so are not valid, legitimate miracles.

Now consider what spiritual gifts were for. What purpose did the Spirit intend for them to accomplish? Do we need miraculous spiritual gifts today to accomplish these purposes?

We emphasize that the reason for studying such subjects is not just to win an argument or to make someone look bad. The purpose is to help people serve God faithfully and avoid being misled by error and false teaching. At the same time, we can come to a fuller appreciation of the purpose of true spiritual gifts and see how fully they have accomplished their purpose.

Gifts of Direct Revelation

The Purpose of Gifts of Prophecy Was to Make Known God's Will to Man.

Today we have the Bible to teach us God's will. But how did the people who wrote it know what to write? And how did people know God's will while the Bible was being written but was not yet complete? The purpose of direct revelation was to meet these needs.

Deuteronomy 18:18,19 – God predicted He would raise up another prophet like Moses. He would put His words in the prophet's mouth, so the prophet would speak what God commanded. The purpose of prophecy was to reveal God's will. (This was fulfilled in Jesus – Acts 3:22,23.)

Matthew 10:19,20 – The Spirit spoke directly through inspired men. (Note that this promise was directed to the twelve apostles – verse 5.)

John 16:13 (14:26) – The Spirit would guide the apostles into **all truth**. 15:27 shows that this too was addressed to the apostles (without Judas). (See 13:1,2 and 18:1ff with Matthew 26:20; Mark 14:17; Luke 22:14; Acts 1:21,22.)

Ephesians 3:3-5 – The Spirit revealed to the apostles and prophets the mystery of the gospel which had previously been unknown. These men then wrote it down so others could know.

2 Peter 1:21 – Holy men of God spoke as they were moved by the Holy Spirit. This is the origin of Scripture (verse 20).

So the purpose, served by gifts of prophecy and direct revelation, was to reveal the very will of God to inspired men. These men taught that message by word of mouth to people in their own day. Then they wrote it down so it could be preserved for future generations (1 Corinthians 14:37; Ephesians 3:3-5; 2 Timothy 3:16,17; etc.). This is how we received the Bible to guide us today and how people knew the will of God in the age before the Bible had been completely written.

(1 Corinthians 14:37; 2:10-13; Galatians 1:8-12; 1 Thessalonians 2:13; 2 Timothy 3:16,17; Luke 10:16; See part I for other passages.)

The Purpose of These Gifts Has Been Accomplished.

Note that the purpose of gifts of direct revelation pertained to the age **before** the Bible was complete. These gifts enabled inspired men to write the Bible and to know God's will until the Bible was complete. Now that we have the Bible, do we still need these gifts, or is our need for revelation completely met by Scripture?

Notice what the Bible itself says about the revelation we have in Scripture:

1. It is complete.

John 16:13; 14:26 – The Spirit guided apostles into **all** truth. (Matthew 28:20)

Acts 20:20,27 – Paul declared the "**whole** counsel of God," keeping back nothing that was profitable.

2 Peter 1:3 – God's power granted to them **all** things that pertain to life and godliness.

2 Timothy 3:16,17 – This inspired message from God was then written in the Scriptures. As a result, the Scriptures now provide us **completely** to **all** good works.

All spiritual truth that God intended for men to ever receive was delivered to inspired men in the first century and then recorded in the Scriptures. There is absolutely no new truth left to be delivered to men from God today.

Galatians 1:6-9; 2 John 9-11 – This is why no one may teach anything different from the gospel delivered in the first century. There simply is no more truth to be revealed from God. To teach as doctrine things that the apostles did not receive would be to imply that they did not receive all truth. (Matthew 15:1-14; Revelation 22:18,19)

So we do not need direct revelation today to reveal new truth from God. There are no new truths to be revealed. The Scriptures completely meet out need for revelation from God.

2. It is understandable.

The teaching of Jesus and His apostles was directed to the multitudes of common people, not to an elite, specially educated clergy. Those to whom it was addressed were expected to understand it.

Mark 7:14 – Jesus addressed the multitude and said that every one of them should **understand** what He taught.

1 Corinthians 14:33 – God is not the author of confusion. But He is the author of the record written by inspired men (verse 37). It follows that the Bible is not the cause of confusion. It can be understood.

Ephesians 3:3-5 – Paul wrote so men who read can understand.

2 Timothy 3:16,17 – The Scriptures are **profitable** to teach and instruct us in righteousness and provide us to all good works. The Scriptures would not be profitable to us if we could not understand them.

Acts 17:11 – Those who do study the Bible diligently ("daily") with an open or ready mind can and will understand it sufficiently to distinguish truth from error.

So, we do not need direct revelation today to in order to help men understand God's will for us. All truth has already been revealed in a way that honest people can understand. The Scriptures completely meet our need for revelation that we can understand.

(Ephesians 5:17; Isaiah 55:11; 2 Timothy 2:7; Colossians 1:9ff; Matthew 13:23; Psalm 119:104,105,130; 1 Timothy 2:4)

God of the Bible

3. It is eternal and indestructible.

2 Peter 1:12-15 – The Scriptures were written so that, even after inspired men died, people would have available to them the message those men revealed. The revelation they received was written down to guide future generations.

1 Peter 1:22-25 – The word given us in the gospel will live and abide forever. It is not like plants that spring up and then die.

2 John 2 – The truth will be with us forever.

John 12:48 – Jesus' words will be present even at the Judgment as the standard by which our destinies will be determined.

Psalm 119:152,160; Isaiah 40:8; 30:8 – These same promises were made regarding the Old Testament. The promises were fulfilled so completely that the message was preserved hundreds of years till Jesus' lifetime. It was so perfect then that He and His apostles repeatedly cited Scripture as Divine authority without ever once implying anything was missing or inaccurate.

These same promises have now been made regarding the entire written word; so we can be sure that God, by His power has likewise kept this promise. The record written by the inspired men will always exist and be available to guide honest people.

So, we do not need direct revelation today to renew to us truths that have been lost over the years. No truth has been lost. All the truth that was revealed to the apostles has now been preserved for us today in the Scriptures. The Bible completely meets our need for accurate revelation today.

(Matthew 24:35; Psalm 12:6,7; Jude 3)

4. It is powerful.

Romans 1:16 – The revealed word has the strength to lead to eternal life all who believe and obey it.

James 1:25 – God's word is perfect. It reveals the message of God that perfectly meets our need in every way.

Scripture provides a complete and perfect guide that reveals all we need to know to be saved and have eternal life. What more could we need?

The gifts of revelation were needed until the Bible was completed. Now that the Bible has been completed, it serves as a thoroughly adequate and sufficient guide. No gifts of direct revelation are needed any longer. When people today seek or claim direct revelation, they show a lack of faith in the perfection of Scripture.

Do you and I appreciate the Scriptures as God's complete and perfect revelation for us today? Do we trust it as our perfect guide from earth to heaven? If so, then we will not seek for further Divine revelation.

(1 Peter 1:22-25; Ephesians 6:10-18; Hebrews 4:12; John 20:30,31; Acts 20:32)

Gifts of Miraculous Confirmation (Signs)

The Primary Purpose of Miraculous Signs Was to Confirm God's Truth.

As discussed earlier, Satan always offers lying counterfeits for every good thing God gives. Specifically, Satan has sent false prophets who claimed to have messages from God when they did not really.

When a man claimed to be inspired of God, how could listeners determine whether the message really was from God or was a counterfeit? This was the main purpose of miraculous signs (though other benefits sometimes occurred). If a man had power to accomplish supernatural acts, people would know God was working through him, so they should believe his message.

Evidence for the main purpose of miracles

Exodus 4:1-9,29-31 – When Moses wanted evidence to convince the people that God had really sent Him, God empowered him with miraculous signs.

Deuteronomy 4:32-40 – God did great signs and wonders among the Israelites, so they would know He is the true God and would obey the commands given through Moses.

1 Kings 17:24 – When Elijah raised the son of the widow of Zarephath from the dead, she said that by this she knew he was a man of God and that the word of the Lord was in his mouth.

1 Kings 18:36-39 – Elijah called down fire from heaven (which the prophets of Baal could not do) so people would know to believe in the true God and that Elijah was acting by God's authority.

John 20:29-31 – Jesus' signs give people reason to believe that He is God's Son, so we can have life in His name. (John 5:36; Acts 2:22; Matthew 9:6)

Mark 16:20 – Jesus sent apostles to preach (verses 14,15); and as they did so, He worked with them, **confirming the word** by the signs He gave them (verses 17,18).

Acts 14:3 – As prophets taught, God **bore witness** to the word, granting signs and wonders to be done by their hands.

2 Corinthians 12:11,12 – Signs, wonders, and miracles were **signs** to confirm that one was an apostle.

Hebrews 2:3,4 – God bore **witness** to the message of salvation by signs, wonders, etc.

This purpose became especially clear when a prophet from God did miracles that a false prophet could not duplicate (as discussed previously). See Acts 8:5-13; 13:6-12; Exodus 8:17-19; 1 Kings 18:20-40; Daniel 2; Acts 19:11-17.

Some folks claim that miracles served primarily as acts of "compassion" to provide some blessing or benefit for people in need. We will see later that, while some miracles did have this effect, not all did. If the primary purpose of miracles was to bring blessings on people in need, how do we explain miracles that actually harmed or punished people? But all miracles accomplished the purpose of confirming some truth about God or some message from God.

Confirming God and His revelation was the primary purpose of miracles in that every miracle served to accomplish this purpose, and it was the determining purpose as to whether a miracle would or would not be done.

(John 10:37,38; 14:10,11; 4:48; 3:1; 1:47-51; 2:11,23; 6:14; 9:16,25-38; 11:4,15,40-48; 12:9-11; Matthew 11:1-6; 14:32,33; Acts 1:3; 10:1-11:18; 9:1-19, 33-42; Romans 1:4; Joshua 3:5-17; 2 Peter 1:16-21; Numbers 16:28-35; chapter 17; Exodus 7:1-5,17; 8:10; 9:14-16; 10:1,2; 14:4,14-18,21-31)

Tongue speaking served a dual purpose.

Tongue speaking involved teaching an understandable message in a language that the speaker had never learned but that people who knew the language could recognize and understand.

Since the tongue conveyed a meaningful message, when the message was properly interpreted, it would serve to instruct and edify by giving revelation from God (1 Corinthians 14:5,12-14,26-28; Acts 2:11).

When people knew the language so they could tell it was accurately spoken though the speaker had never learned it, the tongue would serve as a sign to confirm the message was from God (Acts 2:4-11; 1 Corinthians 14:22).

So miraculous tongues served both as direct revelation and as a sign to confirm that the revelation was from God.

Note that miracles were needed to confirm a new covenant or further revelation, not to reconfirm a previous covenant that was already confirmed.

Luke 16:27-31 – By the time Jesus lived, the Old Testament had been adequately confirmed and did not need reconfirming. No further miracles were needed to convince people to believe it, so God refused to give them. People were expected to believe on the basis of the proof that had been given. It follows that the miracles done by Jesus and the apostles were intended to confirm, not the Old Testament, but the New Testament.

John 20:30,31; Mark 16:15,20; Ephesians 3:3-5 – So, Jesus and apostles plainly stated that their miracles served to confirm who Jesus was and that His **gospel** really was a message from God. This was a new covenant with new commands and truths not previously revealed.

There comes a time when a Divine covenant has been adequately revealed and confirmed by miracles. When that time comes, no further miracles are needed to confirm it. Further miracles would be needed only if God sent new revelation.

(John 5:36; Hebrews 2:2-4; Acts 14:3,7; 2 Corinthians 12:11,21)

The Purpose of These Gifts Has Been Completely Accomplished.

Even for us today, the gospel message stands completely confirmed as being from God by means of the miracles of Jesus and His apostles and prophets in the first century.

Eyewitness testimony is sufficient evidence to confirm historical events.

John 8:17 – Satisfactory testimony of several witnesses is sufficient evidence. Compare this to witnesses in a court trial or witnesses to a will or a wedding, etc. Several witnesses may be needed to confirm that an event truly occurred; but once we have a number of witnesses, more witnesses are not needed.

(Matthew 18:16; Deuteronomy 19:15; 17:6; 2 Corinthians 13:1; 1 Timothy 5:19)

Once a covenant or contract has been written and confirmed, it does not need to be reconfirmed throughout its existence.

Galatians 3:15 – This is true both of human and Divine covenants.

* Suppose you sign a document such as a contract to buy a house. When it has been notarized (attested by witnesses), you don't need to sign it again every year or so. The original confirmation remains valid till the contract has been fulfilled.

* Suppose a man makes a "last will and testament" and has it confirmed by witnesses. Afterward, it need not be reconfirmed yearly to remain valid. The will would need further confirmation only if he decided to change it.

* When a couple marries, their marriage is legally attested by the witnesses. The couple does not need to renew their vows from time to time to make them binding. They remain valid on the basis of their original vows, and any who seek proof can refer to the testimony of witnesses.

* Do you believe the Constitution is the fundamental law of this country? Were you there when it was written? Do we need to vote to reconfirm it every year? It was written and confirmed centuries ago; we believe on the testimony of witnesses recorded in history. If we amend or change it, then the changes need to be ratified; but only the changes need to be ratified, not the main document.

Galatians 3 says these examples illustrate how God deals with His covenants and promises. Once they have been revealed and adequately confirmed by miracles, they need not be repeatedly reconfirmed. If we can accept this for human covenants, why not Divine covenants?

So the Old Testament was delivered and then confirmed by miracles.

Luke 16:27-31 – By the time Jesus lived, the Old Testament had been adequately confirmed and did not need reconfirming. Jesus said that the written record of what prophets wrote was as good as having the living prophets themselves. He and His apostles quoted it as valid authority.

Adequate miraculous evidence had occurred during the Old Testament period to confirm that Old Testament covenant. This evidence was recorded in the Scriptures. No further miracles were needed to convince people to believe it, so God refused to give further evidence.

This principle demonstrates that there comes a time when a Divine message has been adequately revealed and confirmed. When that time comes, no further miracles will be given to confirm it. People are expected to believe on the basis of the proof already given. If they will not believe, then they would not really believe if more evidence were given.

Likewise with the gospel, we have established that all truth was revealed and confirmed in the first century.

Consider the eyewitness testimony recorded by the following writers:

Luke

Luke 1:1-4 – Luke appealed to this principle of witnesses to demonstrate the trustworthiness of His account of Jesus' life. He said he wrote an orderly account of what had been delivered to him from eyewitnesses; therefore, we may know the certainty of the things instructed. It follows that miracles are needed to confirm new revelation. But once sufficient evidence has been given, no further evidence is needed; people are expected to believe on the basis of the eyewitness testimony.

Other New Testament writers

Paul – 1 Corinthians 15:1-8
Peter – 2 Peter 1:12-18
Matthew – Gospel of Matthew
Luke – Book of Acts.

And these are just New Testament examples. Many others are found in the Old Testament.

Old Testament prophecies

These also served to confirm New Testament events – John 5:39; Acts 2; etc.

John

Note especially John 20:29-31 – We do not need to be personal eyewitnesses of the miracles (like Thomas was) in order that we may believe. We are blessed if we believe on the basis of the **written record** of those who were eyewitnesses. This is adequate evidence to lead to faith in Christ and thereby to eternal life. What more is needed?

Conclusions

Men who could do miraculous signs never argued or used testimony as proof they had the power. They just did the signs.

Eyewitness testimony as evidence is needed only after sufficient miracles have been done and have ceased. You and I need eyewitness testimony or miracles today because miraculous confirmation has accomplished its purpose and ceased. But if people claim miracles still exist today, they should convince us by performing them like apostles did. If they attempt to prove their miracles by offering testimony instead of doing miracles, they are in effect admitting that miracles have ceased. If we have the miracles, eyewitness testimony is not needed!

Since the time of the apostles no miracles are needed because no new truths have been revealed from God.

The apostles received all truth in the first century. Further miracles would be needed today only if God changed His testament and revealed new truth. But God has already completely revealed His will, so He will not send new truth. And the truth we have received has been abundantly confirmed by the miracles of the first century. It follows that we need no further miracles to confirm that the gospel is from God. Now we must believe on the basis of the written record of the eyewitness testimony in the Scriptures.

Do we appreciate the fact that, not only has God completely revealed His will for us in the Scriptures, but that we have abundant miraculous proof that it is from God? God has provided everything needed in order for us to know His will and to know that it really is His inspired message. When we understand that, we will accept His message based on the evidence we have received. To demand further miracles as evidence today is to deny the sufficiency of the revelation God has given in the Scriptures.

Yet Some Hold Mistaken Views of the Purpose of Miracles.

These views are often defended in an effort to prove that we still need miracles today.

1. *Some people claim miracles are still needed today to persuade people to believe in Christ or to confirm that their church or doctrine is true, etc.*

But all truth was revealed and adequately confirmed in the first century.

Therefore, no new revelation will occur, and no further confirmation is needed. Remember, miracles confirm **new** revelation (see above). Miracles are needed today only if God is giving a new covenant or adding to His covenant. But we have already proved that He gave it all in the first century.

Contradictory groups base their claims on indistinguishable "miracles."

Mormons, Catholics, Pentecostals, Charismatics of all denominations, Christian Science practitioners, etc., thoroughly contradict one another in doctrine; yet all claim miracles on the basis of "testimonies," and their "miracles" cannot be distinguished.

Galatians 1:8,9; 2 John 9-11 – It follows that some of these groups must be teaching error. Is the Spirit confirming all these false and contradictory doctrines?

1 Corinthians 1:10,13; 14:33; John 17:20,21 – These groups are divided from one another, contributing to religious confusion. If the Spirit confirmed them all, wouldn't this make the Spirit the author of confusion and division?

In Bible examples, true prophets were distinguished from false prophets in that false prophets could not do works as great as those of inspired men. But there is no way to distinguish the "miracles" of various modern groups. All make identical claims and give similar testimonies, but none actually do miracles like those in the Bible. Whose teaching is being confirmed? The conclusion must be that none are being confirmed and none are making true claims!

Some admit their miracles are not greater than those of false teachers. But they say you can tell which miracles are true by comparing their teaching to Bible.

This is just backward from true miracles! In the Bible, **miracles** confirmed that the **message** was from God in an age when the Bible had not been written. Today the Bible has been written, and people use the **message** to confirm the **miracle**!

By appealing to the Bible to prove they are right, modern "miracle workers" are admitting that the Bible is an adequate guide. If so, then their revelations and miracles are useless.

Since modern "miracles" do not distinguish true teachers from false teachers, to claim that they are still needed to "confirm the word" is to misuse the purpose of miracles.

2. Others claim that miracles are needed today to produce unity.

They say people in different groups will be drawn closer together because they all have "charismatic gifts."

Possession of spiritual gifts did not lead to unity in Corinth!

1 Corinthians 1:10-13; 3:3,4; 11:18,19 – The Corinthian church had abundant gifts (1 Corinthians 12-14), yet it was one of the most divided churches in the Bible.

In fact, they had major division over the use of miraculous gifts – 1 Corinthians 12-14!

So even when people did possess miraculous powers, they did not necessarily produce unity.

Bible unity requires understanding and obedience to God's word.

Ephesians 4:3-6 – True "unity of the Spirit" is based on one faith and one body, just like there is one God and Father.

1 Corinthians 1:10-13; Galatians 1:6-9 – There must be no division, but all speak the same doctrine. We must teach the doctrine delivered by inspired men, not another doctrine.

John 17:17,20,21 – We are sanctified and made one by the truth, God's word.

The "unity" of the Charismatic movement is not Bible unity at all. People worship differently, teach different plans of salvation, have different forms of organization, etc. And all of them contradict the Bible on one or more of these points. If all of them had gifts of the Spirit, then the Spirit would not be producing true unity, but would be confirming and justifying *division*! This is a false concept of unity.

In fact, one of the most divisive controversies of our day is the question of whether or not people today have miraculous powers!

The very fact some people claim to have these powers is one thing that divides them from those who deny the existence of the powers!

So despite their claims, various groups that claim to have miraculous powers still remain greatly divided from one another and from those who don't claim to have the gifts. Unity is based on studying and accepting God's word, not on claiming miracles, especially when those claims don't measure up to Bible miracles.

3. Others claim miracles are needed today to help people with their problems.

We are told that God gave miracles to help people with their problems because of His love and compassion (Matthew 14:14; 15:32; etc.). God still loves people and He is no respecter of persons (Acts

10:34,35), so He must still work miracles. So when people today have illness, financial debts, lack of job, family problems, or perhaps some deep emotional need in their lives, they are taught to "expect a miracle." However:

Even in the age when miracles were being worked, problems were not solved for all believers.

2 Timothy 4:20 – Paul left Trophimus sick at Miletus.

Philippians 2:26,27 – Epaphroditus was sick nearly to death – so sick that people far away heard about it.

1 Timothy 5:23 – Timothy often had stomach infirmities. Why didn't Paul do a miracle and heal him? Why recommend a natural remedy?

2 Corinthians 12:7-9 – Paul himself had a thorn in the flesh, which he even prayed to God to remove. But God decided to leave it.

If compassion and love were the main reasons for miracles, why weren't these people all miraculously healed? Didn't God love these people? Was He a respecter of persons in these cases?

We have learned that the primary purpose of miracles was to meet a need greater than physical needs.

We have proved that the main purpose of miracles was to **confirm** God's **word,** so people could believe and be saved. This was more important than physical needs. No miracle was performed unless this greater need would be met.

* Many miracles solved no physical need at all.

Exodus 7:10-12 – Aaron's rod turned into a serpent and back again.

Numbers 17 – Later his rod produced blossoms and almonds.

Matthew 14:22-31 – Jesus and Peter walked on the water.

1 Kings 18:30-39 – Elijah called down fire to consume a sacrifice.

What physical problem did these miracles solve? None! But they did serve confirm truth that had been revealed from God.

** When it was clear that miracles would not lead to faith, they were **not** performed, even though physical needs would have been met.*

We already listed cases of sick people who were not healed. Consider other cases:

John 6:26-31,36 – Jesus refused to miraculously feed people when He realized they did not appreciate the miracle as proof of who He was.

Matthew 4:1-7 – When tempted by Satan, Jesus refused to do miracles for His own physical benefit.

Matthew 13:58 – Jesus refused to do miracles in His own hometown, because He knew already that no one would believe. (Compare 12:38-42.)

Luke 4:23-27 – Jesus expressly cited Old Testament examples in which miracles were not done, though they would have produced physical benefits for people in need.

Again, did God not love these people? Do these cases prove God is a respecter of persons? If not, then why would it show lack of love or respect of persons if He refuses to do miracles today?

* *In fact, some miracles even caused physical* **problems** *or punished people for sin.*

Numbers 16:28-35; 2 Kings 1:9-12; Acts 5:1-11 – Sometimes people were struck dead.

Acts 9:8,9; 13:6-12 – Some people were struck blind.

1 Kings 13:1-6 – Jeroboam's hand was shriveled.

Exodus 7-12 – God miraculously brought the ten plagues on Egypt.

Were these acts of compassion to relieve peoples' physical problems? Clearly not, but all did serve the purpose of confirming truth that had been revealed from God.

God still does meet His children's needs, according to natural law.

Consider some examples that show the difference between miracles and answers to prayer through natural law:

* *Food*: A blessing from God through natural law would be praying for daily bread (Matthew 6:11) then getting a job and working for it (Ephesians 4:28). But a miracle would be: (1) using a boy's lunch to feed thousands of people and having more food left over than you started with (Matthew 14:13-21), or (2) manna coming directly from heaven (Exodus 16:14-16), or (3) turning water to wine (John 2:1ff).

* *Human reproduction*: Natural law would be a man and his wife conceiving a child by natural procreation (Genesis 4:1,2). If they had prayed for a child, that would be a blessing from God in answer to prayer through natural law (1 Samuel 1). A miracle would be making a woman from a man's rib (Genesis 2:21,22), or causing someone to be conceived in the womb of a virgin (Matthew 1:18-25).

* *Health*: Likewise, if we pray for good health (3 John 2), we may heal by natural body processes, perhaps aided by medical treatment, diet, exercise, etc. (2 Kings 20:1-7) This would be a blessing from God in answer to prayer through natural law. Miraculous healings, however, are those we have described, which clearly did not occur according to natural law.

The fact God does not do miracles today would not prove that He lacks love or compassion nor that He is a respecter of persons. He still helps His children in answer to prayer (Matthew 6:33; James 1:17). But He answers through natural processes, not by miracles.

When we pray, sometimes God gives what we asked for, and sometimes He does not, just like some people were healed by miracles and others were not. This is because sin in is the world, and all must suffer as a consequence. (References saying God is no respecter of persons are talking about salvation, not physical blessings. Otherwise, God would have to physically bless all His people exactly the same. See Matthew 5:45.)

When the primary need is caring for His children's **physical** problems, God can meet that need by **natural** processes in answer to prayer. Miracles were used only when the primary need was to **confirm truth revealed from God** (though physical blessings often occurred as a secondary benefit). The determining factor in whether or not a miracle would be done was whether or not the word needed to be confirmed.

But the word today has been completely confirmed, so miracles are not needed at all. To claim miracles just to meet physical needs is to misuse the purpose of miracles.

4. Some want spiritual gifts to prove they are spiritually acceptable or mature.

Whether they consciously realize it or not, one of the main reasons people want to experience "miracles," especially tongue-speaking, is to provide them some tangible sign that convinces them they are acceptable to God. Time and again I have seen people who are shown by the Bible to be in error on some point (even on the conditions of salvation), yet they respond that they must be right with God else why would He give them these miraculous powers?

"Miracles" convince other people that they are spiritually mature, because they have something other people don't have.

But spiritual gifts have never been a sign of spiritual acceptability or maturity.

The Bible contains many examples of people who received or did real miracles, yet they were neither acceptable nor mature spiritually. Surely not everyone who received a miracle in his life was pleasing to God. As described earlier, many did not even have faith.

Numbers 22:28-33 -- God spoke through Balaam's donkey. Was the donkey in God's fellowship? Was it spiritually mature? Later God spoke through Balaam, though he was displeasing to God. (Compare Numbers 24:1; 31:8,16; 2 Peter 2:15,16; Revelation 2:14; 1 Samuel 19:18-24; John 11:49-53).

The Corinthian church had abundant gifts (1 Corinthians 12-14) but was one of the most displeasing and immature churches in the New Testament (1 Corinthians 12-14; compare chapter 1-4,5,11, etc.). In fact, the way they used their spiritual gifts was one of the main areas in which they displeased God and demonstrated immaturity (1 Cor 12-14). Many of them were rebuked for using their gifts as the basis of an ego trip, just like many today view them.

(King Saul – 1 Samuel 19:18-24; Caiaphas – John 11:49-53)

As previously described, people of all different faiths claim to have miracles and give similar testimonies.

Yet in doctrine and practice they contradict one another and even contradict the Bible (such as on the requirements of salvation as per Mark 16:16; Acts 2:38; 22:16; etc.).

Galatians 1:8,9; 2 John 9-11 – Again, it must be that some of these groups are teaching error. Is the Spirit confirming the salvation of members of all these false and contradictory groups?

1 Corinthians 14:33; 1:10,13; John 17:20,21 – Obviously, these groups are divided from one another, contributing to religious confusion. If the Spirit confirmed the salvation of them all, wouldn't this make the Spirit the author of confusion and division?

Not all saved people had miraculous gifts.

1 Corinthians 12:29,30 – Some did not speak in tongues, some had illnesses that were not healed, etc. (see above).

If miracles were a sign of God's favor, why did He not give the sign to all saved people? This **would** make God a respecter of persons in an area that pertains to salvation!

The true way to know whether or not God accepts us is by comparing our lives to Bible teaching.

1 John 2:3-6 – We know whether or not we know God, not by experiencing miracles, but by our obedience to God (revealed in His word – 1 Corinthians 14:37).

Matthew 7:21-28 – Like some today, these people claimed that their miraculous powers proved they were pleasing to God. But Jesus said he never knew them, because they worked iniquity. Those who enter the kingdom will be those who do the will of the Father.

2 Timothy 3:15-17 – The Scriptures make us wise to salvation, instruct us in righteousness, and provide us to all good works. (Acts 17:11)

Galatians 1:6-9 – We know whether or not we are following true doctrine by whether or not it agrees with the gospel taught by inspired men, recorded in the Scriptures. (1 John 4:1-6)

2 Corinthians 5:7; Romans 10:17 – We walk by faith, not by sight. Faith comes by hearing God's word, not by receiving miraculous powers. To seek some personal experience as our assurance is to fail to trust God's word: it is walking by **sight**, rather than by **faith**. This kind of thinking characterizes other people, such as those who worship idols: instead of being satisfied with God's word, they want some visible proof of God.

John 20:29-31 – When Thomas demanded personal evidence of a miracle, Jesus responded that, in the future, this would not be the way people would develop faith. Spiritual assurance today – real faith and

God of the Bible

real spiritual maturity – come by faith based on the written word, not on personally seeing signs!

To view miracles as a sign of God's favor again is to misuse the purpose of spiritual gifts.

5. *Some view miraculous powers as a source of financial profit.*

Most "faith healers" frequently beg for money – usually **before** the "healing" begins. The doctrine of "seed faith" and similar tactics imply that one must give a gift before he can expect a miracle, or that larger gifts will lead to greater miracles. Many faith healers have become fabulously wealthy as a result.

When did Jesus, His apostles, or any Bible prophet ever ask for a contribution from those they healed or take up a collection at a healing service?

2 Peter 2:3,15 – God warned about covetous false teachers who exploit those they teach. Like Balaam, they love the hire of wrongdoing.

2 Kings 5:14-16,20-27 – Having miraculously healed Naaman of leprosy, the true prophet Elisha refused to accept a gift from him. When Elisha's servant used the healing to take a gift, the servant was struck with leprosy.

Acts 3:6 – Peter said he had no silver or gold, nor did he ask for any. Yet he healed a man who had never walked.

Acts 8:18-21 – Peter was offered money in exchange for power to give miraculous gifts. He not only refused the money, he rebuked the man who offered it saying his heart was not right.

Matthew 8:20 – Jesus did great miracles, but never asked for money from those He healed, nor did He become wealthy as a result.

It is a shame that many "faith healers" have become fabulously wealthy by taking money from those who can least afford to give it, including people whose diseases have already driven them into poverty. Such preachers are guilty of materialism and greed. They leave the impression that God's blessings are for sale. This is a gross perversion of the purpose of spiritual gifts and illustrates why this subject really matters.

(Faithful preachers often did accept financial income as payment for the spiritual work they did in preaching the gospel, but never in return for doing miracles. See 1 Corinthians 9:4-14; 2 Corinthians 11:7-9; Philippians 4:14-18; 1 Timothy 5:18; Luke 10:7.)

Conclusion

A lack of appreciation for the all-sufficiency of the Scriptures is at the heart and core of the desire for modern-day miracles. When one understands that the Bible gives a complete and perfect revelation and confirmation of God's will, then one will see that modern miracles are not needed. People desire miracles today only when they fail to understand the purpose of miracles and so lose faith in the adequacy of the Bible.

Do you trust the Bible as evidence for your salvation and eternal hope?

The Imparting of Spiritual Gifts

By what means did people receive spiritual gifts? How were the gifts bestowed?

As we study note carefully: (1) There are only **two** possible methods mentioned anywhere in the New Testament by which anyone could receive miraculous gifts of the Spirit. (2) Both methods required the personal involvement of **apostles**. (3) Neither method exists today.

Holy Spirit Baptism

By definition, Holy Spirit baptism was a complete immersion or overwhelming in the power of the Holy Spirit (not really in the Spirit Himself, since the Spirit is a person).

The New Testament often mentions the Holy Spirit, but remember that the Spirit did many things and gave many different gifts. Whenever some people see the Holy Spirit mentioned, they assume without proof that it refers to Holy Spirit baptism or spiritual gifts. But not all references to the Spirit refer to Holy Spirit **baptism**. Also, the Bible refers to several kinds of baptisms, but not all references to baptism refer to **Holy Spirit** baptism.

Who Received Holy Spirit Baptism?

The Bible describes two and **only two** events as Holy Spirit baptism:

1. The apostles on the occasion of the first Jewish converts – Acts 1 and 2.

Note Acts 1:2-8.

* Jesus spoke to the **apostles** (verse 2). Note that they are called "**men of Galilee**" (verse 11).

* He said they would be baptized in the Holy Spirit, as God promised through John the Baptist (verses 4,5). Note that Holy Spirit baptism is separate and distinct from water baptism (verse 5).

* This promise would be fulfilled in Jerusalem "not many days hence" (verses 4,5).

* The Holy Spirit would give them power to bear witness for Jesus (verse 8).

* He told them to "wait" for the promise to be fulfilled (verse 4).

* All this was decided by God (verses 4,5,7,8). Note that those who received the baptism had no control over when, where, how, or on whom it came.

This was a promise to a specific group of people to be fulfilled at a specific time and place. No one today can claim that this promise is addressed to them; it was only for **apostles** waiting in **Jerusalem**, "**not many days**" after Jesus' ascension.

We may as well build arks like Noah or sacrifice our sons like Abraham as to claim Holy Spirit baptism today based on this passage. God surely could choose to give Holy Spirit baptism to others if He so chose, but no one else can claim **this** promise for himself or herself.

Now note Acts 2:1-21,33.

On the day of Pentecost the Holy Spirit came on the apostles as promised (verses 4,33). As a result they received power to speak in tongues (verses 4-11) and to preach and bear witness to the people (verses 14ff). This must be the fulfillment of the promise of Acts 1, since it came on the apostles in Jerusalem not many days after Jesus' ascension, just like Jesus promised (2:1,5,14; compare 1:12). Peter said it fulfilled the Father's promise to send the Spirit (verse 33; compare 1:4,5).

Some refer to the 120 disciples in 1:15 and claim that, in addition to the apostles, all of the 120 received Holy Spirit baptism. But note:

* As already mentioned, the promise was addressed to the apostles (1:2-8), no one else.

* The pronoun "they" in 2:1-4 should refer to the nearest antecedent (unless there is clear evidence otherwise), and that would be the 11 apostles plus Matthias (1:26).

(Much intervened between 1:15 and 1:26. The "they" of 1:26 is the "us" of verse 22 (apostles). "They" (the apostles of verse 22) cast lots (verse 26) and with Matthias became the "they" of 2:1. The 120 lacked the qualifications of 1:21,22, so were not included in the group discussed from then on.)

God of the Bible

* The purpose for which Jesus promised Holy Spirit baptism was to give the apostles power to bear witness for Christ (1:8). Those who spoke on Pentecost were the 12 apostles and all did bear witness (2:14,32,37). The 120 were nowhere included among those who spoke or testified. Why should they receive the baptism if they were not going to accomplish its intended purpose?

* Those who spoke were all Galileans (2:7). This agrees with the descriptions of the apostles in 1:11 and 13:31.

On this occasion, Holy Spirit baptism came on the apostles and only the apostles.

2. Cornelius' household on the occasion of the first Gentile converts – Acts 10 and 11 (read 10:44-48; 11:15-18).

Several miraculous events convinced Peter to preach to Gentiles (10:1-43; 11:1-14). As he preached, the Spirit fell on the hearers and they spoke in tongues (verses 44-46; 11:15-17). Peter cited this as fulfilling the promise of Holy Spirit baptism, and said it was a "like gift" to what he and others received "at the beginning" (11:15-17).

Peter concluded Gentiles could be baptized in water, and other Jews agreed (10:46-48; 11:17,18; 15:5-11). Note again that Holy Spirit baptism was a separate and distinct baptism from water baptism. Cornelius received **both** (10:44,48; 11:16).

Again, God decided who, how, when, and where people would receive Holy Spirit baptism. Those who received it had no control over these matters.

Note that an apostle (Peter) was personally involved and played an essential role in this occurrence of Holy Spirit baptism.

Acts 2 and Acts 10 are the only recorded occurrences of Holy Spirit baptism. This was a special promise involving specific people in special cases. Nowhere did God promise or require all people or all of His children to be baptized in the Spirit.

(This case did not fulfill the same purpose as Jesus described in Acts 1, but Peter said it did have a unique purpose that fit no other case. God gave Holy Spirit baptism as suited His purpose, but always it met a special, unique purpose, and always apostles served an essential role.)

3. Some people claim that Holy Spirit baptism was also for other people.

Consider some evidence they may present:

Matthew 3:11 (Mark 1:8; Luke 3:16)

Some claim John promised Holy Spirit baptism to the multitude (or all disciples). However:

* John's promise said Holy Spirit baptism would come on some people present, but nowhere said that **all** of them would receive it.

* Pharisees and Sadducees were present and were firmly rebuked (verses 7-10). Did they receive Holy Spirit baptism too?

* Some were promised baptism in fire, but the context shows this refers to eternal damnation (verses 10,11,12). Did John promise this baptism to everyone present? What he meant was that some would receive one baptism but others a different baptism.

* Jesus and Peter later specifically quoted John's prophecy and explained how and to whom it would be fulfilled. As we have seen, it was for the apostles and Cornelius – Acts 1:5; 11:16.

Acts 2:38,39

Some claim this says Holy Spirit baptism was for all whom the Lord will call. However:

* The passage does not mention "Holy Spirit *baptism"*; it says "the *gift* of the Holy Spirit." The Spirit has given many gifts. We must not assume this is Holy Spirit baptism without proof.

* The gift mentioned here is for all who receive remission of sins (verses 38,39). But it contradicts Scripture to say that every saved person must have Holy Spirit baptism (see the next point).

* All who received Holy Spirit baptism spoke in tongues (Acts 2:4; 10:46). But not all saved people spoke in tongues (1 Corinthians 12:7-11,29,30). Therefore, the "gift of the Spirit," which was for *all* people, cannot have been Holy Spirit baptism.

* If this gift is Holy Spirit baptism, then *all* saved people would receive *two* baptisms: one baptism was necessary to receive remission and the other came afterward (verses 38,39). The apostles and Cornelius did receive two baptisms, but they were special cases. By the time Ephesians 4:4-6 was written, and since that time, there is only *one* baptism.

* If people have Holy Spirit baptism today, like the apostles did, then they must preach the same gospel that the apostles preached. This would require preaching water baptism is necessary to salvation (2:38). Water baptism, not Holy Spirit baptism, is the one baptism for today.

But many, who claim Holy Spirit baptism, do not preach baptism is necessary to salvation. So, they preach a different gospel from what the apostles preached: something the Holy Spirit would never guide anyone to do (compare Galatians 1:8,9).

* The "gift of the Holy Spirit" in Acts 2:38 best fits the description of the *indwelling* of the Spirit. This is a different work of the Holy Spirit, and is definitely *not* Holy Spirit *baptism*. (Some say the "gift" is salvation. But since the indwelling is just fellowship with the Holy Spirit, this has the same effect, since only those who have salvation have fellowship with the Spirit.)

1 Corinthians 12:13 (John 3:3,5)

To be in the body (or kingdom), one must be baptized by (or born of) the Holy Spirit. Some claim this means Holy Spirit baptism is for everyone.

God of the Bible

* But the body (kingdom) is the church (Ephesians 1:22,23; Matthew 16:18,19), and membership in the church is essential to salvation (Ephesians 5:22-26; Acts 20:28; Colossians 1:13). So, this argument would make Holy Spirit baptism essential to salvation, which is not true (see notes above and below).

* Again, if everyone in the church has Holy Spirit baptism, then all must speak in tongues. But this same chapter shows **not** all church members spoke in tongues (12:7-11,29,30). So the "Spirit" in verse 13 is not Holy Spirit baptism.

* Again, this plus water baptism would make two baptisms for all people. But Ephesians 4:4-6 shows this is no longer so.

* "By the Spirit" can mean different things in different contexts. Regarding baptism into the body or kingdom, it means **in accordance with the teaching** of the Spirit, who commanded us to be baptized (compare John 3:3,5 to Ephesians 5:25,26; 1 Peter 1:22,23; Romans 1:16; Ephesians 6:17).

What Was the Purpose of Holy Spirit Baptism?

1. It gave miraculous powers.

The apostles spoke in tongues – Acts 2:4-11.

Cornelius' house spoke in tongues – Acts 10:44-46; 11:15-17.

All who were Holy Spirit baptized immediately spoke in tongues. But we learned earlier that miraculous powers served their purpose and are no longer needed. So Holy Spirit baptism is no longer needed for this purpose.

2. It gave the apostles direct guidance in teaching and bearing witness of Jesus.

See Acts 1:8; 2:14-36. See also John 16:13; 14:26.

This power was needed when the Scriptures were not complete. But as has also been discussed earlier, the Scriptures are now complete, so we no longer need this power.

3. It confirmed that the Gentiles could obey the gospel.

See Acts 10:44-48; 11:1-18.

But this truth is also now clearly confirmed and revealed in the Bible. So Holy Spirit baptism is no longer needed for this purpose.

What purpose then would Holy Spirit baptism serve today? All its purposes have been accomplished. It is no longer needed at all. This is why it was given only on a few special occasions. Like Noah's flood, it served only a special, temporary purpose and is no longer being repeated.

Who Administered Holy Spirit Baptism?

1. Human agents administered some forms of baptism.

This is the case with water baptism: a man immerses another man into the element.

The man who administers the baptism is acting by the authority of the one who commanded the baptism, so he is said to act "**in the name of**" the one who gave the command – Acts 8:35-39; 10:47,48; Matthew 28:19; 3:11,6,13; etc.

2. Jesus himself was the administrator of Holy Spirit baptism.

No human agent was involved, but the Spirit came directly from heaven upon the subject who received it (Matthew 3:11; Mark 1:8; Luke 3:16; John 1:33; Acts 2:1-4; 10:44-46; 11:16).

Is Holy Spirit Baptism Essential to Salvation?

The Bible commands a "baptism" that is essential to salvation – Mark 16:16; Acts 2:38; 22:16; Romans 6:3,4; etc. Some say this is Holy Spirit baptism. But God's word mentions more than one baptism (note Matthew 3:11; etc.). Which baptism is the one that is essential?

The baptism essential to salvation was a command addressed to all people.

See Mark 16:15,16; Acts 2:38; 22:16.

But Holy Spirit baptism was not a command. It was a **promise** fulfilled in certain select cases – Acts 1:2-8; chapter 2 and chapter 10.

Water baptism, however, was a **command** – Acts 10:47,48.

Baptism for salvation did not give miraculous gifts.

1 Corinthians 12:7-11,29,30; Acts 8:12-24; 19:1-7

But Holy Spirit baptism immediately gave power to speak in tongues – Acts 2:4; 10:44-46.

The baptism essential to salvation was administered by men in the name of God.

See Matthew 28:19,20 (with Mark 16:16); Acts 2:38.

This fits the pattern of water baptism – Acts 8:35-39; 10:47,48.

But as discussed earlier, Holy Spirit baptism was not administered by men. It came directly from heaven without the involvement of any human agent – Matthew 3:11; Acts 2:1-4; etc.

People had to decide for themselves whether or not to be baptized for salvation.

See Mark 16:15,16; Acts 2:38; 22:16.

This fits the pattern of water baptism – Acts 8:35-39; 10:47,48.

God of the Bible

But **God** decided who would receive Holy Spirit baptism, when, where, etc., regardless of the people's choice – Acts 1:2-8; chapter 2; 10:44ff.

People who chose to be baptized for salvation were told not to wait.

They were baptized immediately – Acts 22:16; 2:38-41; 16:31-34.

This fits the pattern of water baptism – Acts 8:35-39; 10:47,48.

But people who received Holy Spirit baptism had to **wait** till God sent it – Acts 1:4,5.

No passage anywhere states or implies that Holy Spirit baptism is essential to salvation. The one baptism that is for today (Ephesians 4:4-6) and that is essential to salvation is **water** baptism. Holy Spirit baptism has accomplished its purpose and is no longer needed at all.

Laying on of Apostles' Hands

Laying on of hands was a common practice for various purposes. Sometimes it had a religious significance. Other times it was a customary sign of special dedication or honor. We will study only cases where spiritual gifts were imparted. But in many cases, no spiritual gifts were involved in the practice at all – Leviticus 3:2,8,13; 16:21; 24:14; Numbers 27:18,23; Genesis 48:14,17,18; Mark 6:5; 16:18; Acts 28:8; Matthew 19:13,15; Acts 13:3; Matthew 9:18,25.

Examples in which Apostles Laid on Hands to Impart Miracles

Acts 8:14-21 – The Holy Spirit was given through the laying on of **apostles'** hands (verse 18). Although Philip could perform miracles (verses 6-13), yet the people he converted did not receive the Holy Spirit till the apostles came from Jerusalem and laid hands on them (verses 14,15). (Compare Acts 6:6.)

Acts 19:1-7 – Men received Holy Spirit and spoke in tongues when Paul laid his hands on them.

Romans 1:9-11 – Paul desired to come and see them to **impart some spiritual gift**. An apostle had to personally visit them in order for a gift to be imparted to them. If miraculous powers could come by Holy Spirit baptism or some other way, why would Paul need to go?

2 Timothy 1:6 – Timothy received a gift by the laying on of Paul's hands.

(Compare 1 Timothy 4:14 – "**with** [μετα] the laying on of hands of the presbytery" to 2 Timothy 1:6 "**by** [δια] the putting on of my hands." Apparently the elders laid hands on Timothy to endorse Paul's act and to encourage Timothy's work – Acts 13:2-4. But the spiritual gift was bestowed **by** Paul's hands.)

Although other people besides apostles **possessed** miraculous powers, only the **apostles** could **bestow or impart** gifts to others.

But the Church No Longer Has Apostles Living on Earth.

1. Apostles had to be chosen personally by Jesus.

The original apostles were directly chosen by Jesus – Luke 6:12-16.

Matthias was chosen by Jesus to replace Judas – Acts 1:24-26.

Paul was chosen personally by Jesus – Acts 26:16; Galatians 1:1.

2. Apostles had to be eyewitnesses of the resurrected Christ.

All the 12 were eyewitnesses – 1 Corinthians 15:4-8; Acts 2:32; 3:15; 4:33; 5:32; 10:39-41; etc.

Judas' replacement had to be an eyewitness – Acts 1:21,22.

Paul was an eyewitness – 1 Corinthians 9:1; 15:8; Acts 22:14,15; 26:16.

However, living eyewitnesses are no longer needed, because we now have the written record of the eyewitnesses (John 20:30,31; etc.).

Paul said Jesus' appearance to him was "last of all" and "out of due time" (1 Corinthians 15:8). It came after Jesus' Ascension (Acts 9), whereas other apostles had seen Him before the Ascension (Acts 1). Jesus had to come back to make an exceptional appearance to Paul. If Jesus is continuing to appear to men, then Paul would not have been "out of due time" at all, for there would be many more like him. In fact the original 12 would be the **exceptions**!

3. Apostles were guided directly by the Holy Spirit in their teaching.

See John 16:13; Matthew 10:19,20; Ephesians 3:3-5; 1 Corinthians 14:37; etc.

But we have seen that this power is no longer needed, because the Scriptures now completely record God's will.

4. The apostles performed miracles by the power of the Spirit to confirm their message was from God.

See 2 Corinthians 12:11,12. (Acts 5:12; 14:3; Hebrews 2:3,4; Mark 16:20)

But again, this power is not needed today because the New Testament record of miracles is adequate evidence. And no one today does signs with the characteristics of true miracles.

The work of the apostles pertained to the **foundation** of the church – Ephesians 2:20. They accomplished their work, so they are no longer needed on earth, just like Jesus accomplished His work and is no longer needed on earth.

Nevertheless, just as people in Jesus' day "**had**" Moses and the prophets (Luke 16:29-31), so we "have" apostles today. We have the end product of their work: the complete Scriptures.

Conclusion

There are only **two** ways people in the gospel age received spiritual gifts: Holy Spirit baptism and the laying on of apostles' hands. Both of these methods required personal involvement of apostles. *Scripture records no instance in the gospel age in which people received miraculous powers without the direct, personal involvement of apostles. But there are no apostles living on earth today to impart these gifts.*

Furthermore, the purpose of spiritual gifts has been fulfilled, so there is no need for either Holy Spirit baptism or laying on of hands today. This harmonizes with the evidence we studied earlier showing that there is no need for spiritual gifts today. The **means** of imparting the gifts is no longer needed, because the gifts have accomplished their purpose.

Again, the key point is faith in the Scriptures as the perfect, all-sufficient revelation of God's will for man today. Do you understand that the Bible contains everything we need in order to believe, obey, and be saved? If so, then you understand why we do not need Holy Spirit baptism, apostles, or miraculous gifts today. You will be content to just follow the Scriptures. And you will be equipped to answer those who believe otherwise.

The Duration of Spiritual Gifts

We have learned that the purposes served by spiritual gifts were to reveal and confirm God's will for man. And that work was completed during the lifetime of the original apostles.

Our purpose now will be to consider whether, when that work was completed, were the gifts to continue or did God cause them to cease? Some people believe that miracles and direct revelation still occur today. Is this correct, or have the gifts ceased?

Evidence that Spiritual Gifts Have Ceased.

No Modern Events Have the Characteristics of Bible Miracles.

We have already studied the characteristics of true revelations and true miracles. Consider the application to the existence of miracles at all today.

Modern "revelations" have the character of false prophecy, not true prophecy.

The Bible warns about false prophets:

Matthew 7:15; 2 Corinthians 11:13-15; 2 Peter 2:1; 1 John 4:1; etc.

We learned that we can distinguish false prophets from true prophets by their characteristics.

God of the Bible

The teachings of true inspired men always agreed with Scripture, and their predictions of the future always came true.

False prophets could be distinguished from true prophets, because teachings of false prophets did **not** always harmonize with scriptures and their predictions did **not** always come true (Deuteronomy 18:20-22; Galatians 1:6-9; 2 John 9-11).

When the revelations of modern "prophets" are examined, invariably some of their teachings contradict the Bible and/or some of their predictions fail.

We earlier cited many examples of this. To demonstrate this to be true in any specific case, simply study their "revelations." If some of their teachings differ from the Bible or their predictions sometimes fail, then they are not truly from God. They must be false prophets, not true ones. When this is done with modern "prophets," invariably they fail the test.

Modern "miracles" have the characteristics of false miracles, not true miracles.

The Bible warns about false miracles:

2 Thessalonians 2:9-12; Acts 8:9-13; Matthew 24:24; etc.

As already studied, every true miracle had all the following characteristics:

* There was conclusive evidence that the event really occurred.

* The event occurred suddenly (or in exactly the limited time period God specified).

* There were never any failures when miracles were attempted (by Jesus or by His apostles after they received Holy Spirit baptism).

* The results always completely and perfectly accomplished the intended purpose.

* So the event was clearly **impossible** by natural law.

Men who had true miraculous powers could be distinguished from those who worked false miracles by comparing the characteristics of the works performed.

To prove they were really from God, men with truly miraculous powers were willing to work miracles even in the presence of false teachers, and all their miracles always had all the characteristics of true miracles. False miracle workers were known by the fact their works lacked the characteristics of true miracles. See Acts 8:5-13; 13:6-12; 19:11-17; 1 Kings 18:20-40; Exodus chaps 7-12 (especially 8:17-19) and other examples previously listed.

On close examination, the works of all modern "miracle-workers" are found to lack some or all of the characteristics of true miracles.

We earlier gave examples of this. Again, to demonstrate it in any particular case, simply compare the events people claim are "miracles" to the Bible characteristics.

In practice, when people today are asked to do miracles, so they can be compared to the Bible characteristics of miracles, they will usually refuse. Often they say they cannot work miracles in the presence of those who don't believe or those they claim are "false teachers." They rely instead on "testimonies" of their "miracles." But this simply proves they are false, for men with true miracle power repeatedly did miracles in the presence of unbelievers and false teachers.

We continually hear people who claim they have received miracles today. If so, there should be many examples that have the characteristics of true Bible miracles. But all we ever find are the frauds who claim to do miracles but without the true characteristics. So we must conclude that the gifts have ceased, and all those who claim to possess the gifts are false. (Remember that we are speaking here about true Bible miracles. God still answers prayers through natural law, but not by miracles.)

Spiritual Gifts Are Not Needed, Because They Fulfilled Their Purpose.

We earlier studied the purposes of the gifts and the fulfillment of those purposes.

See earlier notes for the specific evidence.

Some gifts served the purpose of delivering the revelation of God's will.

This work was completed by the end of the lifetime of the original apostles. The apostles received all truth that God gave in order for man to know how to please God and be saved. Then they recorded this message in the Scriptures.

God then promised to preserve the message in the written word throughout all ages. So, we today have the complete revelation of God's will in the Scriptures (2 Timothy 3:16,17).

We need no further revelation today. The purpose of the gifts of direct revelation has been fulfilled. All this we thoroughly documented earlier in this study from the Scriptures.

Some gifts served the purpose of confirming truths that God revealed.

The gifts may have served other secondary purposes, but confirming truth from God was the primary purpose and was the determining purpose in whether or not miracles occurred. When miracles were not needed to accomplish this primary purpose, they did not occur.

John 20:29-31 – The Bible not only records the revelation of God's will, it also records the eyewitness testimony of the miracles that confirm the message to be from God. We do not need miracles today to convince us to believe in God and the Bible, because we now have adequate evidence in the written word. We have thoroughly documented this point earlier in this study.

It follows that when direct revelation was no longer needed, then the gifts of confirmation would no longer be needed. This work was completed during the lifetime of the original apostles, therefore none of the spiritual gifts are needed any longer.

Throughout the Bible, whenever a work of God had fulfilled its purpose, it ceased.

Whenever a work of God was no longer needed, God stopped doing it. Consider examples:

* Creation of the world – Genesis chaps 1,2 (note 2:1,2).
* Universal flood – Genesis chaps. 6-9 (note 9:8-17).
* Sacrifice of a son – Genesis chapter 22.
* Animal sacrifices – Hebrews 10:1-18
* Circumcision – 1 Corinthians 7:18-20; Galatians 5:2-8; etc.
* Virgin birth – Matthew 1:18,20; Luke 1:35
* Earthly life and death of Jesus – Hebrews 9:26,28; 10:10; 7:26,27; etc.
* Resurrection of Jesus – Romans 1:4.

All of these are works God once did but has ceased because their purpose was accomplished. And note that many of them involved miracles. Can you name any work that God continued to do after it had fulfilled its purpose, when it was no longer needed?

We earlier studied some attempts of people who claim miracles are needed today, but those claims are not valid. They are claiming either things that are no longer needed according to the Bible, or things that never were the intended purpose of miracles.

The clear pattern is that God ceases to do works, including miraculous works, when their purpose has been accomplished. All miracles have now accomplished their purpose, so it follows that God has ceased all miracles.

There Is No Means by Which People Today Can Receive These Gifts.

As we studied earlier, the means no longer exist today for people to receive the gifts.

People received power to do spiritual gifts by two possible means.

1. Holy Spirit baptism

Holy Spirit baptism was **never required or even promised to all people**. Only two instances are recorded in Scripture. God never implied He would continue to give it to people throughout all ages.

The **purpose** of Holy Spirit baptism was to give people miraculous powers. But those powers fulfilled their purpose and are no longer needed. Since the gifts themselves have ceased, it follows that Holy Spirit baptism is no longer needed to give the powers.

Ephesians 4:3-6 – **There is one baptism today**. We learned that this one baptism is water baptism, which is commanded for people of all ages. In fact, nearly all groups today practice some form of water baptism, including those who also claim Holy Spirit baptism.

But Holy Spirit baptism and water baptism are two separate and distinct baptisms (Acts 1:5). And Ephesians 4 expressly says that, when Paul wrote the book of Ephesians, there was only **one** baptism. We can no more practice two separate and distinct baptisms today than we can worship two Heavenly Fathers!

So, whereas there **have been** several baptisms practiced at various times, yet by the time Ephesians was written, all these baptisms had ceased except **one**. But water baptism was to continue for all ages, so Holy Spirit baptism must have ceased before Ephesians was written.

2. Laying on of apostles' hands

People also received spiritual gifts by having apostles lay hands on them. But we have seen that only **apostles** could impart gifts in this way. Even if other people had received gifts from an apostle, they could not in turn **impart** or pass on spiritual gifts to others.

This means of receiving the gifts has also fulfilled its purpose and ceased, as we will see, since there are no apostles today.

Apostles were always involved, whenever people received miraculous powers.

Whether by Holy Spirit baptism or by laying on of apostles' hands, no one ever received miraculous powers after Jesus' resurrection except with the direct, personal involvement of an apostle. But we have also seen that no one today meets the qualifications of apostles.

* No one works the true signs of apostles.

* No one is directly guided by the Spirit as apostles were.

* No one is a personal eyewitness of the resurrected Christ like apostles had to be.

* No one has been called directly by Jesus to serve as an apostle.

So apostles were always involved whenever anyone received miraculous powers of the Spirit, but there are no apostles today. Therefore, there is no way for people to receive the gifts today; Holy

God of the Bible

Spirit baptism and laying on of apostles' hands both ceased in the first century. So, the gifts themselves must have ceased around the time when all apostles had passed away. This harmonizes with all the other evidence we have studied.

The Bible Teaches that Miracles Would Cease When Their Purpose Was Fulfilled.

1 Corinthians 13:8-11 – A prophecy that spiritual gifts would cease

The context – chaps. 12,13, and 14 all discuss spiritual gifts.

Chapter 12 lists the gifts (12:4-11) and shows they all had a useful purpose at the time they existed. But 12:31 contrasts the gifts to a "more excellent way."

Chapter 13 shows the "more excellent way" is **love**. Love is greater than spiritual gifts primarily in that love will **endure**, whereas the gifts were temporary and would **cease**.

Chapter 14 gives regulations regarding the proper use of the gifts for the temporary period when they continued to exist.

Why and when would spiritual gifts cease? – 13:8-10

The gifts would cease **because they were "in part"** (verses 9,10) – in some sense they were incomplete and imperfect.

They would cease **"when that which is perfect is come"** (verse 10). "Perfect" here means "complete" (NKJV footnote). Note: "That which is perfect" is contrasted to "that which is in part" (spiritual gifts). "That which is perfect" in some sense completes or perfects that which is incomplete or imperfect about spiritual gifts. If we can determine in what sense spiritual gifts were "in part," then we will understand when and why they would cease.

In what way were the gifts "in part"?

The only sensible answer is that, at the time Paul wrote, **the gifts had only partly accomplished their purpose**. The gifts were then in the process of **delivering** the will of God (as chapters 12-14 frequently mention). But the delivery was not complete when Paul wrote.

Since "that which is perfect (complete)" is contrasted to "that which is in part", we conclude "that which is perfect" must refer to the **complete revelation of all truth.** When the revelation was delivered completely, the purpose of spiritual gifts would be accomplished and they would no longer be needed, so they would cease.

When did this occur? Near the end of the lifetime of the original apostles, as we have seen! Remember the gifts were needed because people did not have the written word. In fact, the gifts were needed to **give** men the written word. When the scriptures were complete, direct revelation was no longer needed, so it ceased.

James 1:25 describes the gospel as the "**perfect** law of liberty" – "that which is perfect."

Verse 11 – an illustration: childish conduct vs. mature conduct

A child cannot speak or walk well. It drinks only milk, needs its diaper changed, etc. As it grows up, it ceases these childish acts. So, when God first began to reveal the gospel, gifts of prophecy, tongues, etc., were needed to deliver the message. But when the message became mature – i.e., completely delivered – then those gifts, that had been needed to accomplish its delivery, would no longer be needed and so would cease.

Note that this means spiritual gifts were the immature state of God's revelation, but the completed Bible is mature. To insist that spiritual gifts are needed today is to go back to immaturity. When people understand that the Bible as God's completed message, they will rely on it for spiritual guidance and will not seek to go back to that which is partial or incomplete.

A similar illustration: While a man is **building a house**, he needs to hammer and saw, etc. When the house is **complete**, the hammering and sawing are no longer needed, so they cease. Likewise, spiritual gifts were needed while the gospel was being revealed, but they ceased when the revelation was complete.

Some think "that which is perfect" refers to Jesus' second coming (either Jesus Himself or some other event at Jesus' return).

* Where does the context refer to Jesus' return? How would spiritual gifts ("that which is in part") contrast to Jesus ("that which is perfect")? Jesus second coming fits neither the context nor Paul's logic.

* The three spiritual gifts listed (prophecy, tongues, and knowledge – verse 8) are contrasted to three **abiding** qualities: faith, hope, and love (verse 13). The spiritual gifts are **temporary** – they **cease** "when that which is perfect" is come (verse 10). But faith, hope, and love are **abiding** compared to the gifts: they do **not** cease "when that which is perfect is come." So spiritual gifts would cease "when that which is perfect" came, but faith, hope, and love would not cease.

This means "that which is perfect" cannot refer to Jesus' second coming, since **faith and hope will cease then** (Romans 8:24; 2 Corinthians 5:7; Hebrews 11:1). To say spiritual gifts will last till Jesus returns would be to say that the gifts are as enduring as faith and hope; but this is the opposite of what the passage says. So spiritual gifts must cease **before** Jesus' second coming. The truth, as we have seen, is that the gifts ceased when the scriptures were completed.

God of the Bible

To insist we need spiritual gifts today would be to deny the sufficiency of Scripture! It would be as unreasonable as dressing a full-grown man in a diaper and feeding him from a baby bottle!

Jude 3 – The faith (gospel) was "once" delivered to the saints.

"Once" is translated "once for all" (New King James Version, American Standard Version, English Standard Version, and others). It is "used of what is so done as to be of perpetual validity and never need repetition" – Thayer.

Note Hebrews 9:26,28; 10:10; 7:26,27; 1 Peter 3:18 – "Once" (same Greek word) describes Jesus' death in contrast to animal sacrifices.

Old Testament sacrifices did not completely remove sins, so they continued to be offered. But Jesus' death was **perfect** and sufficient to completely remove all sin for all men of all ages, so it happened only "**once**". It did not need to be repeated, so it never will be repeated. To say we need more sacrifice for sin would be to deny the perfection of Jesus' sacrifice.

Likewise, the faith was delivered "once" (for all).

Spiritual gifts continued as long as God's perfect testament had not been perfectly and completely revealed. But the perfect New Testament was perfectly and completely delivered to men in the first century. It does not **need** to be delivered again, so it never will be delivered again. Therefore, the spiritual gifts by which it was delivered have ceased. To say we still need spiritual gifts would be to deny the perfection of the New Testament!

Everything Jesus did was perfect. He gave us a perfect sacrifice for sin; when that sacrifice had accomplished its purpose, it ceased and was not repeated. He also gave us the perfect New Testament to tell us how to receive forgiveness (Hebrews 1:1,2; James 1:25). That perfect revelation was perfectly delivered "once for all" by means of spiritual gifts in the first century. That delivery will not be repeated, because it was done perfectly. The revelation we have needs no improvements, just like Jesus' death will never be repeated because it needs no improvements.

Every person who seeks spiritual gifts today is saying (perhaps unintentionally) that he lacks faith in the Bible as the complete and perfect revelation of God's will. Those who are satisfied with the Scriptures will appreciate that they need no other revelation; so they believe God when He says there will be no other revelation.

Answers to Evidence that Spiritual Gifts Are for Today

Those who believe spiritual gifts exist today naturally attempt to justify their view. We have already answered many such arguments, but here are a few remaining ones:

Those Who Seek Signs Are a "Wicked and Adulterous Generation" - Matthew 12:38,39.

This objection is offered when we challenge people who believe in miracles to prove their claims by doing miracles (see also Matthew 16:1,2; John 2:18; 6:26-30; 1 Corinthians 1:22).

1 John 4:1 – God commands us to test prophets to see if they are from God.

We have cited many examples showing that one way to test prophets is by comparing their works to Bible miracles. God's true prophets often deliberately worked signs to prove they were from God. They did so in the presence of false teachers and unbelievers, so people could see the difference between their words and false miracles.

Evidently true prophets did not believe that it was "wicked and adulterous" for people to ask for signs, in the age when they did exist. On the contrary, we have cited many Scriptures showing that the purpose of miracles was to confirm the message.

Do those who make this argument seriously believe that everyone who asked Jesus for a miracle was "wicked and adulterous"? We have abundantly proved that was not the case.

Jesus rebuked people for requesting more signs only after they had already received adequate evidence.

He did not condemn people for sincerely wanting signs so they could determine whether He was from God. The people He rebuked had already seen many signs, but instead of believing and repenting (verse 41), they attributed His miracles to Beelzebub and demanded more signs (see Matthew 12:9-14,22-24; note chaps 4-12).

But this is not our case. We have not seen any real signs at all! One is "wicked and adulterous" only when he has **already received enough evidence** yet still refuses to believe and demands more evidence.

Jesus never offered testimonials or arguments in place of doing miracles.

When we challenge those who believe in modern miracles, they respond by citing a string of testimonials and arguments to try to prove that they really do have miracles. Some have conducted many public debates to try to prove miracles still exist!

When did Jesus or His apostles ever debate, argue, or give testimonials to prove they could do miracles? The very fact that people today offer such debates and arguments proves they do not have the same power as Jesus and the apostles had!

If Jesus knew people needed the opportunity to see miracles, He just **did** the miracles. If He knew people had already seen sufficient evidence but still did not believe, He rebuked them and left. But He never tried to **argue** to convince anyone He could do miracles.

Even the doubters were still given another sign: the resurrection (verses 39,40).

Jesus offered the wicked and adulterous generation yet another sign: He arose from the dead. That sign will satisfy us. If people today will just raise someone from the dead, where we can see and know it has happened, we won't ask for any more miracles afterward!

If Matthew 12 rebukes anyone today, it is those who still want miracles.

Today we have in the Scriptures adequate evidence of the miracles that confirm God's word, so we can have eternal life (John 20:30,31). But some people today are not satisfied with those miracles, so they continue to ask for more! That is the problem that Jesus rebuked.

We are not asking for miracles to convince us to believe in Jesus and the Bible. We ask for miracles only when people tell us they still exist today, and we are testing the prophets like the Bible teaches us to do. We are satisfied with the miracles Jesus and His apostles and prophets already did as recorded in the Scriptures. The people who claim miracles still exist today are the ones who are not satisfied with the miracles God has already done!

Jesus Is the Same Yesterday, Today, And Forever - Hebrews 13:8.

Since Jesus worked miracles "yesterday," some say this verse proves He must do so "today."

Note that the verse also says He is the same "forever."

So, if the verse means Jesus must do miracles today, then He must also do them **forever**. That flatly contradicts 1 Corinthians 13:8-10, which surely teaches miracles will cease someday.

God has ceased doing many things that He did in the past.

Previously in this study we have listed many things that God has ceased doing, including many miracles. The whole point of the context of Hebrews 13:8 is that, in the New Testament, God has ceased doing many things that He did under the Old Testament.

If it does not violate Hebrews 13:8 to believe that God ceased doing many works, including many miracles, why would it violate the verse to believe that He has ceased doing all miracles?

Hebrews 13:8 says Jesus is the same, not that He does the same.

God's basic **character** remains unchanged. He is always loving, merciful, just, all-powerful, etc. – this does not change. But His **deeds** and His **will** for men have changed. That is the point of the book of Hebrews: God ceased binding the Old Covenant because we now have the New Covenant. Likewise, He has ceased doing miracles, because we have the completed Scriptures.

To Say Spiritual Gifts Have Ceased Would Limit God's Love and Make Him a Respecter of Persons (Acts 10:34,35).

We are told that God's miracles demonstrated His love and blessings in Bible times. To say He has stopped would mean that He is a respecter of persons who lacks love for people today.

Even in the age of spiritual gifts, not all people were equally gifted – 1 Corinthians 12:28-30,4-11.

Even then, some believers possessed no spiritual gifts at all; those that did possess them, differed in their gifts. Some people in that day received miracles (such as healings) and others did not. (See our notes on the purpose of miracles for specific examples.)

Did God not love all those people? Was He a respecter of persons then? If not, then the fact God does miracles for some people but not for others does not prove He lacks love or is a respecter of persons.

Among people today who claim spiritual gifts, are all equally gifted?

Do all believers today possess all the miraculous powers just the same as all other believers? Do all believers today receive miracles the same as all other believers?

If not, does that make God a respecter of persons? Does He not love everyone the same today? Why is it that people can understand that God would not be partial and unloving if He gave different gifts to different people today, but if we claim that everyone is the same today (no one has any gifts), then we are accused of making God partial and unloving?

This objection is based entirely on a lack of appreciation for the Scriptures.

Those who make this argument assume that we, who have the Bible today, are at some disadvantage to people who had spiritual gifts. It is true that we don't have gifts as those people did; but it is also true that we do have the **completed Scriptures,** which they did not. In fact, the reason the gifts ceased is that we now have the Scriptures, so the gifts are not needed.

We are at no disadvantage to the people who received miracles, so God has shown us no lack of love nor any respect of persons. To say otherwise is to belittle the blessing of the Scriptures. This argument simply proves again that those who want miracles today do not appreciate the Bible. They think that which is "in part" (gifts) is better than "that which is perfect" (the Bible).

Love and impartiality mean that God offers salvation to all men equally; it never required Him to give all men equal blessings in this life.

Acts 10:34,35 – God's impartiality pertains to whether or not we are **accepted** by Him, not to the abilities or blessings we have in this life.

No Scripture promises that God will give **equal abilities** or **equal blessings** to all. If love and impartiality require Him to do miracles today as in the past, why not argue that He must equally bless us in all other ways? Must we all have the same abilities, health, material prosperity, etc.? People have always differed in these ways.

1 Corinthians 12 & 14 emphasize that God did give different gifts to different people and some had no gifts at all; they were commanded to accept this, not resent it. Paul rebuked Corinth because people resented the fact that other people had different gifts from them. But this is the same mindset people have today when they think they are at a disadvantage if they have no miracles today!

To argue that love and impartiality require God to give equal gifts to all is to flatly contradict the Scriptures that discuss spiritual gifts! God's love and impartiality are demonstrated in that He offers salvation to all on the basis of obedient faith according to the gospel.

To Deny Miracles Today Is to Deny God's Power.

We are told that God is all-powerful, so He can always do miracles. If we claim He does not do them today, then we are denying or limiting His power.

We have already proved that God did many things in the past that He no longer does.

Previously in this study we have listed many such acts, including many miracles. If God ceased to do them, does that prove He lacks the power to do them?

Do you deny that God has ceased to do these works? If you agree that God is not doing some of these works, then are you limiting God's power?

If you can understand how God can still be all-powerful even though He ceased doing the works we have listed, then you can just as easily understand how He can still be all-powerful even though He has ceased doing miracles.

The issue is, not God's <u>power</u>, but God's <u>will</u>.

God has the **power** to do many things that He **chooses** not to do. Of the works we have proved that God ceased doing, the reason He ceased them is that He **wills** not to do them. He does not lack the power to do them.

We have shown repeatedly that God ceases to do works, when their purpose is accomplished. It is not that He lacks the power to do them, but they simply no longer accomplish His purpose. So He stops.

We have shown by the Scriptures that one of the works God does not will to do today is miracles. And we have shown why He does not work them.

We don't deny God's power. If it was His will to do them, He could do them. But is it not His will. The problem is not that we are denying God's power. The problem is that insisting on miracles for today is a denial of God's **will**!

Mark 16:17,18 Says Miracles Will Follow Them That Believe.

We are told that this refers to those believers who are saved (verse 16). People still believe today, so we are told that the signs of verses 17,18 must still exist today.

This argument requires that miracles must continue as long as faith continues.

Yet 1 Corinthians 13:8-13 definitely says that the gifts would **cease** at a time when faith continues to abide. This argument on Mark 16 flatly contradicts 1 Corinthians 13!

This argument also requires that all saved people must do miracles.

If "them that believe" in verses 17,18, means all saved believers (verse 16), then the signs listed **shall follow** all saved believers.

It follows that those who don't do the signs must be unbelievers, and unbelievers are **condemned**! This means that anyone who does not do miracles stands condemned as an unbeliever. Do those who make this argument really believe that?

In fact, many people who make this argument know many people who don't do miracles, yet they believe many of those people are saved. Many of them do not do miracles themselves!

Even in the first century there were saved believers who did no signs (1 Corinthians 12; Acts 8; etc.)

So Mark 16:17,18 cannot refer to all believers, else we have a contradiction in Scripture.

God of the Bible

Most modern "miracle-workers" attempt only 1 or 2 of the signs of Mark 16.

If these signs shall follow those who believe, and those believers are the saved people of verse 16, then all these signs should be present among all believers. Yet many who make the argument do not drink poison or take up snakes, nor have they seen others do so. Why not?

The purpose of the signs was to confirm the message preached (verse 20).

Yet many, who claim modern miracles, don't truly believe what verse 16 says about the necessity of baptism, or they contradict other Bible teachings. Are the signs confirming false teaching?

Further, those who claim to do signs often contradict one another, yet they all tell similar testimonies. Whose preaching is being confirmed? Does the Spirit confirm false teaching?

We have shown that the truth has been fully confirmed, so the signs are no longer needed.

Verses 17,18 were fulfilled in the apostles who needed faith to preach the gospel.

Verses 17,18 cannot mean that the signs will follow all saved people. So, what does it mean?

Those who **heard** the gospel (verse 16) were not the only people in the context who needed faith! Verses 11-15 mention another group of people who lacked faith: the people whom Jesus here commanded to **preach** the gospel were told to believe just as surely as were those who **heard** the gospel. Which group of believers was Jesus saying would do the miracles of verses 17,18?

Verse 20 answers by showing how the promise was **fulfilled.** Jesus was speaking here to the **apostles** (verse 14). The **preachers** had shown lack of faith, but they needed faith to preach and confirm their message by signs. Verse 20 says *"they"* were the ones who fulfilled verses 17,18 by doing the signs. The **purpose** of the signs was to confirm the word of the **apostles.**

So Mark 16:17,18 simply means that the apostles needed faith, so they could preach and do miracles. Then verse 20 confirms that they were the ones who did them. This harmonizes with all the other teachings on miracles we have already studied. To claim that the passage is promising that all believers can do miracles would be to contradict the context and other passages.

Conclusion

So, miracles and spiritual gifts were essential to God's plan. They were necessary to reveal the word of God, record it in the Scriptures, and confirm it to be God's will. However, when the message was completed, the gifts were no longer needed, so they ceased. To believe otherwise is to misunderstand God's will. Many false doctrines have been believed and practiced as a result.

What we believe about miracles for today is ultimately determined by whether or not we respect the Bible as the perfect and complete revelation of God's will. Those who claim we still need miracles invariably demonstrate a lack of faith and appreciation for Scripture. Those who truly respect the Bible know that miracles are no longer needed. Which view do you choose?

The Indwelling of the Holy Spirit

Introduction:

The Holy Spirit is a topic of current interest among religious people. Some folks believe they have Holy Spirit baptism, miracles, tongues, or direct guidance. Some preachers have become fabulously wealthy by claiming to have such powers or to give such powers to others.

On the other hand, many people are quite confused about the work of the Holy Spirit.

The Bible mentions many different works done by the Holy Spirit at various times in history.

The Holy Spirit is a living spirit Being, one of the three members of the Godhead. As such He has been active throughout Bible history.

* He was active in creation and in sustaining the universe (Genesis 1:2; Psalms 104:30; Job 26:13; 33:4).

* He conceived Jesus in Mary's womb (Matthew 1:18,20; Luke 1:35).

* He revealed God's will to men who then taught this message to others (1 Corinthians 2:10-14; Ephesians 3:3-5; Mark 13:11; John 14:26; 16:13; 2 Peter 1:21).

* He then empowered these men to perform miracles to confirm that their message was from God (Hebrews 2:3,4; 1 Corinthians 12:4-11; Acts 2:4; 10:44-46; 14:3).

* He teaches, convicts, and sanctifies sinners (John 16:8-11; 1 Corinthians 6:11; John 3:3-5; Ephesians 2:18; 1 Corinthians 12:13; 1 Peter 1:2).

* He gives Christians joy, comfort, unity, love, etc. (Romans 5:5; 14:17; 15:13; Ephesians 4:3; Acts 9:31; Galatians 5:22-25; 1 Thessalonians 1:6).

Note that some of these activities continue to occur today, but others have reached completion and ceased. The fact the Spirit once did a work does not necessarily prove He is continuing to do it today.

The purpose of this study is to consider the indwelling of the Holy Spirit.

The Bible definitely teaches that the Spirit does dwell in people today.

1 Corinthians 3:16 – We are a temple of God, and the Spirit of God dwells (Greek οικεω) in us.

1 Corinthians 6:19 – Our body is a temple of the Holy Spirit, which is in us because we are bought with a price. Everyone who has been purchased (redeemed) by the blood of Christ also has the Spirit of God dwelling in him.

(Note: This verse has no word for "dwell," but simply says He is "in" us – Greek εν. The parallel in 1 Corinthians 3:16, however, shows this means the same as the Spirit "dwelling" in us. Note similar examples below.)

Romans 8:9 – We should be led by the Spirit of God. If the Spirit of God (Christ) does not dwell (Greek οικεω) in us, we do not belong to God.

These verses teach the following (please remember these points as our study proceeds):

1) The Spirit does dwell in some people today.

2) In fact, He dwells in **all** true children of God.

3) And He begins to dwell in us at the moment we become God's children.

(See also Acts 2:38; 5:32; James 4:5; Romans 5:5; Ephesians 5:18.)

Why is this subject important?

People of all different faiths make conflicting claims about the Holy Spirit: Catholics, Pentecostals, Mormons, Lutherans, and even some former members of churches of Christ. Surely we need to know the truth about the Holy Spirit.

Some people conclude that, if the Holy Spirit dwells in them, then they must have the supernatural manifestations of the Holy Spirit: Holy Spirit baptism, miracles, and tongues.

Others are convinced that – in addition to the teaching of the Scriptures – the Holy Spirit guides them directly in daily decisions, or perhaps especially in spiritual decisions.

But remember that the Holy Spirit has done many different things at different times. When a passage mentions the Holy Spirit, the only way to know what He is **doing** is from the context.

God of the Bible

So, let us consider what the indwelling of the Holy Spirit involves, and how it compares to other works of the Spirit.

Is the Indwelling the Same as Holy Spirit Baptism, Direct Guidance, and Miracles?

We agree that, in times past, the Holy Spirit gave people Holy Spirit baptism, direct guidance, and miracles. Are these the same as the indwelling of the Holy Spirit, and are they occurring today?

All Christians Received the Indwelling, but NOT All Received Holy Spirit Baptism, Direct Guidance, or Miracles.

We already showed that all Christians have the indwelling of the Spirit. However:

Not all people received direct revelation and miracles.

1 Corinthians 12:29,30 – Were all people apostles or prophets? No. Likewise, not all had tongues, miracles, etc. (Note verses 4,7-11.)

Holy Spirit "baptism" was a special work that was never promised to all people.

Only two cases in the Bible are described as Holy Spirit "baptism."

Compare Acts 1:2-8 to 2:1-11. The **apostles** received Holy Spirit baptism when the **Jews** first received the gospel. Note the reference to "men of Galilee" in 1:11 and compare to 2:7,14.

Acts 10:44-46; 11:15-18 (15:7-9) – **Cornelius' household** received Holy Spirit baptism when the **Gentiles** first received the gospel.

No other incidents in Scripture are referred to as Holy Spirit baptism.

Everyone who received Holy Spirit Baptism spoke in tongues, but not all Christians spoke in tongues though they had the indwelling.

In both of the cases of Holy Spirit baptism listed above, the people immediately spoke in tongues (Acts 2:1-11; 10:46). But not all Christians spoke in tongues, even though all had the indwelling (see 1 Corinthians 12:4,7-11,29,30 above).

Whereas all Christians possess the indwelling, not all Christians received Holy Spirit baptism, direct guidance, or miracles. It follows that these are not the same work of the Spirit.

The Indwelling Is Received at Conversion, but Spiritual Gifts Came by Other Means at Other Times.

Acts 22:16 – Remember, people have the indwelling as soon as they are forgiven of sin. But they are commanded **not** to wait to be forgiven.

But people were told to wait for Holy Spirit baptism.

Acts 1:4,5,8 – Jesus told the apostles that, in order to receive Holy Spirit baptism, they had to "wait" till God chose to give it to them.

We have the power to choose whether and when we will be saved and receive the indwelling. But those few who received Holy Spirit baptism had no control over when or who. It follows that the indwelling is not the same as Holy Spirit baptism.

Likewise, some people received miraculous gifts through the apostles' hands at a different time from conversion.

Acts 8:12-19 – The Samaritans believed and were baptized (verse 12), so they were saved (Mark 16:16; Acts 2:38; etc.). As we have learned, they would have immediately received the indwelling.

However, the Spirit had not yet fallen on them (verses 15,16). The Spirit was indwelling them, yet in another sense they did not receive the Spirit till the apostles came and laid hands on them (verses 14-19). Other examples of laying on of apostles' hands show that this involved bestowing miraculous powers, tongues, etc. (Acts 19:1-6; 2 Timothy 1:6; Romans 1:8-11).

Again, these people received the indwelling at conversion, but did not then receive miraculous powers. And when people did receive them both, they came at different times and in different ways. So clearly the two are not the same.

Today No One Does Miracles Like Those in the Early Church.

The indwelling must exist today just like in the first century, since all saved people have it. But no one today duplicates the miraculous powers of the first century.

True miracles can be distinguished from frauds.

1 John 4:1 – We must test people who claim miracles or direct guidance, because many are frauds. (Matthew 7:15-23; 24:24; 2 Corinthians 11:13-15; 2 Peter 2:1; Deuteronomy 18:20-22; Acts 8:9-13; 2 Thessalonians 2:9-12; Revelation 2:2)

God of the Bible

Today when we "test" the claims of "miracle-workers," they almost never attempt to show us miracles. Instead they offer arguments and testimonials.

Acts 8:5-13 – However, true miracle workers exercised their gifts in the presence of false teachers. Instead of offering testimonials or arguments, they just **did** the miracles so people could observe for themselves.

Acts 4:14-16 – Even opponents of true prophets could not deny the miracles that occurred.

(Note John 11:47,48; Exodus 7-12 (especially 8:17-19); Numbers 16 and 17; 1 Kings 18:20-40; 13:6-12; 2 Kings 1 and 6; Daniel 2; Daniel 3; Daniel 6; 1 Kings 13:1-6; Jeremiah 28.)

Modern "healings" differ from true healings.

When we examine modern so-called miracles, they do not measure up to Bible miracles.

John 11:38-45 – Bible healings involved obvious organic diseases that were healed obviously, instantaneously, and completely. They never involved relapses, partial improvements, or gradual healings requiring days or weeks.

Further, Jesus and his apostles (after they received Holy Spirit baptism) always succeeded. No disease was too hard to heal, nor did they fail in any attempt to heal.

So-called miracles today lack many characteristics of Bible miracles. True miracles were evident to everyone. Modern "miracles" are not convincing, but have the characteristics of frauds.

(Note 9:1,7,18-25; Acts 3:2-10 and 4:22; 5:12,15,16; Luke 13:11-17; 7:11-17; Mark 1:40-45; 2:10-12; 5:25-29, 35-42; Matthew 4:23,24; 14:34-36; 12:10-13.)

Modern "revelations" differ from true guidance of the Spirit.

Matthew 10:19,20 – True guidance of the Spirit gave men the infallible will of God, which could be expressed in exactly the words God wanted. The message was precise even in great detail (Matthew 22:32; Galatians 3:16).

However, modern so-called direct guidance involves vague leadings, impressions, feelings, and undefined urgings. Instead of stating the revelation clearly, people often say it is "better felt than told" and "you cannot understand until you experience it."

Further, modern "revelations" often contradict one another and contradict the Bible. But the Holy Spirit does not contradict Himself (1 Corinthians 14:33; 1:10-13; Galatians 1:8,9; 2 John 9; etc.).

True revelations from God could always be distinguished from frauds by objective evidence. This was the primary purpose of miracles. But there is no objective evidence to prove any modern "revelations" are from God or to distinguish the true ones from the false ones. This implies they are human, not divine, in origin.

The indwelling of the Spirit continues today unchanged, but modern so-called miracles clearly differ from what existed in Bible times.

(Note: 1 Corinthians 14:37; 2:10-13; Deuteronomy 18:18-22; 2 Peter 1:21; 2 Samuel 23:1,2; Ephesians 3:3-5.)

The Purposes of Holy Spirit Baptism and Spiritual Gifts Have Been Fulfilled.

As we have seen, the indwelling continues today, since without it we do not belong to God.

Holy Spirit baptism and spiritual gifts were given to reveal new truths and to confirm that those messages were truly from God.

Matthew 10:19,20; Acts 14:3 – Spiritual gifts of direct guidance revealed new truths in the age when the Scriptures had not yet been completed.

Mark 16:20; Hebrews 2:3,4 – Miracles confirmed that those messages were really from God.

Today, direct guidance and miracles are not needed, because we have the completed Scriptures.

2 Timothy 3:16,17 – The Scriptures reveal all that we need to know to please God, in a way that any honest person can understand. (2 Peter 1:3; Acts 20:20,27; Ephesians 3:3-5; Acts 17:11; 1 Corinthians 14:33; 1 Peter 1:22-25; 2 John 2)

John 20:30,31 – Furthermore, the Scriptures contain eyewitness testimony of the miracles that confirm the message is from God. No further miracles are needed to confirm the message. (Luke 1:1-4; 1 Corinthians 15:1-8; 2 Peter 1:12-18)

Galatians 3:15 – Once a covenant has been confirmed or ratified, it does not need to be continually re-confirmed.

Miraculous confirmation was needed as long as new truths were being revealed. But since the apostles received all truth, there is no new truth to be revealed (John 16:13; 2 Peter 1:3; Acts 20:20,27; 2 Timothy 3:16,17). So, direct guidance of the Spirit and miraculous confirmation are not needed today. They have served their purpose. But the indwelling continues.

Holy Spirit Baptism and Spiritual Gifts Have Ceased.

Remember that all people who belong to God will have the indwelling. But consider the evidence that Holy Spirit baptism and spiritual gifts have ceased.

Holy Spirit baptism and spiritual gifts were never promised to all people.

Even in the first century, not all saved people had them. There is therefore no reason to expect people to need them today.

God of the Bible

The purposes of miraculous powers have been fulfilled.

As we have seen, Holy Spirit baptism and spiritual gifts existed to reveal and confirm the revelation from God. Since God's word was adequately revealed and confirmed in the first century, we no longer need direct guidance or miracles. The gifts fulfilled their purpose.

The means of bestowing miraculous powers and direct revelation have ceased.

Whenever anyone received miraculous powers in the New Testament, apostles were always present and directly involved. Since Pentecost, not one case can be named in which anyone received these powers apart from the direct involvement of apostles.

But there are no apostles today, since no one today is an eyewitness that Jesus was raised from the dead (Acts 1:22; 1 Corinthians 9:1; 15:8; etc.). So, no one can obtain these powers today. This agrees with the fact that no one needs these gifts now.

No one today practices the kind of miracles and powers done in the early church.

We have seen that the miracles claimed for today do not have the characteristics of true miracles but instead have the characteristics of frauds. True Biblical miracles are no longer being done because they are not needed.

Ephesians 4:4-6 – There is only "ONE baptism" today.

Holy Spirit baptism and water baptism are two separate and distinct baptisms (Matthew 3:11; Acts 1:5). But by the time Ephesians was written, one or the other had ceased.

Some folks today claim to practice both water baptism and Holy Spirit baptism. But there can no more be two baptisms today than there can be two Gods.

Water baptism, administered by men in Jesus' name, is clearly still for today, since all men need it to be saved (Matthew 28:19; Mark 16:16; Acts 8:36-39; 10:47,48; 2:38; 22:16; 1 Peter 3:21). But Holy Spirit baptism is entirely different. It has accomplished its purpose and has ceased.

The Bible predicted that miracles would cease when their purpose was fulfilled.

1 Corinthians 13:8-11 – Prophecies, tongues, and miraculous knowledge are three of the gifts the Spirit used to deliver God's will (12:7-11). But love (chapter 13) is "more excellent" than these gifts (12:31). Why? Because the gifts served a temporary purpose and would cease (verses 8-10), whereas love, faith, and hope would abide because they continue to be needed (13:13).

Spiritual gifts would cease because they were "in part" (verse 9), and they would cease when "that which is perfect" or complete would come (verse 10). Note: "that which is perfect" is contrasted to the gifts that were "in part."

In what sense were spiritual gifts "in part"? At the time Paul wrote, the gifts had only partially completed their purpose of revealing God's will. The revelation was delivered by means of these gifts, but that work was not yet completed at the time Paul wrote.

"That which is perfect" must, therefore, refer to the completed or mature revelation of God's will ("the perfect law of liberty" – James 1:25). When it had all been completely and adequately revealed, the spiritual gifts would cease because they had fulfilled their purpose.

But all truth was revealed to the apostles and recorded in the Bible in the first century (John 16:13; 2 Timothy 3:16,17; 2 Peter 1:3). After that, spiritual gifts were unneeded, so they ceased. Now the written word is the only inspired means we have to learn God's will.

Jude 3 – The faith was "once for all delivered to the saints" (NKJV). The phrase "once for all" is used elsewhere to describe Jesus' death, which occurred only one time, in contrast to animal sacrifices which were continually repeated because they could not really remove sin (Hebrews 9:26,28; 10:10; 7:26,27; 1 Peter 3:18). Jesus' sacrifice was so perfect that it did not need to be repeated. (See Thayer's definition.)

Likewise, the gospel was delivered to God's people only "once." When it was complete or perfect, it did not need to be repeated. We may as well affirm that Jesus' sacrifice needs to be repeated as to affirm that people still need spiritual gifts today.

So, the indwelling of the Holy Spirit is different from Holy Spirit baptism, miracles, and direct guidance. The indwelling still exists, but Holy Spirit baptism and the miraculous gifts have ceased.

How Does the Spirit Lead Men Today?

People sometimes wonder, if there is no direct guidance from the Spirit today, then how does the Spirit instruct us to know God's will?

The Spirit Instructs Men through the Scriptures.

All spiritual truth about God's will was delivered to men in the first century and recorded in the Scriptures. This message has been preserved, so we today can know the will of God through the Spirit's message in the written word.

John 14:26; 16:13 – Speaking to the original apostles (compare 13:1,21,22; 16:17 to Matthew 26:20,26), Jesus promised that the Holy Spirit would guide them into all truth. The direct guidance of the Spirit did this for them, but this was never promised to all men.

God of the Bible

1 Corinthians 14:37 – The inspired men then wrote down the message that the Spirit revealed to them. So, the Scriptures now contain the message of the Spirit in written form. (11:23)

Ephesians 3:3-5 – What Paul received by revelation, he wrote down so others could read and understand it.

2 Timothy 3:16,17 – The inspiration of the Holy Spirit guided the inspired men to record all good works in the Scriptures, the written word. In this way, the Scriptures are profitable to teach and instruct men in righteousness, etc.

John 20:30,31 – The written word tells enough that we can receive eternal life. (Compare 1 John 1:1-4; 2:1-6.)

2 Peter 1:12-15— Having received all things pertaining to life and godliness (1:3), Peter wrote so that, even after he died, others could be reminded of the words and commandments of Jesus' apostles and prophets. (3:1,2)

Today, we need no further revelation because the Bible completely reveals all we need to know to please God and be saved. Any religious doctrine taught today, which was not recorded in the Bible by the apostles and prophets in the first century, is not true, since those men received and wrote down all truth.

(See also 1 Corinthians 11:23; 2:10-14; 15:3; 2 Thessalonians 3:6,14; Jude 3; Revelation 1:11; Acts 20:20,27; Galatians 1:8-12; James 1:25; Matthew 28:20; Colossians 4:12; Hebrews 13:20,31.)

Whatever the Spirit Does in Leading Men, the Word Is Said to Do the Same.

Holy Spirit	Work	The Word
Ephesians 5:18,19; 1 Corinthians 6:19	Dwells in us	Colossians 3:16; 2 John 2
Romans 8:14; Galatians 5:18	Leads or guides	Psalm 119:104,105; 2 Timothy 3:16,17
2 Thessalonians 2:13	Sanctifies	John 17:17,19
Galatians 5:22,23	Bears fruit	Colossians 1:5,6,9,10; Luke 8:11,15
Romans 15:13; Ephesians 3:16	Gives power	Romans 1:16; Hebrews 4:12
Romans 8:16; Ephesians 1:13,14	Testifies we are God's	1 John 2:3-6; 1 Peter 1:23
Acts 9:31	Comforts	Romans 15:4; 1 Thessalonians 4:18
Hebrews 2:3,4	Gives evidence	John 20:30,31

Ephesians 6:17 – The word is the sword of the Spirit. The Spirit and the word are two separate things – they are not the same. But the

word is the instrument the Spirit uses through which to reveal His will and lead men to obey Him today (compare Hebrews 4:12,13).

There is no means for knowing God's will today apart from the Scriptures. This is why so many passages exhort us to study and teach God's word (Acts 17:11; 8:4; Matthew 28:20; 22:29; 2 Timothy 3:16,17; 2:2,15; Psalm 19:7-11; 1:2; etc.).

Indeed the Spirit does dwell in every Christian today. But this is not the means by which the Spirit leads men to know God's will. The indwelling is a different work from that of revealing God's will or guiding men.

When a man claims the Holy Spirit guides him today in ways in addition to the Scriptures, whether he realizes it or not, he is not satisfied to simply follow the Bible. He wants something else in addition to what the Bible says. He has rejected the Scriptures as a complete and perfect guide.

What Is the Indwelling of the Spirit?

If the indwelling of the Holy Spirit does not give miraculous powers or direct guidance, then what is its nature? What does the gospel mean when it says that the Holy Spirit dwells in all children of God?

The Holy Spirit Dwells in Us Like the Father and the Son Dwell in Us.

Many people become completely flustered trying to grasp the idea that the Holy Spirit dwells in them, yet they seem to have no problem whatever with the fact the Father and Son also dwell in them! Consider what the Bible teaches:

The Father dwells in us and we in Him.

2 Corinthians 6:16 – We are a temple of God (the "Father" – verse 18). He dwells (Greek: form of οικεω) in us and walks in us, if we are His children, His people.

1 John 4:14-16 – The Father sent the Son. If we confess Jesus to be the Son of God (the Father), then God dwells (Greek: μενω) in us and *we in Him*. (Compare also verses 12,13.)

Christians are not just a temple of the Holy Spirit who dwells in us; we are likewise a temple of the Father who dwells in us. And we dwell in the Father. Who would claim that this is a direct, personal indwelling? Does the heavenly Father somehow inhabit our bodies? (Ephesians 2:20-22; 1 John 2:24)

God of the Bible

The Son dwells in us and we in Him.

Ephesians 3:17 – Christ dwells (Greek: form of οικεω) in our hearts by faith.

John 15:4-6 – As a branch abides in the vine, so disciples abide (Greek: μενω) *in Jesus and He in us*.

2 Corinthians 5:17 – If anyone is "in Christ" (Greek εν) he is a new creature. Old things are passed away and all are become new.

Romans 8:1 – There is no condemnation to those "in Christ." (Greek εν. Note the references in context to the Spirit "dwelling in" us – verses 9-11.)

Galatians 3:27; Romans 6:3,4 – We are baptized *into* Christ. But baptism is essential to be forgiven of sins and become a child of God (Mark 16:16; Acts 2:38; 22:16; 1 Peter 3:21; etc.). Therefore, all who are forgiven of sins are in Christ.

Note that these concepts are usually taught to people even before they become Christians, yet no one finds them particularly difficult or confusing. And no one assumes that these passages refer to some kind of direct, personal inhabiting of our bodies by Jesus' spirit.

Just as the Holy Spirit dwells in us, so also Jesus dwells in us and we in Him.

(Compare 2 Corinthians 13:5; John 6:56; 14:20; 1 John 3:24; 2:5,6,24,27,28; 5:20; Colossians 1:2,27; Romans 16:3,8-13; 8:10; Revelation 14:13; Galatians 1:22; Ephesians 1:1; Philippians 1:1,14; 1 Thessalonians 4:16; 1 Peter 5:14.)

The Father and Son dwell in One Another.

John 14:10,11 – We should believe that the Father dwells in Jesus and Jesus is in the Father. (Greek μενω and εν)

John 14:20 – Jesus is in the Father, and we in Jesus, and Jesus in us. (Greek: εν)

John 10:37,38 – We should know and believe that the Father was in Jesus and Jesus in the Father. (Greek: εν)

The Father and Son are distinct individuals, just as we disciples are separate beings from one another. Yet the Son was in the Father, and the Father in the Son.

(Note John 17:20-23.)

Christians are in one another.

2 Corinthians 7:3 – Paul said to the Corinthians, "You are in our hearts." (Greek: εν)

Philippians 1:7 – "I have you in my heart." (Greek: εν)

So the Spirit does dwell in faithful Christians. But the Father and Son also dwell in us, and we dwell in them. And Christians are even in one another.

If we can believe without confusion that the Father and Son dwell in us, why are we so confused by the fact the Holy Spirit dwells in us? If we can understand how the Father and Son dwell in us and we in them, then we can understand how the Spirit dwells in us, since the same language is used for all these cases.

(Notice that Satan can also enter a person and fill his heart – Luke 22:3; John 13:27; Acts 5:3. Is this a direct personal indwelling? Does it not simply describe the fact that a person has put himself in fellowship with Satan as a result of submitting to his influence and guidance – John 8:44; 1 John 3:8-10; 1 Timothy 5:15; 2 Timothy 2:25,26)

(Note: To do some **action** "in" Deity may have a slightly different connotation from dwelling or being in one another. It could mean we act "by" God: by means of His power. John 3:21; 1 Thessalonians 2:2.)

The Indwelling Is Not a Direct, Personal Habitation.

The human spirit dwells directly and personally in the human body as in a temple or tabernacle. In that sense our spirits inhabit our bodies, and Jesus' spirit inhabited His body. Note 2 Corinthians 4:16; 5:1,4; John 2:21; James 2:26; Hebrews 10:5; 2 Peter 1:13,14; Luke 23:46. Is this how the Holy Spirit dwells in us?

Do the Father and Son personally indwell us, etc.?

If the Spirit personally dwells in us, then the Father and Son personally dwell in us, we dwell in them, and Christians dwell in one another, etc. (since the same language is used in Scripture for all these relationships). Do our spirits inhabit God's body, etc.? Do all these spirits inhabit our bodies? I know no one who believes such, because there is no reason to believe this is what the language means.

Some people will argue at length that the Holy Spirit "personally" indwells Christians, yet they almost never argue that the Father and Son "personally" dwell in us or we in them. Why not? Why do we not see just as much effort to prove a personal indwelling of the Father and Son as for the Holy Spirit? Why not argue that we personally dwell in the Father and Son?

Evidently we all know the Father and Son do not personally dwell in us, we in them, etc. So why conclude that the parallel language for the Spirit means a personal indwelling?

Consider the consequences of "God in the flesh."

When Jesus' spirit dwelt in His body, that was an example of personal, direct indwelling. But He was God in the flesh. If the Holy Spirit personally and directly inhabits our bodies (and so do the Father and Son), then wouldn't that make us God in the flesh like Jesus was? If our spirits personally dwell in the Father, wouldn't that make us God? Surely such ideas would be blasphemous, and no one really believes these things to be true. So why claim that the Spirit dwells in us directly and personally?

What work does the Spirit do that would require a direct, personal indwelling?

He does not do miracles today, as we have seen. What does He do that would require a personal indwelling?

Some emphasize that the Spirit intercedes for us (Romans 8:26,27). But why would this require a personal, direct indwelling? This is not a work done *in* us, but a work done in heaven on our behalf. (And remember that Jesus also intercedes for us. Does this require a personal indwelling?)

There is no Bible evidence that the Spirit directly, personally indwells us, but there is considerable evidence against it. The concept of personal indwelling does not fit the terms used in Scripture.

At this point we know that the indwelling of the Holy Spirit is *not*:

(1) Holy Spirit baptism or miraculous powers

(2) Direct guidance apart from the word or

(3) A direct, personal inhabiting of our bodies.

Furthermore, whatever explanation we give for the indwelling of the Spirit, that explanation must harmonize with these facts:

(1) The indwelling is not any of the things we have just listed.

(2) The indwelling is for all Christians from the moment of conversion on.

(3) The Spirit dwells in us like the Father and Son dwell in us, etc.

The Indwelling Involves Fellowship with the Spirit Based on the Influence of God's Word and Resulting in the Fruits of the Spirit.

The indwelling involves fellowship or a close relationship with the Spirit, including all the blessings that are associated with such a relationship.

John 17:20-23 – Disciples are "in" the Father and the Son, they are "in" us, and they are "in" one another. The passage explains that this means to be "*one*": a close spiritual relationship of harmony, unity, and fellowship.

John 15:1-6 – We "abide in" Jesus as a branch abides in the vine: close contact. It is the opposite of being cut off or separated from Him (verses 2,5,6).

2 Corinthians 6:14-18 – God dwells in us as His temple if we are He people, His sons and daughters. The point in context is *fellowship* in contrast to *separation*. We must fellowship God or sin: one or the other. If we separate from sin, God will fellowship us: He will dwell in us as His temple and we will be His sons and daughters.

1 John 1:3,6,7; 2:3-6 – The subject in context is how to fellowship the Father and the Son, and how to know we are right with them. This is called "*fellowship*" in 1:3,6, and is also called "knowing" God or "*abiding* in" God in 2:3-6.

Ephesians 2:1-5,11-22 – We are a temple or habitation of God in the Spirit. Again, He dwells in or inhabits us. In what sense? The whole context shows we now have *fellowship* or union (reconciliation) with Him – access to Him – where before conversion we were **separated** or alienated from Him.

This fits what we have learned, because sin is what keeps us from having fellowship with God (Isaiah 59:1,2). As soon as sin is forgiven, we have fellowship with the Father, Son, and Holy Spirit. But we have learned that this is exactly when and how the indwelling of the Spirit begins.

When the Bible says the Father and Son "dwell in" us and in one another, etc., it means we have a close relationship of unity and fellowship with them. Associated with this relationship are all spiritual blessings (Ephesians 1:3). Why assume it means something different when used for the Spirit dwelling in us?

Many other Scriptures talk about having fellowship with the Spirit. Note 2 Corinthians 13:14; Philippians 2:1; Hebrews 6:4.

(Note: This concept is also confirmed by lexicons that define "dwell" and "in.")

This fellowship results from the influence of the Holy Spirit through the word.

The indwelling begins the moment we are forgiven of sins by obeying the gospel, God's word. Note other verses that tie indwelling to the word.

1 John 2:3-6 – We know we know God and are "*in* Him" if we **keep His commands**.

1 John 3:24 – If we keep His **commands**, He **dwells** in us and we *in* Him (compare 2:24).

Ephesians 3:17; Romans 10:17 – How does Jesus dwell in our hearts? By *faith*. But faith comes by hearing God's word.

Ephesians 5:18,19; compare Colossians 3:16 – These are parallel passages. One says, "Let the **word** ... dwell in you..." The parallel says to be "filled with the **Spirit**" (this is not miracles but the indwelling, since all Christians are commanded to do it). So, we are filled with the Spirit when God's word dwells in us.

Ephesians 6:17 – The word is the sword of the Spirit. The word is not the Spirit, but is the agent used by the Spirit. If we know and obey the word, then we have fellowship with the Spirit and the Spirit continually directs and influences our lives through the word. (Compare John 8:31; 15:7-10; 2 John 9.)

This harmonizes with the fact we earlier learned that the Bible says the word does whatever the Holy Spirit does in instructing and leading men. As we are led by the word, we are led by the Spirit Who revealed the word. As a result, we have fellowship with Deity, with all the blessings that come with that fellowship.

God of the Bible

Following the word of God, not only leads to fellowship with God, but also results in the fruits of the Spirit.

Galatians 5:22-25 – When we are **led** by the Spirit (verse 18), our lives produce the "fruits" or qualities listed.

Colossians 1:5,6,9,10; Luke 8:11,15 – This fruit, however, is produced, not by some mystical, miraculous, unexplainable influence of the Spirit, but through the influence of the word.

John 15:1-6 – When we abide in Jesus as branches in the vine, we bear fruit. This occurs because we let Jesus' **word** abide in us and we keep His **commands** (verses 7-10).

Galatians 2:20 – Christ lives in me. When I live by the rules or principles He lived by, it is as though He were living His life through me. (4:19)

When a child acts like its parents, we say, "You can sure see his Daddy in him." Paul Overstreet wrote a song entitled "I'm Seein' My Father in Me." So, when we are in fellowship with the Father, Son, and Spirit, and we let their word work in our lives, then we bear the fruits of their teachings. People can truly say, "You can see Jesus in him," or "You can see the Spirit of God in Him."

Would anyone object if someone said that he has fellowship with God as he obeys God's word, is influenced by God's word, and produces fruit in his life by God's word? Could anyone prove that having the Father dwell in him involves something more than that? If not, then why not conclude that this is the sense in which the Holy Spirit dwells in us?

(Note: Some say "The Spirit dwells in us through the word." I do not disagree with that but have attempted to give a fuller, more detailed understanding of what this means.)

Conclusion

Do the Father, Son, and Holy Spirit dwell in you? To have God in your life, you must obey the word revealed by the Spirit so your sins will be forgiven. The teachings of the Spirit say that, to be forgiven you must hear the gospel, believe, repent, confess Christ, and be baptized (Mark 16:15,16; Acts 2:38,42; 22:16; Romans 1:16; 10:17; 6:3,4). Then you must continue serving God faithfully, developing the fruit of the Spirit (Romans 6:16-18; 1 Corinthians 15:58; 1 John 2:3-6).

I conclude that the indwelling of the Spirit is not nearly so mysterious as many people make it out to be. Nevertheless, it is a great blessing, and you should be sure you have that fellowship with God by receiving forgiveness and developing the character that His word can produce in you.

Printed books, booklets, and tracts available at
www.gospelway.com/sales
Free Bible study articles online at
www.gospelway.com
Free Bible courses online at
www.biblestudylessons.com
Free class books at
www.biblestudylessons.com/classbooks
Free commentaries on Bible books at
www.biblestudylessons.com/commentary
Contact the author at
www.gospelway.com/comments
Free e-mail Bible study newsletter –
www.gospelway.com/update_subscribe.htm

Made in the USA
Middletown, DE
16 April 2022

64336513R00119